happy
birth
day

The National Childbirth Trust

happy birth day

how to have the best possible pregnancy and birth

Foreword by Dr Richard Porter FRCOG

Mitchell Beazley

Contents

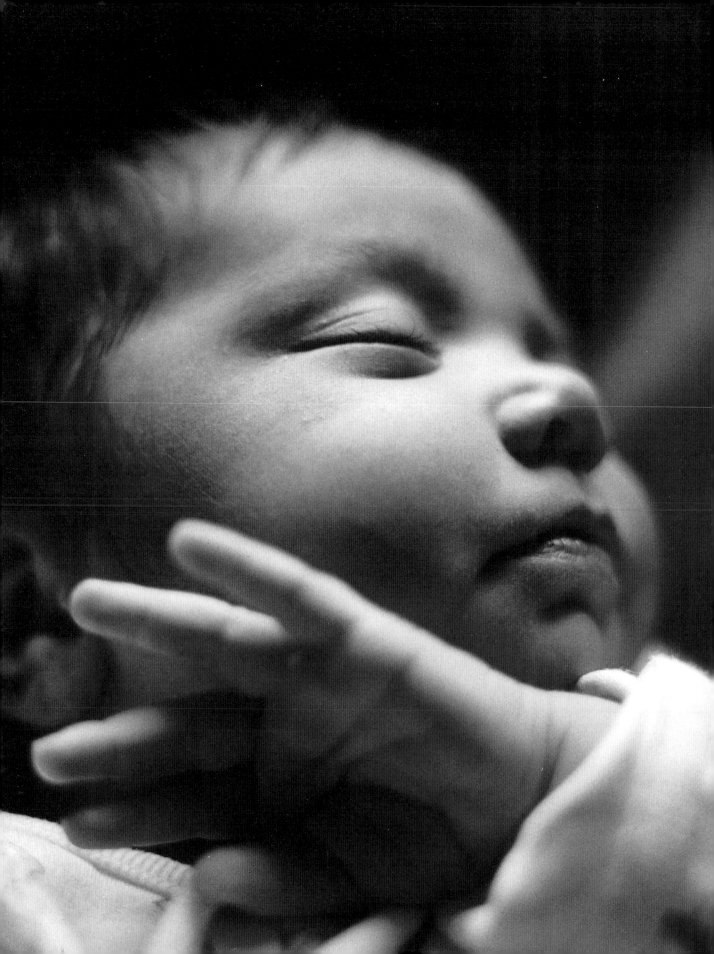

Foreword

Pregnancy and childbirth are momentous events, and this book takes the approach of considering the choices available at all the points in the journey. It is clearly centred on the people making that journey – the mother, the baby, and the family.

There is a lot of information here, but it is presented in such a way that all of us, from the "total beginner" to the "expert" in the field, can gain from it.

As we all know, choice is a prerequisite of freedom – and knowledge is power. And so it follows that those who read this splendid book will be empowered, and will be better able to exercise their freedom, during one of the most important times of their lives.

I am delighted that The National Childbirth Trust, for so long a source of strength for mothers-to-be in this country, should have produced this book. It is a credit to them. Countless mothers will gain enormously from reading it, either by dipping into it or by reading it from cover to cover, and I cannot recommend it too highly.

Dr Richard Porter FRCOG

1 Becoming a parent

Journey to birth

Giving birth is often called "the everyday miracle", and nothing could be more true. The creation of a new life begins with the mixture of two sets of genes that grow from the meeting of egg and sperm and combine to make a unique human being.

This everyday miracle develops from a microscopic bundle of cells into a fully grown human baby ready to be born. Some cells grow to become legs, while others gradually develop into arms, eyes, hair, lungs, and brain. Inside the mother's uterus the baby waits patiently – listening, seeing, sucking his thumb. Meanwhile the mother's body feeds the baby, filters out harmful substances, and keeps him safe inside a fluid-filled protective bubble. Then follows the beautifully designed process of labour and birth, which allows this new baby to emerge from his mother's body, now able to sustain life alone.

This phenomenal task is accomplished in only nine months (or 40 weeks). It is nothing less than incredible, and is how each of us began. But of

your birth year

testis starts to form in boy babies | tiny skeleton has formed | you may now be able to feel your baby kicking

FIRST TRIMESTER | **SECOND TRIMESTER**

1 2 3 4 6 7 8 9 10 11 12 13 14 15 16 17 18 19 20 21 22 23 24 25 26

conception takes place | arm buds then leg buds begin to develop | fetus looks like a baby now | by week 15 ovaries have formed in baby girls | by weeks 21–25 your baby can recognize your voice

course, for women, preparation for this process started many years earlier. As a young girl at the onset of menstruation, you begin releasing eggs ready for fertilization and each month your uterus prepares for the possibility of a baby.

Humans are literally made for love: men's and women's bodies are designed for sex, for creating new life. And once pregnant, a woman's body knows how to nourish and protect a growing baby (or babies) and how to give birth.

Pregnancy is one step on a journey that began for each of us long ago, and it is a journey common to women across the world. Historically, across all cultures, women have supported each other through the process of pregnancy and birth, with older, more experienced mothers passing on their wisdom to young mothers pregnant for the first time. During the birth itself, women were encouraged and supported by other women who had been through childbirth, and that knowledge gave them strength.

Young women grew up surrounded by pregnancy, birth, and breast-feeding, so these processes were familiar to them.

This book aims to give you back some of that women's wisdom about pregnancy and birth. There is nothing to be afraid of. You are following the well-trodden footsteps of millions of women on your journey – let them guide your way.

your baby is now perfectly formed and has eyebrows and eyelashes | your baby now has very little space in the uterus

THIRD TRIMESTER

BIRTH AND FIRST 3 MONTHS

| 27 | 28 | 29 | 30 | 31 | 32 | 33 | 34 | 35 | 36 | 37 | 38 | 39 | 40 | 41 | 42 | 43 | 44 | 45 | 46 | 47 | 48 | 49 | 50 | 51 | 52 |

your baby's eyes are open he can blink, and his lungs are capable of breathing | by weeks 35–37 baby will turn toward light | week 40 (term) only about five per cent of babies arrive on their due date

From child to adult

The transformation of a child to woman or man is an extraordinary process. In girls it begins any time between the age of about eight and 14. Over the next four years she'll grow about 30cm (1ft) taller, her body changes, and her periods start. For boys adolescence starts about two years later than for girls.

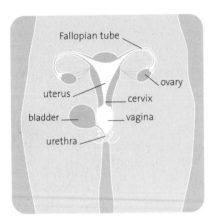

Fertilization usually *takes place in the Fallopian tube as the egg journeys towards the uterus.*

Puberty for girls

The physical maturation of puberty for girls is a complex interaction between the brain, the pituitary gland, and her ovaries and is influenced by social, cultural, and environmental factors. It begins with a rapid spurt of growth and usually follows a predictable order, with breast buds coming first and some skeletal growth, followed by the arrival of pubic and armpit hair, the development of rounded breasts, and a final growth spurt.

The first period indicates that levels of hormones are adequate to allow the uterus to develop, although ovulation will not start yet.

First signs of ovulation

Girl babies are born with all the eggs they need for their adult life. The eggs lie dormant in the follicles of the ovaries, which in an adult woman are almond-shaped and 3–4cm (1¼–1½in) long. The outer layer of the ovaries contains the egg-holding follicles, which also produce the female hormones oestrogen and progesterone.

Ovulation (the release of an egg) usually occurs about ten months after a girl's first period. More than half of a girl's early menstrual cycles do not result in the release of an egg. After around five years, the incidence of cycles where no eggs are released has decreased to about 20 per cent.

What happens in ovulation Near the ovaries, projecting from the top of the uterus on either side, are two Fallopian tubes (named after the Italian anatomist who first described them, Gabriello Fallopio). These are about 10cm (4in) long and end in finger-like projections, known as fimbriae, near the ovary. These projections wave back and forward to attract the egg released at ovulation into the opening of the Fallopian tube. Once inside, muscular contractions and the waving of small hair-like structures called cilia that beat toward the uterus, help transport the egg along to the narrower part of the tube, the isthmus. Where its transport is held up by about 30 hours. If fertilization occurs, it usually takes place here.

The adaptable uterus The womb, or uterus, is a hollow muscular organ that sits in the lower

"We replicate because our cells replicate. They replicate because their molecules replicate. Everything about us seems to want to replicate. All the time…. That's why we love life, love children, and love sex."

part of your abdomen. It is about 7cm (3in) long and 5cm (2in) wide across its upper part, which is known as the fundus. The lower part is called the neck, or cervix, and this projects down into the stretchy muscular vagina. Roughly every 28 days the uterus prepares to receive a fertilized egg as the lining, known as the endometrium, thickens to form the site for implantation of the egg.

If fertilization doesn't take place, the thickened lining of the uterus is shed and the whole process starts all over again. If the uterus receives a fertilized egg, it then shelters and nourishes it for nine months (40 weeks) before the involuntary muscular contractions of labour open up the cervix and the baby is ready to be born.

During pregnancy, the uterus increases in weight from around 50g (1³/₄oz) to 1kg (just over 2lb), stretching and growing in thickness and length to accommodate your growing baby. It then shrinks back to its original size by six weeks after the birth.

All girl babies *are born with eggs ready and waiting in their bodies. From puberty, hormones start to prepare a girl for motherhood. Approximately ten months after a girl's first period, ovulation occurs, but more than half of these early cycles do not release an egg.*

THE PROTECTIVE PELVIS

A woman's reproductive organs are held safely within the protective circle of the bony pelvis. The pelvis (the word means basin in Latin) is a bowl-like structure . You can feel the bones that form it. The ilia or hip bones at the sides are what you feel when you put your hands on your hips. The sacrum is the triangular section that ends in the coccyx, or tail bone, at the back. The ischia, or sitting bones, are at the base. You can feel these if you put your hands under your bottom when you are sitting. The ischia sweep up from either side, in a shallow curve in a woman, to form the pubis at the front.

During birth, your baby has to negotiate a tunnel that bends back toward your tail bone and then turns forward under your pubic arch. Being in an upright position or on all-fours during labour gives your lower spine and sacrum the freedom to move, allowing your baby room to descend.

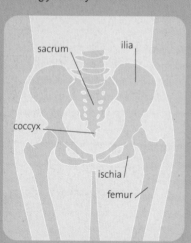

Your pelvis is the heaviest *part of your bone structure. The strong, protective circle holds a woman's reproductive organs safely.*

How hormones prepare the body for pregnancy

Every day, from puberty onward, a few follicles on the ovary restart their development, taking about three months to get to the stage where they are mature enough to respond to follicle-stimulating hormone (FSH) – the hormone that is released early in a woman's menstrual cycle.

About 15 to 20 follicles will increase in size and develop protein stores, ready for fertilization, as well as a transparent jelly coating that plays an important role in helping sperm to bind and penetrate. The egg-holding follicles also produce the hormone "oestrogen" in increasing amounts, the more mature follicles producing the most.

By around eight to 16 days into your menstrual cycle, one dominant follicle will form a 2cm (1in) bump on the surface of the ovary and the other follicles will wither away. A surge of a luteinizing hormone will help this follicle to mature and around 36 hours later it ruptures, releasing its egg, which starts its journey to the uterus. Having taken years to reach maturation, each egg is then only viable for fertilization for about a day.

Back at the ovary, after the follicle collapses it fills in to form the corpus luteum, or "yellow body", which produces another hormone, progesterone. Meanwhile, oestrogen has also changed the composition of the cervical mucus – which now becomes copious, clear, and receptive to sperm penetration – and in addition has prepared the uterus to receive a fertilized egg. Oestrogen has also stimulated the glands in the lining of the uterus to encourage arteries and veins to grow. The lining thickens ten-fold in a few days. Progesterone finishes the job of blood-vessel growth and stimulates the glands to produce nutrients ready for the nourishment of the fertilized egg before it implants.

All this is to no avail if fertilization doesn't take place. The corpus luteum shrinks back, levels of progesterone fall, the uterus lining sinks lower, the glands regress, and the spiral arteries and veins are coiled tighter and compressed, cutting off their blood supply. Eventually the superficial layers of the lining of the uterus are shed in your "menstrual period".

The second phase of this cycle, from ovulation to menstruation, lasts about 14 days. This can be a helpful predictor of ovulation if your periods are regular.

Physical development in boys

There is no difference between male and female development during the first six weeks of life in the uterus. If the Y chromosome is present, however, the "unisex" genital of the embryo will develop into a testis at about six weeks. In a female embryo, no development occurs at this time – instead the enlargement happens at about 12 weeks when the outer part of the genital develops into an ovary.

In a boy baby, testosterone is produced by the testes and this hormone remains in your baby's bloodstream to complete the development of his male genitals. After birth, a boy baby still has high levels of testosterone in his body for a while and it is believed that this has the effect of delaying

During the first six weeks of life in the uterus, there is no difference between male and female development. The testes of a male baby start to develop at six weeks, producing testosterone, which completes the development of his male genitals.

SPERM DEVELOPMENT AND EJACULATION

The ability to produce sperm is something a boy can do from puberty and it then continues throughout his adult life. Although the amount, and the quality, of sperm diminishes from middle age, men in their 80s, and even 90s, have fathered children. At times of sexual activity, men produce more sperm. In fact, every second, a man can make on average, 1,000 sperm, but the quantity will go down with very frequent ejaculations.

Over a lifetime, a man may produce as many as 12 trillion sperm. Each sperm is about $^1/_{25}$ of a millimetre long, the "tail" being ten to 15 times longer than the "head".

Having been released into the vagina at ejaculation, semen initially coagulates, which helps the sperm stay put and buffers them against the acidic environment in the woman's vagina. The alkaline seminal fluid also nourishes the sperm, as does the watery cervical mucus produced by the woman at ovulation. This means sperm remain able to fertilize an egg for up to five days.

male brain development both before and after birth; the knock-on effect also means that puberty occurs later in boys than in girls.

Sexual development for boys begins and ends, on average, two years later than puberty for girls. At some time between the ages of 11 and 13, levels of the hormone testosterone increase in a boy's body, resulting in a growth spurt that stretches his arms and legs. The penis and testes start to grow from around the ages of 11 to 13 and a boy is able to ejaculate semen about a year after this happens, although at first the ejaculate contains no sperm. At age 14, testosterone levels are at their peak, which is on average when the larynx enlarges and a boy's voice "breaks".

The sperm is one of the smallest human cells. Shaped like a long-tailed tadpole, its 23 chromosomes, including the X or Y chromosome that will determine the sex of the new baby, are carried in its "head". The head of the sperm also contains digestive enzymes that will help the sperm burrow into the egg. Unlike the female egg, which is passively washed along the Fallopian tube, sperm can move actively, propelled by their "tails".

From conception to birth

During the nine months of pregnancy, a baby develops from one single cell – formed from the fused nuclei of one sperm and one ovum – into your moving, breathing, sleeping, waking, crying, feeling, recognizable offspring.

THE BABY'S LIFE-SUPPORT SYSTEM

The early embryo is contained in an outer sac called the chorion, which sends out tiny branches that grow into the thickened, blood-filled lining of the uterus. These grow and branch throughout early pregnancy and develop into the placenta. Inside the branches are small, thin-walled blood vessels through which substances are transferred, for example, nutrients and oxygen from the mother, and waste products from the baby. The development of this placenta is vital for the survival of the baby. By the end of pregnancy (described as "term") the placenta is about 18–20cm (7–8in) thick. The umbilical cord links the baby to the placenta and contains blood vessels. This gets longer as pregnancy progresses and becomes your unborn baby's first "toy". By the end, it's normally 50–60cm (18–24in) long.

Loosely joined to the chorion is the inner "amnion". This is a sac that produces fluid to cushion the baby, allow easy movement, keep body temperature constant, and provide protection from many bacteria. However, some bacteria and viruses are able to cross the placenta, as are drugs, carbon monoxide from smoking, and other harmful substances.

Fertilization and conception

When a man and woman make love and a man ejaculates, between 40 and 500 million sperm are released. However, most sperm never even enter the woman's uterus, and only a hundred or so reach the Fallopian tubes within a few hours of sex. The sperm are chemically attracted to the egg and they progress through the uterus stimulated by a substance that makes their tail movements whiplash-like so they can "swim" upstream into the Fallopian tube. Once there, sperm bore into the egg. The first one to penetrate the outer layer fuses with the egg membrane beneath. Immediately, changes in the membrane prevent other sperm entering the egg. This is fertilization and the process of an egg and sperm uniting is known as conception.

From single cell to full-term baby Fertilization takes 18 to 24 hours, and the first cell of a unique human is called a "zygote". The joined sperm and egg contain all the genes responsible for passing on various characteristics from the parents. The zygote begins to divide and takes four to six days to travel down the Fallopian tube to the uterus. At first, cells divide around every 15 hours, but that rate of cell division slows down. At birth a baby has around 60 billion cells that have divided around 40 times.

During the first three weeks of development the cells separate into the layers from which all future organs and tissues develop. From weeks four to eight the embryo starts to look like a tiny human being. After week eight it is now called a fetus. Week nine to birth is mostly a time of growth, development, and refinement.

As many of us are not aware of exactly when conception took place (although you might have a good idea) pregnancy is officially dated from the first day of your last period (called your LMP date), and it's assumed that conception takes place at the end of the second week. This puts the average length of pregnancy at 280 days (40 weeks), at which stage the baby is actually 266 days (38 weeks) old.

"When I discovered myself once again in the pickles aisle, selecting the largest jar of pickled onions, I just knew I was pregnant again [for the third time]"

YOUR PREGNANCY WEEK BY WEEK: FIRST TRIMESTER

Weeks 1–2 The thickened lining of your uterus is shed as a fertilized egg has not implanted, and menstruation occurs. The uterus then prepares to receive a fertilized egg and the endometrium (the lining of the uterus) starts to thicken all over again. At ovulation, a new egg is released from the ovary and starts on its journey to the uterus.

Weeks 3–4 Egg and sperm have met in a Fallopian tube and fertilized. The resulting single-celled zygote begins journeying to the uterus. By the time it reaches the uterus, a blastocyst, or hollow ball of cells that contains an inner cell mass, has been formed. The blastocyst, about 0.1mm across, implants in the lining of the uterus, usually at the upper end. Cell division in the blastocyst is frequent. By week four, the beginnings of the umbilical cord appear, and the placenta starts to form.

Week 5 Three layers begin to form: the ectoderm, mesoderm, and endoderm, which will give rise to all the tissues and organs of the body. (For example, the nervous system comes from the ectoderm.) The digestive tract, brain, heart, and nervous system begin developing and the beating heart is the embryo's first movement.

Week 6 At around 27 days old, the embryo is a shrimp-shaped little being, a bit less than .6cm (^{1}/4in) long and visible for the first time to the naked eye. It has a definitive head and tail. The arms buds are beginning to form, followed by leg buds.

Week 7 There is rapid brain development and head enlargement. In a five-week embryo, a more mature and rhythmic heartbeat replaces the earlier form. Facial prominences appear and eyelids have begun to form a protective layer over the eyes. The embryo has elbows and finger areas. Ridges indicate the position of the primitive kidneys.

Week 8 The tiny skeleton has been fully formed, at this stage not of bone but of cartilage. The head is proportionally large, the joints of the arms appear, and the beginnings of fingers are evident. All five distinct toes are in place, although there is webbing between them, and the legs have developed knees. The external ear is formed.

Week 9 The embryo has the foundations for all the organs needed as an adult. The fingers are partially separated and the liver is prominent. He can now make very simple movements of a single arm or leg joint, or wrist, elbow, or knee. If the baby's hand or foot touches something, the fingers or toes will curl.

Weeks 10–12 The embryo is now a fetus. Fingers have separated and the beginnings of toes are visible. A little arm and leg movement occurs, and bones form in the legs. The sex is not identifiable, although genitalia are visible. At around 11–12 weeks the fetus will start yawning.

TWINS

One in 70 births in the UK results in twins. Around two-thirds of these are non identical (dizygotic), and the rest are identical (monozygotic).

Non-identical twins result from multiple ovulation and two fertilized eggs implanting in the uterus, while identical twins come from one fertilized egg, which either splits within hours, at the two-cell stage (see opposite) or, most commonly, at a later stage.

Non-identical twins have separate chorions, amnions, and placentas, as have identical twins who have split at the two-cell stage. Twins that result from splitting at the later stage share chorions and placentas and either have their own private amniotic sac or they share everything.

At the end of the first trimester, your baby has the beginnings of all its organs and limbs. Your bump though will still be hardly noticeable.

YOUR PREGNANCY WEEK BY WEEK: SECOND TRIMESTER

Weeks 13–14 The fetus now looks like a tiny baby and growth accelerates. His head is still much larger than his body, it's about one–third of his length. By now he will be able to open his mouth in response to touch, suck his fingers, and starts developing the muscles he'll use for swallowing.

Weeks 15–18 There is rapid growth and there are co-ordinated limb movements, although you won't feel them yet. In girl babies, the ovaries have appeared. The baby's sex can be identified on a scan and the eyes and ears are closer to their normal positions. Eye movements will begin between 16 and 18 weeks of pregnancy and the baby will start to make sound vibrations in the uterus.

Weeks 19–20 You may begin to feel your baby kick or roll over because your growing uterus has now reached your abdominal wall. The baby can step, and hold himself erect. From week 20 onward there will be slight differences in the baby's activity between morning and night, with the busiest being toward midnight. The baby's skin is now covered in protective waxy "vernix", which is held in position by downy hair. This prevents the skin becoming waterlogged. Brown fat, a special fat that is easily processed by the body to produce energy, is laid down now.

Weeks 21–26 The baby's hearing has developed well enough to be able to recognize your voice. Teeth buds have now formed under the gums, and hair is starting to appear on his head. The baby's lungs are beginning to mature. The baby can grasp and, in fact, babies are often seen on ultrasound scans holding their umbilical cord. He is also starting to put on weight now, though is still quite skinny. After 24 weeks, the baby is sufficiently well developed to have a good chance of survival if he was born now, provided he received expert specialist care.

Your growing bump *will be very obvious now. Your size will depend on your build. You will feel your baby's movements and may even get rib pain as your ribs spread outward.*

YOUR PREGNANCY WEEK BY WEEK: THIRD TRIMESTER

Weeks 27–29 The baby's nostrils have opened, the lungs are capable of breathing, and the central nervous system can control breathing. The eyes are open and toenails are visible. The baby is able to blink and does so in response to external sound. He often moves the eyes as if looking for something to see. White fat is deposited and wrinkles in the skin smooth out. The muscles are becoming well developed and you will probably feel kicks and punches as he tries them out.

Weeks 30–34 Babies are perfectly formed at this stage and by week 32 their heads are fully in proportion with their bodies. Your baby now has delicate eyebrows and eyelashes, his eyes are now open, and the pupils react to light. The skin is smooth and the arms and legs are chubby. Your baby is starting to develop an immune system to fight off germs as the placenta has been taking up antibodies from your bloodstream. Babies will borrow their mothers' immunity to a whole range of diseases until they can develop their own immunity; this process is boosted after his birth by your colostrum and breast-milk. Sleep and waking become more differentiated, and when awake your baby opens his eyes, is alert, and kicks.

Weeks 35–37 Your baby has a firm grasp and his fingernails cover the nailbeds – babies can sometimes scratch themselves in the uterus. He turns his head towards light and the circumference of his head and abdomen are about equal. The skin appears bluish-pink.

Weeks 38–39 The baby is well rounded, with good skin tone. There is now very little room for manoeuvre in the uterus and you may feel your baby's feet pressed hard up against your diaphragm under your ribs and odd energetic kicks may take your breath away.

Weeks 40–42 By 40 weeks or "at term", your baby has grown to seven times taller than he was at 12 weeks and is nearly 200 times heavier. Close to term, a baby makes vigorous squirming movements as he tries to stretch his arms and legs as well as his spine. The average full-term baby is about 55cm (21in) long and weighs 3,300g ($7^{1}/4$lb). Nobody quite knows what starts the process of birth known as labour. One theory is that hormonal "messages" go between you and the baby until a biochemical switch is triggered.

How labour and birth work

Women give birth instinctively – before labour starts, you cannot know how you will react. As you go into labour it's important to be be open-minded and prepared to trust your body to go with an involuntary process that is both hard work and painful. But it is pain with a purpose, not the pain of injury, and if you understand the process of birth, the pain becomes meaningful.

What happens?

Every woman is different and every labour is unique. You will never experience the same labour twice, no matter how many children you bear. When friends tell you their stories, you read birth accounts, or watch videos, bear in mind that your birth experience is not likely to be the same. Remember, however, that your body is designed to do the work of labour and you will have the love and support of a friend or partner and your midwives as companions on your journey.

Labour is divided into three stages just to help midwives make judgements about its progress, but the lengths of individual stages and labours vary widely. There are, however, some landmarks that will happen to all women in a certain order. During the first stage, the cervix (exit) at the neck of the uterus must soften and begin to open (dilate), getting wider until it is wide enough for the baby to leave the uterus (10cm/4in). In the second stage, your baby will travel down the birth canal (vagina) to be born. The third stage occurs when the afterbirth (placenta) is expelled. The stages are sometimes further divided into:

First stage
- Pre-labour (or the "latent" phase)
- Early labour (until the cervix is 3–4cm/1¼–1½in dilated)
- Active or strong labour (4–10cm/1½–4in)

Transition
- Preparing to push

Second stage
- Pushing
- Birth

Third stage
- Delivery of the placenta.

The first stage of labour

Often the first sign of labour starting will be regular tightenings or contractions. These can feel like period pains (anything from mild to quite severe), like backache or twinges and aches inside your uterus, bottom, and hips. How can you tell early labour from the "practice" Braxton Hicks

THE UTERUS DURING LABOUR

In order to squeeze the baby out, the uterus has three layers of elastic, spiralling muscles. During labour, contractions begin at the top of the uterus, which has the highest density of muscle fibres, and travel in a wave downward and inward, toward the cervix, becoming less strong. The muscle fibres of the upper uterus do not return completely to their full length between contractions and gradually get shorter and thicker with each contraction. Thus, the less active lower uterus is pulled up toward the shortening upper part.

Sitting on a birth ball *makes it easier to rock your pelvis as you breathe through a contraction, and holding onto something (wall bars, chair back, partner) means you can lean forward to find the most comfortable position.*

contractions you may have had over the past weeks? The answer is the "real" contractions become gradually stronger, longer, and closer together as time passes. They tend to build to a peak of intensity and then die away. You may have anything from about five to 30 minutes between them.

Alternatively, you may have a "show". In pre-labour, the neck of the uterus starts to soften and thin out under your baby's head and the plug of mucus that has sealed the uterus during pregnancy can come away, bringing with it a little blood. You may notice a pinkish discharge.

Finally, you'll know you are in labour if your waters break (that's the bag of amniotic fluid surrounding your baby). There may be a distinct "pop", then a gush of warm fluid, or you may just notice a gentle trickle.

All these are signs that the cervix (the neck of the uterus) is beginning to dilate. This dilatation can take a short time, or hours – every birth is unique. The dilatation continues until, finally, the cervix is almost fully open. By this time your contractions may be less than a minute apart, or they could also be five minutes apart all the way through. You could have a long contraction followed by a short one. Contractions are involuntary, but distractions can cause them to slow down.

Transition stage

This is the bridge between the first and second stage of labour. It can last a matter of seconds or minutes, or, occasionally, hours. In some cases, the stages simply blend together. Sometimes at this point, there is also a lull in contractions – known as the "rest and be thankful" stage – just before you feel the urge to push.

The second stage of labour

This is the "pushing" phase, and it can last anything from a few minutes to a couple of hours (or longer). It begins when the baby's head moves out of the uterus into the birth canal. As the baby's head starts to stretch your pelvic floor, you will find the urge to push irresistible. As you breathe in before pushing, your diaphragm is lowered and your abdominal muscles contract, assisting the contractions. During a contraction the baby's head advances forward, and between contractions it slips back slightly.

Some women find the second stage of labour less painful than the first. At this point, dilatation of the cervix is complete and progress is faster.

> "I really felt in tune with my body and that I was doing the right stuff. I used the gas for a couple more contractions, then Maria said she could see the head and asked if I wanted to touch it, which I did."

Getting into the right position helps greatly. If you are lying on your back, you will have to push your baby through the L-shaped bend of the birth canal, against gravity. If you're upright, on all-fours, or lying on your left-hand side if tired, you will find pushing easier.

During the second stage, as your baby's head passes through your pelvis the pressure on certain nerves sometimes causes cramp or shooting pains down your legs. As your baby's descent continues, his head, which has been tucked with his chin toward his chest, turns further and his neck extends so that the back of his neck turns under your pubic bone in front. This may take some time and the turning is usually complete before the back of his head shows at your vaginal opening – which is called "crowning".

Stretching of the vulva is now at its maximum. When you feel a burning pain, or numbness, around your vagina, try to stop pushing and pant to help ease the head out. With further contractions the baby's head will come out and his body will turn again so that the head is in line with the shoulders: first one shoulder, then the other is born.

Some mothers want to hold their new baby immediately and put him to the breast, but don't worry if you feel too tired or disorientated to do so.

Your newborn baby's most developed sense is touch. His ears are still full of amniotic fluid to protect him from the loud noises outside your uterus, but he will still be able to hear and recognize your voice.

The third stage of labour

This is the stage when your placenta is delivered and it usually happens within an hour or so of the birth of your baby. After the birth, the elastic-walled uterus contracts and, as it does so, the shortening muscle fibres tighten around the mother's blood vessels, literally binding them off. The placenta is not elastic and it is sloughed off the "wrinkling" wall of the uterus. Fibrinogen, a protein that helps with blood clotting, is then deposited in a mesh over the site of the placenta. Meanwhile, your baby begins to breathe independently and after anything up to about ten minutes, the umbilical cord will stop pulsating. (The placenta and cord continue functioning until breathing is fully established, to guarantee the baby a supply of oxygen.)

This stage of labour can be "natural" or "managed". With a natural third stage, the baby's umbilical cord is not cut. You put your baby to the breast and encourage him to suckle. This stimulates your body to produce more oxytocin, which makes your uterus contract and push the placenta out.

When the third stage is managed, you will be given an injection of syntometrine (synthetic, or artificial, oxytocin) as your baby's shoulders are being born. As soon as your baby is born, the cord is clamped in two places and cut in between so that he is no longer attached to you. The syntometrine makes your uterus contract strongly to expel the placenta.

Giving birth in your own home

"I saw that there was no reason why I shouldn't give birth at home – it seemed a positively sensible choice."

A first-time mother's birth story

"My midwife and I agreed on the local maternity unit for my first birth. After my antenatal class, I looked around the unit. It was lovely, but the thought of having to get into a car and travel to hospital when I would be in pain was terrible. At the next class I said I could see why people chose home birth. The teacher asked if I was considering it and gave me a couple of books to read. I saw that there was no reason why I shouldn't give birth at home – it seemed a positively sensible choice. I discussed it with Steve and our only misgiving was that if I gave birth in hospital I would have more recuperation time. However my husband is eminently capable and in fact, I wouldn't want anyone else looking after me. That left me with just two fears: the neighbours and the upholstery!

On the day

Four days before my due date my waters broke. The midwife Annie came out and checked I was OK and then left. She hardly got home before the contractions started. I expected to be baking cakes in between contractions; so going straight into active labour was a surprise. I had a bath and Steve made the bed with some plastic and a charity shop sheet!

We called Annie and I knelt against the bed swaying my hips during contractions. The midwife arrived and laughed when I asked if I was in second stage – and when I said that I was going to hospital to get some drugs. I remember being annoyed that the baby's heartbeat was calm, because if it hadn't been, I would have got a lift straight to some painkillers! As I became tired, the midwives, Annie and Rosie, encouraged me on to the bed to rest. After a while I got back on to my knees leaning on the headboard. I soon needed to push but resisted it – it was going to hurt! I lay on my side, with one leg on Rosie's shoulder.

Alegria was delivered onto my breast, and Steve cut the cord. She latched on almost immediately, and my happiness was complete. The midwives made Steve find the camera, and took a couple of shots for me to remember that moment by. Annie and Rosie cleared up and left. They were great and I was lucky to have them. Steve rang our relatives and I had a bath with Alegria.

The days afterwards were easy. On the first day we had a lot of visitors but after that, one a day. The doctor arrived and found me, breast-feeding. 'So, you had her at home?' was his surprised comment.

I tell everyone what a good idea home birth is. The reaction is 'how brave!' but for me, brave is getting into a taxi in labour – not brave – mad. As for my fears, my neighbour asked if we'd had the baby because all she could hear was laughter, and there isn't a spot on the upholstery!"

The same story from the father's viewpoint

"After some investigation, and then chatting to our antenatal teacher and community midwife, it was clear that there were some definite advantages to having a baby at home. Instead of running the risk of hitting a birth rush- hour and having to share your midwife with others, we would get not one but two midwives all to ourselves.

My biggest concern was the recuperation period. In our hospital you get that nice three-day cooling-off period of being a parent. A little bit of time to ease yourself into it. Midwives helping you out with feeds and nappy-changing, and most importantly uninterrupted sleep for the father at home. It was clear that this was not going to happen with a home birth, and that the midwives would be out of there as soon as possible, leaving you to cope on your own. They were however very clear about the fact that they would be taking away all of the 'waste'.

It would take too long to recount all the happenings of that night. Needless to say like all men wherever it happens I had that feeling of helplessness. Wanting to help out and share the pain but just not being able to. At one point we were both kneeling, leaning against the bed, Kathryn was recovering from a contraction and I was rubbing her back. Suddenly she looked down at the floor and cried out 'Where did you get that pillow?' In the heat of the moment I had not realized that she had been kneeling on the hard floor for an hour whereas I had whipped a pillow off the bed. Well, that can really hurt your knees, can't it?

After about seven hours of heroic effort the time was nearly upon us. Now was my moment and I was sent to get the towels. In hindsight, I did panic a bit and instead of bringing the old, ordained towels I picked up the best, fluffiest towel in the house. On my return Kathryn was in the throes of another contraction, this time not tempered by the Entonox. 'Not that one!' she screamed through clenched teeth, and I could see in her eyes that she was already regretting allowing her DNA to get involved with something from my shallow end of the gene pool.

And then there were three

But it all went well in the end. Baby born, photos taken, midwives removed all the waste, and it was time to say our goodbyes. This was the bit I was dreading. Just the three of us in the house. No support, no one to take over, no one to give advice. And do you know what? That was the best part. We all snuggled up on the bed together (the sheets had been changed) and we just revelled in the fact that we were a family.

And there was a definite feeling that if we can do this with little outside assistance then it was always going to be so, and what's more it was all going to be all right."

A man's experience of home birth

"We all snuggled up on the bed together and just revelled in the fact that we were a family."

2

Choices for your care

Planning your care

Choosing where your baby will be born, and who is going to care for you during pregnancy and birth, are important decisions that you will have to make now.

For most women, the first health professional they see when they become pregnant is still their family doctor or general practitioner (GP), but women can go directly to a midwife. While some doctors are very knowledgeable about local maternity services, others are not aware of all the choices you have now.

The choices you do have will depend on your local area, but at the very least you should be able to choose between a consultant unit at your nearest hospital and a home birth. Some areas may have several hospitals with maternity units, some with a midwife-led unit alongside, or there may be a separate midwife-led birth centre. Most maternity provision in your area will be run by the National Health Service (NHS), but

your birth year

tell your GP or local midwife that you are pregnant

around weeks 8–10, first booking appointment with your midwife

at 18–20 weeks you will be offered detailed anomaly scan

FIRST TRIMESTER

SECOND TRIMESTER

| 1 | 2 | 3 | 4 | 6 | 7 | 8 | 9 | 10 | 11 | 12 | 13 | 14 | 15 | 16 | 17 | 18 | 19 | 20 | 21 | 22 | 23 | 24 | 25 | 26 |

conception takes place

look at website www.birthchoiceuk.com to find out about local maternity services

at 8–14 weeks routine early dating scan may be offered

if you're planning a home water birth, research where to hire your birth pool in many regions, you will also be able to hire the services of an independent, or private, midwife. Some maternity hospitals also provide private care. For information on your local options look at www.birthchoiceuk.com. If you want a private midwife, look at www.independentmidwives.org.uk.

At the beginning of your pregnancy, the maternity care system can seem like a maze. Some simple facts can help you through:

- Pregnancy and birth are normal natural processes. For a healthy woman with a healthy baby, medical assistance is not usually necessary.
- Continuity of care throughout your pregnancy and birth, together with continuous support during labour, have been shown to reduce reliance on medical pain relief and other interventions (1).
- Midwives are trained to care for women during labour and birth and typically will attend a woman in labour. Unless there are complications, no other health professional need be present.

- If you wish, you can arrange your midwifery care directly with your local midwives, rather than through your GP. Do this by contacting the Supervisor of Midwives at your local hospital.

Many great advances have been made in obstetrics to deal with complications in pregnancy and emergencies. However, most women with the right support and environment can give birth without the need for medical assistance (2).

antenatal classes start around week 28	antenatal checks weekly from now	Keep important phone numbers handy and make sure you know how to contact your midwife or maternity unit

THIRD TRIMESTER   **BIRTH AND FIRST 3 MONTHS**

27	28	29	30	31	32	33	34	35	36	37	38	39	40	41	42	43	44	45	46	47	48	49	50	51	52

ask for a tour of the unit if you're planning a hospital or birth centre birth	prepare for a home birth or pack your bags for labour in hospital	accept offers of help with your newborn

The role of your midwife

The word "midwife" means "with woman". Midwives are specialists in normal pregnancy and birth, and are qualified to look after a pregnant woman and her baby throughout the antenatal period, during labour and birth, and for up to 28 days after the baby has been born.

If you book a home birth, *your midwife may be able to visit you at home during pregnancy for your antenatal appointment.*

What does a midwife do?

You can go directly to a midwife for antenatal care. If you don't know how to contact your midwife, ask your health centre, or write to the Supervisor of Midwives at the local hospital. You do not need to see an obstetrician (a doctor who specializes in childbirth) while you are pregnant or giving birth. As long as everything is normal, a midwife can provide all your care. If complications arise, a midwife will refer you to a doctor who is trained to deal with special situations. Within the NHS there are hospital and community midwives. There are also private midwives who work independently of the NHS though there may be regulatory changes affecting how independent midwives practice in 2008.

Hospital midwives These are midwives who are based in a hospital obstetric, or consultant, unit, and they staff the antenatal clinic, labour ward, and postnatal wards.

Community midwives These midwives often work in teams and provide a degree of continuity of care. They see you antenatally either at home or at a clinic. When you go into labour they are available for a home birth, or they may come into the labour ward in the hospital to be with you. Once your baby is born, they'll visit you at home for about ten to 28 days after birth. Community midwives also provide postnatal care for women who have been looked after during labour by hospital midwives.

Your relationship with a midwife

It is important that you and your midwife have a good relationship. You need to work together and she needs to support you in all your choices. In order to help you give birth, your midwife needs to be respectful, responsive, unintrusive, and accepting. This will help to make you feel safe and enable you to relax, which in turn allows the labour hormones to work.

Childbirth may be the most powerful life experience you undergo. With a midwife's full support you can tap into enormous reserves of strength during the birth process and learn that you are capable of so much more than you realized – a valuable discovery as you become a mother.

What training has my midwife had?

Some midwives have trained as nurses before becoming midwives, but it's now possible to qualify as a midwife without qualifying as a nurse first. Student midwives are based at university, and are studying for either a diploma or a degree in midwifery. The course contains a mixture of theory and practice. Courses vary across the country, but are designed to prepare a student for the responsibilities of being a midwife.

Once qualified, a midwife must be able to care for women throughout pregnancy, birth, and during the postnatal period too, as well as care for newborn babies. She must be able to detect problems and summon medical help if needed, and be trained in emergency procedures herself. She also has a role in health education and preparation for parenthood, such as teaching antenatal classes.

Midwives also have to stay up to date in order to keep their registration, which is reviewed every three years. This includes having to work a minimum number of hours as a midwife and attend study events.

Your care in pregnancy

You will see a midwife regularly throughout your pregnancy and she will let you know how to contact her, if you need to. Your first visit will be at around eight to ten weeks of pregnancy. This is known as your "pregnancy welcome visit" or, more often, your "booking appointment". Your midwife will spend quite a long time finding out all about you and your pregnancy. She will ask you questions about your medical history, any previous pregnancies and also about your current pregnancy (see box, right). If she is a midwife you will be seeing regularly, this is an opportunity for you to get to know each other and for her to find out about your hopes for the pregnancy and birth. She will answer all your questions and should also be able to help you with any concerns.

Your midwife can also advise on diet, exercise, and dealing with minor discomforts of pregnancy. She will outline what your options are for antenatal tests and screening and explain the purpose of each test. You will be provided with information about the various tests which you can take away and consider, so that you and your partner can decide whether you wish to have any of them.

At every antenatal appointment your midwife will, with your consent, routinely take your blood pressure, test your urine for glucose and protein (see box), and feel your abdomen to see how your baby is growing. She will write everything down in your maternity notes. You'll be given a copy of your own maternity notes to look at, keep, and to bring to appointments.

When the baby has grown enough, your midwife may listen to the baby's heart rate with a hand-held device that uses ultrasound waves (if you are happy to have ultrasound). Later in pregnancy the baby's heart rate may be heard using a Pinard stethoscope. Once your baby is big enough for you to feel movements, your midwife will ask if the baby is active. Toward the end of pregnancy it will become more important for your midwife to

FIRST MIDWIFE VISIT

Your midwife will ask you about your current state of health; lifestyle habits (whether you smoke or drink), and your and your partner's medical history. She will ask about previous pregnancies and the date of your last period.

She will check your blood pressure and take your height and weight. If you are ten weeks pregnant or more, and there's a query about dates, the midwife may palpate (feel) your tummy to see if she can feel the fundus (top of the uterus). This gives an indication of gestation. An internal vaginal examination is not usually necessary.

Urine: You will be asked to give a urine sample. This is tested to see whether you have any sugar or protein in your urine and for signs of any infection.

Blood tests: Different areas have different policies. In general, several "bloods" are taken to:
- identify your blood group
- check your rhesus factor
- rule out anaemia
- check your immunity to rubella (German measles)
- make sure you're not producing any unusual antibodies
- screen for syphilis and hepatitis
- measure your blood glucose level.

You will be offered HIV testing with counselling and certain genetic disorders, such as sickle-cell anaemia and thalassaemia, may also be checked. Some places screen automatically for neural tube defects too.

Ultrasound scans: A routine ultrasound scan is offered at eight to 14 weeks to accurately date the age of your unborn baby, and his expected due date, and to check whether you are expecting more than one baby.

establish which way the baby is lying in your uterus. At certain points further blood tests will be done with your consent (see box page 42). These checks form the basis of every antenatal appointment a woman will have and they become more frequent as pregnancy progresses.

Your care during labour

If you have booked a home birth, your midwife will come to assess you at home when you go into labour. If you are having a hospital birth, some community midwives do home assessments before you go into hospital, but often you will have to make your own way to hospital at some point during your labour, before you get seen by a midwife.

During labour, your midwife's job is to support and help you. She is also there to support any birth partners you have. Her role includes helping you to give birth in the way that you would like, and to monitor your health and

> "My midwife held my hand, encouraged me to blow and not push, and breathed with me. She knew just what kind of support I needed."

MAKING SENSE OF YOUR MEDICAL NOTES

Your baby's position (or presentation and lie)	Recorded as Ceph or C or Vx (cephalic, vertex, or head down); Br (breech or bottom down); Long (longitudinal or vertical); Tr (transverse, or across your body); Obl (oblique or diagonally). OA = Occiput Anterior (head down, facing your back); OP = Occiput Posterior (head down, facing your front); OL = Occiput Lateral (head down, facing your side). L or R written in front of these indicates which side of your body your baby is lying on. OA is the most favourable position for your baby to be in.
How much of your baby's head is in your pelvis	NE, NEng, Not Eng (not engaged) or "free" means that baby's head is above your pelvis. 1/5, 2/5, 3/5, 4/5 refer either to how much of the head can be felt above your pelvis or to how much of it is in your pelvis (ask your midwife which). Your baby is engaged once 3/5 of the head is in your pelvis. E or Eng = Engaged.
Your baby's movements	FMF = Fetal Movements Felt; F = Felt FMNF = Fetal Movements Not Felt; NF = Not Felt
Your baby's heartbeat	FHH = Fetal Heart Heard; H = Heard FHNH = Fetal Heart Not Heard; NH = Not Heard
Urine test results	Prot or Alb (protein or albumin) and glucose are what are tested for. NAD means Nothing Abnormal Detected; Nil means none found (normal); Tr (trace) means that a small amount of protein or glucose has been found; +, ++, +++ indicate that greater amounts have been found.
Your blood pressure	The average blood pressure for adult women is 110/70. Blood pressure above 130/90 is considered high but if the blood pressure was particularly low at the beginning of the pregnancy, lower levels may be considered to be excessive later on.
Swelling (or oedema)	Oed. Amount recorded as +, ++, +++

that of the baby. She can help you to get into positions that are comfortable and will help labour progress, and she can suggest ways of coping with contractions. If your midwife feels concerned at any point that things are not progressing normally, she will liaise with medical staff.

If you are being looked after by a team of community midwives, you may already know the midwife who is with you during labour. To be cared for during birth by a midwife you have got to know beforehand is helpful. If your labour is long, you may experience a change of shifts; your midwife will go off duty and be replaced by one who is just starting her shift.

Immediately after your baby has been born, your midwife will help you, and your partner, if present, to get comfortable and feed the baby.

Your care after the birth

In the days and weeks following the birth, you will be visited at home by a midwife who will examine you and the baby to make sure that you are both adjusting well. In some areas, the midwife may stop visiting once your baby is ten days old, but in other areas she may carry on visiting for up to 28 days after the birth. She will ensure that the baby is feeding well and beginning to gain weight, and that you are recovering well from the birth.

How can I get continuity of care?

Research shows that to receive care from the same person throughout pregnancy, labour, and the postnatal period provides a better birth experience for a woman, than if she is looked after by lots of different people (1). One way of getting continuity is to book a home birth. Some women book one even if they are not sure that is what they want, and they make their final decision later on during their pregnancy or even in labour. You are also more likely to receive continuity of care if you give birth at a birth centre.

If you are planning to give birth in a hospital unit, it's not always as easy to get to know your midwives. If you arrange to have "shared care" with your GP and the hospital, the majority of your appointments will be at your GP's surgery. While this can be very convenient, your GP will not attend the birth and it means you are unlikely to know the midwives at the hospital when you go in to give birth.

Some hospitals operate a team-midwifery system, usually run by community midwives. If you have only one local hospital, you can ask whether it is possible to have midwifery-led care, and to be looked after by a small team of midwives. If you have several maternity units to choose from in your area, you may need to ask several of them. Some hospitals have teams that operate only in certain areas, which may limit your choice. If you are in any doubt, phone up your local community midwives and discuss it with them.

> "She was superb throughout: minimal fuss, minimal monitoring and maximum care. She helped me birth Adam slowly enough so I didn't tear and all credit goes to her because he was a 9lb baby!"

Choosing an independent midwife

Independent midwives are fully qualified midwives who have chosen to work privately, rather than to be employed by the NHS. Working independently allows them the freedom to practise the midwife's role to its fullest extent, enabling them to be truly "with woman".

What is the difference?

The art of midwifery is to trust in the birth process, helping to create a supportive environment where a woman can relax and find her inner strength and power to give birth. A woman is entitled to choose where she wants to have her baby. Midwives can work with women at home, in hospital, or in separate midwifery-led units. They can work under the umbrella of the NHS or be self-employed.

Independent midwives have more freedom to practise individualized care compared to those working within the NHS, who may be confined by more rules and protocols. Independent midwives are still regulated by the Nursing and Midwifery Council. They are subject to the same supervision as NHS midwives, are required to keep up to date with their practice and are only allowed to act within their sphere of competence as midwives. There are currently approximately 150 independent midwives in the UK. They often work in partnerships or have close connections with other independent midwives, enabling them to provide seamless care to the women who use their services.

Independent midwives form relationships of trust with pregnant women, which then help women to feel safe and supported when they

WHY CHOOSE AN INDEPENDENT MIDWIFE?

Women choose independent midwives for many reasons:

- They want to feel that they are being looked after on an individual basis, with all their needs taken into account.
- They like the continuity of care provided by one or two midwives with whom they can develop a close relationship during their pregnancy.
- They want to be sure that they will know who is at the birth.
- They want to feel they have someone they can call on if they have any worries at all during their pregnancy.
- They want their antenatal care to take place in their own home, or at a time to suit them and their families.
- They can get the type of care they may not be able to access through the NHS, due to low staffing levels or inexperienced

midwives: for example, a home birth or a water birth.

- They may know that they have a higher risk of complications or medical intervention (for example, a breech birth, twins, or a previous Caesarean birth) but they want to avoid an obstetrically managed birth or a Caesarean.
- They may have previously experienced a traumatic birth and/or unsatisfactory maternity care, and want a normal birth without medical intervention, but think that this may not happen using the other local maternity services available.
- They would like some extra care and support after they have had their baby. In particular some women want more help with breast-feeding. Independent midwives can give an excellent service in this area.

"Having an independent midwife was fantastic, I had a fabulous birth and superb support both post- and antenatally, and I would encourage anyone to save, beg, or borrow to pay for one. They are worth every penny. If only the hospital in our area could provide a service even one tenth as good, then I am sure that we would see an increase in uncomplicated happy births and healthier, happier children and mums."

go into labour. Many independent midwives have become very experienced in areas of childbirth that within the NHS are usually dealt with by obstetric management these days. These include breech birth, twins, and vaginal birth after Caesarean (often referred to as VBAC). The majority of births attended by independent midwives are home births, but they can also be present at planned hospital births.

You can book an independent midwife at any stage during your pregnancy, no matter how close you are to your due date. Some will give free consultations to women who are considering all their birthing options.

Practicalities to be aware of

Before you decide to book a birth with an independent midwife, there are several issues you may wish to consider. You can also find out more information about them, including those working in your local area, from the Independent Midwives Association (www.independentmidwives.org.uk).

Cost Independent midwives charge for their services. The amount will depend on where you live and the type of service they provide. You can book their care for the postnatal period too. Most independent midwives will accept payment in installments.

Place of the birth Most independent midwives attend births at home. There is one independent midwifery service in the UK that has its own birth centre. If you are planning a hospital birth or need to be transferred to hospital, you will need to consider the role of your midwife. Very few, if any, hospitals will give "honorary contracts" because of the insurance issue. If you transfer to hospital with your midwife, you will be attended by a hospital midwife, and the independent midwife can remain with you, but only as a birth companion or advocate.

Insurance At the time of writing it's impossible for independent midwives to hold professional indemnity insurance. The midwife should explain this to you in the first discussion as recommended by their regulatory body. They are in conversation with the government to resolve the issue.

Other birth supporters

A woman in labour generally needs companionship and emotional support from a person or people she trusts and feels comfortable with. Research findings have shown one-to-one continuous empathic support has a strong positive effect on the physiology and outcome of labour (1).

Why have a birth partner?

Research over the past 25 years has shown that the constant presence of a supportive birth companion is one of the most effective forms of care that women can receive in childbirth (2).

Constant support during labour is associated with a shorter labour, reduced use of medical pain relief, fewer forceps/ventouse deliveries and Caesareans, and fewer babies needing resuscitation after the birth. Women who had the benefit of uninterrupted support during childbirth have found labour better than expected and generally to be a more positive overall experience (3).

Who should it be? A birth support partner could be your partner, a family member, a friend, trained lay women (such as a doula, see page 39), a student midwife, or midwives. Religious and cultural beliefs are important considerations for some women as in some cultures it is thought shameful for a man to be present during childbirth.

You need to decide what the appropriate support may be for you. Some fathers, in particular, just do not feel comfortable attending their baby's birth. Some people have a fear of hospitals or are terribly squeamish and the emotions can be overwhelming.

Having your mother present also may not be appropriate as the dynamic of the mother–daughter relationship may throw you into the "child" role when you are vulnerable in labour, and not bring out the strength you need to access when giving birth.

Some women will prefer not to have anyone who is close to them present in labour. If you feel like this, you may feel less inhibited with a professional support person, such as a doula. Trials have shown that "the continuous presence of an experienced support person who had no prior social bond with the labouring woman" has beneficial effects on childbirth (4).

You could ask a few people close to you to be your birth supporters and leave the final choice open until the day arrives: you may not be sure who you want with you until labour begins, when you will have a heightened sensitivity about who to invite.

HOW A BIRTH PARTNER CAN HELP

A birth partner's role is to:
- provide empathic support
- be a listening ear
- be positive and encouraging about the woman's ability to go through the process of birth
- keep her refreshed with sips of water
- help by sponging her brow, etc
- make her as comfortable as possible.

All this helps a woman become relaxed enough to increase her levels of oxytocin (the hormone produced in labour) and endorphins (natural pain relieving substances) and to reduce adrenaline – the "fight or flight" hormone produced by anxiety, which inhibits labour.

"My husband massaged my back from when we went in at 10am until I had Matthew at 8pm and never wanted to smell the lavender oil again, but he was brilliant and I could not have done it without him."

Entonox, often called gas and air, gives effective pain relief through a mouthpiece – but being supported by another person as well also helps you deal with contractions.

It is important that others understand this and respect your choice. For labour to progress, you need to be as relaxed as possible, and to feel happy about putting your own needs first.

What does a birth supporter need to do?

It is a tremendous privilege to witness the entry of a new human being into the world and few fail to be deeply moved by the experience. To be asked to be a birth supporter can be very exciting. Some may feel nervous, especially if they are the woman's partner. They may wonder how they will cope especially when they see the woman in pain, if she becomes very distressed, or if things don't go according to plan. It is natural to want to stop another's suffering – feelings of helplessness may come up and a birth supporter may worry that they are not doing enough.

Support during early labour While the contractions are mild, support people can maintain their normal daily activities. Women may wish for time alone to relax and prepare themselves. They can be encouraged to rest and eat and drink to preserve and build energy reserves.

"I think I would have been too scared to do it without my sister, she was brilliant, and we both cried when he was born."

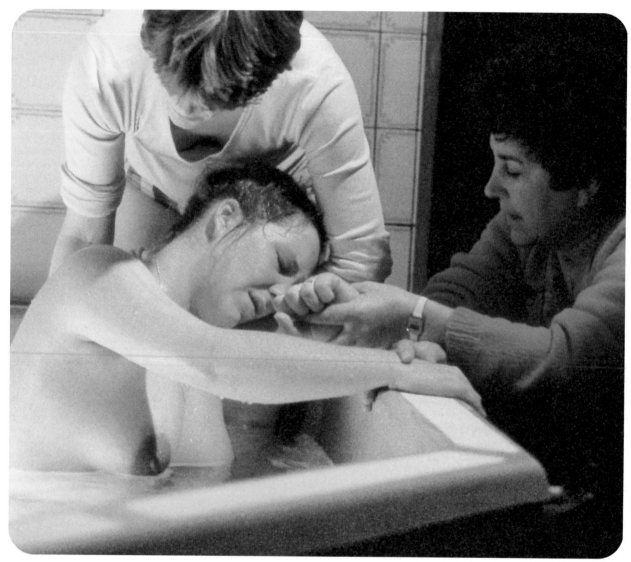

When the hormones *are flowing unimpeded, as the labour advances, a labouring woman becomes less communicative and "goes into herself".*

It may be hours before regular, stronger contractions occur that signal the arrival of established labour, and important changes in the woman's behaviour will indicate this.

Support during active labour When labour is advancing and the hormones are flowing unimpeded a woman usually becomes less communicative, and goes "into herself". She will show signs of withdrawal – such as wanting to rest, sinking toward the floor, closing her eyes, stopping conversation between contractions, and showing a need to concentrate as contractions begin to increase in intensity (1).

Supporters need to mirror her behaviour by quietening down, avoiding chat, and slowing down their movements. A woman may feel conversation, soothing words, massage, or even trying to get eye contact, to be intrusive.

Try to anticipate her needs: if her mouth appears dry, offer her sips of drink with as little disturbance as possible; if she appears cold and shivery, wrap a blanket over her shoulders; if she's hot, mop her brow. Try to encourage her to stay upright, rather than lying on her back, and offer physical support if necessary. Remind her to go to the toilet because this will keep her bladder and bowels empty, which in turn helps labour to progress.

Give quiet support A woman generally labours best when she is undisturbed and has privacy. Every woman is different and will have different needs and these will change at different stages of labour. Being able to provide the right amount of encouragement and physical support has been described as a difficult "juggling act" that requires sensitivity, tact, and insight (2) on behalf of the supporter.

Don't worry if, as a birth partner, you feel redundant. Doing nothing can sometimes be the best thing you can do. Most women when asked, said they simply wanted their birth partner to "be there" (3) – she'll probably tell you if she wants anything. You may feel you're not doing anything, but a labouring woman doesn't need the added pressure of making sure you're comfortable, or finding things for you to do, so that you don't feel helpless.

Be reassured that birth is a normal process and try to stay as calm as possible, however distressed a woman becomes, because a calm presence conveys to a woman that her experience is normal. Your strength is what she needs now. Your quiet presence acknowledges to her that you accept her as she is and this in turn will instil confidence and a feeling of psychological safety in her.

Act as a go-between Being a woman's advocate can also be considered part of a birth supporter's role. A woman can feel very vulnerable during labour and find it difficult (especially in hospital) to express what she wants, so a birth supporter can be helpful in this area and can liaise, if necessary, with medical staff. Being familiar with any particular wishes she might have is advisable as, if you are in hospital, staff may sometimes be too busy to remember her wishes, or there may not be enough time for staff to become familiar with her needs as the actual birth is drawing near.

Be prepared for a long "journey" Supporting a woman in labour can be intensive and can take a long time. It is important for the birth supporters to take snacks and drinks for themselves and to wear loose, comfortable clothing. Some women find it useful to have a couple of birth supporters as they can take breaks and cover for each other.

Giving birth can be seen as a journey and, as with all journeys, it takes courage and determination to keep going when it gets difficult. It follows that how a woman feels psychologically can have a tremendous effect on her labour. The right support in labour acts as a buffer against stress (4) and assists her with coping strategies. With the right support, many midwives firmly believe most women can give birth naturally.

WHAT IS A DOULA?

A doula is a female caregiver who is not a midwife, but has had a basic training in labour and birth. Her job is to provide emotional support and a constant reassuring presence. She has basic skills in massage and is able to explain what is going on if medical intervention is needed. She can be around to support the mother during pregnancy and also after the birth to help with the care of the baby and general household duties. The constant, comforting support of a female caregiver has been shown to reduce the anxiety and the feeling of having had a difficult birth in mothers, and also to have a positive effect on the number of mothers who were still breast-feeding at six weeks after the birth. Continuous support from caregivers such as doulas seems to have a number of benefits for the mother and baby and does not appear to have any harmful effects (5). If you want to find out about arranging for a doula, see Useful organizations on page 245.

see also

The role of your midwife	30–3
Good positions for labour	130–33
Dealing with pain	134–39

Antenatal classes

Becoming a parent will change your life forever – so it can be helpful to meet up with others in your locality who are facing this big change too. Antenatal classes will give you the chance to meet other parents-to-be, and to learn about what to expect during pregnancy, labour, and birth. They can also help you make choices and decisions about your pregnancy and your baby's birth.

Why go to antenatal classes?

Many women who are pregnant for the first time can feel quite isolated. You are at the start of big changes and one useful way of working through these changes is to meet up with other women, or other couples, who are facing the same new experiences. Sharing thoughts, comparing notes, and putting your half-formed worries into words can really help.

So a good way of meeting other pregnant women, making new friends and gaining support, in addition to learning about pregnancy and birth, is to go to antenatal classes. These are usually offered in the last three months of pregnancy, though "early-bird" classes are available in months three or four in some areas. Exercise classes, such as yoga or aquanatal, also provide the opportunity of meeting other pregnant women.

Going to antenatal classes is a good way of getting information about the later stages of pregnancy, labour, and birth, and the early days with your new baby, but they offer lots more as well.

> "The friends I met during the NCT antenatal classes were the greatest support. We continue to have contact four and a half years later."

Information Unlike other sources of information, such as books and magazines, classes give you the opportunity to ask questions about anything that you don't understand or would like to know more about, while learning from the ideas and experiences of other members of the group as well as from the class leader.

Learn practical skills Some classes give you the chance to try practical skills for labour and birth, such as labour positions, relaxation techniques, and massage. You'll also learn some of the practical aspects of looking after your baby, which helps you to prepare and plan for your baby's arrival.

Exercise classes *are a great way to prepare you for the physical demands of labour. In addition you'll meet other pregnant women who may live locally, which can be a great support later.*

Share your concerns If you're unsure about what to expect with regard to your pregnancy and the birth of your baby, what's normal, how to get what you want, what choices you have, sharing your concerns with other women and your class leader can help to clarify things. It can also be helpful simply to talk to other pregnant women about your experiences and how you're feeling and to get support from them.

Make new friends You may make friends about to have babies through the classes who'll support you during your pregnancy as well as after your baby's born. Some lasting friendships are formed at antenatal classes.

Support for partners Most classes are for men as well as women, and these are a good way of helping your partner to feel actively involved in your pregnancy, and, if he's going to be your birth supporter, to learn about what to expect in labour and how he can best support you.

What classes are there?

National Health Service (NHS) classes These are free and are held either at a hospital clinic or local health clinics, or your GP's surgery. They are usually run by midwives, though there may also be some input from others, such as physiotherapists and health visitors. The format of these classes varies from place to place. Ask your midwife how to book them. Due to budget cuts some hospitals have cut their antenatal classes.

National Childbirth Trust (NCT) classes These are led by trained NCT antenatal teachers and held either in the teacher's home or a community centre. There is a charge and prices vary; there is a reduced rate for those on a low income. The classes are small and informal, with the emphasis on the group learning together through discussion and practical activities. A standard course usually consists of eight two-hour evening sessions, but other formats are offered. Contact the NCT head office or your local branch to find out how to book classes. It's advisable to book early.

In general, the following topics will be covered in NCT classes: coping with labour; relaxation techniques; pain management; positions for labour and birth; medical aspects of birth – such as induction, instrumental birth, and Caesareans; recognizing the signs of going into labour and what to do; life with a new baby; breast-feeding; adjusting to parenthood; and the needs and concerns of fathers.

Other pre-birth classes and drop-ins Most Children's Centres offer antenatal drop-in groups for expectant parents. There is also a variety of classes including Active Birth, aquanatal, and hypnotherapy. Active birth classes are yoga-based, and focus on preparing physically for labour. Aquanatal classes are based on exercise in water, while hypnotherapy can help you feel more control of the process. Think about the type of class you might go to and ensure you go to a reputable teacher or organization.

NCT POSTNATAL CLASSES

After the birth of your baby, NCT Postnatal Courses are a really good way to meet other parents and make new friends in your area. They also provide you with somewhere to air your feelings and concerns and help you adjust to motherhood.

The groups are informal and provide an opportunity for you to get together regularly with other new parents to share ideas and talk about the ups and downs of life with a new baby. They cover such issues as:

- the difference between the expectations and the reality of new motherhood
- the pros and cons of returning to work – full time or part time
- balancing your time
- tips for settling a crying baby.

Read more about the NCT on page 247.

Antenatal testing options

Although antenatal testing can identify problems with your pregnancy, assess the chance of your baby having particular conditions, and diagnose specific abnormalities – this increased choice and knowledge can also lead to increased anxiety and confusion.

MATERNAL BLOOD TESTS

At your first antenatal appointment, your midwife will test your urine for sugar and protein (to check for diabetes, infections, and signs of pre-eclampsia, see page 105). She will also check your blood pressure. You will also be offered blood tests to identify:

- your blood group and rhesus factor
- your blood count (to see if you are anaemic or short of iron)
- your immune status for infections such as rubella (German measles)
- hepatitis B and syphilis
- and an HIV test.

The Association of British Insurers has stated that having a negative HIV test, as part of routine antenatal care, is not a valid reason for refusing insurance or increasing payments.

Find out what is available

It may never have crossed your mind that there could be anything wrong with your baby, but as soon as you're offered a test to find out if she is OK, you start to worry. Pregnancy tests fall into two categories: screening tests or diagnostic tests, see opposite, and p.44–47. The decisions that you will need to make about whether to have a certain test and what to do if the result of that test is anything other than normal are complex and emotional. Before you say "yes" or "no" to any tests, do make sure that you fully understand the following points:

- what the test involves
- what conditions it is testing for
- whether it is a diagnostic or a screening test
- how and when you will get the results
- what your options are when you get your results
- who you can talk to when you have received your results.

Talk to other women about their experience of having antenatal tests. And, most important of all, talk to your partner or the person you're closest to, about whether you want the information that tests give you, and what you would do if the results gave bad news.

Although for the majority of women antenatal tests can give reassurance, they can also raise strong feelings. Parents may find themselves making painful decisions including – for a small minority – whether to consider ending the pregnancy.

Your midwife or doctor should provide you with information about any tests you are be offered. Be sure you understand the purpose of all the tests before you take them. Don't be afraid to ask.

Not all tests described here are available everywhere, but you should be given clear information about any test you are offered.

Ultrasound scans

Dating scan Ultrasound used from eight to 14 weeks can establish how many weeks pregnant you are and broadly how your baby is developing. The scan will also confirm whether you have a live baby and show how many babies you are carrying.

Before your early pregnancy scan, you will be asked to drink a lot of water so that your bladder pushes your uterus forward, making the image

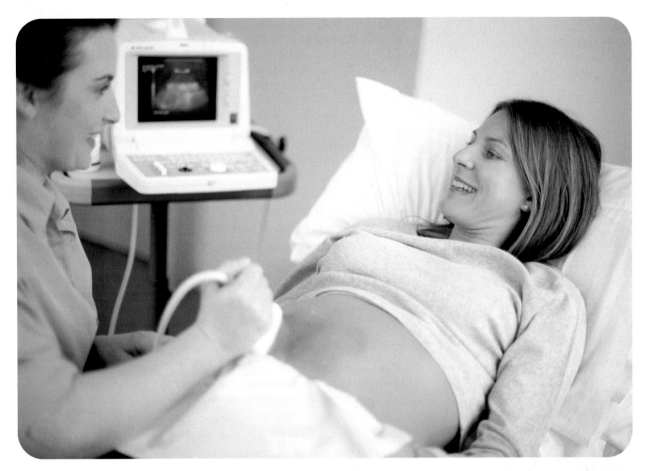

of your baby clearer. The sonographer will spread a gel over your tummy and then roll a small "transducer" over the gel to produce an image of your baby on a screen. Your partner or someone else of your choice should be allowed to sit with you during the scan. While it's exciting to see your baby on the screen, you may feel nervous about what will show up and it's good to have some support with you.

Anomaly scan 18–20 weeks Most hospitals offer a detailed ultrasound scan at between 18 and 20 weeks. This scan will check the structure of your baby and look carefully at her organs, including the brain, spine, heart, and kidneys and take measurements. It is not 100 per cent guaranteed to spot anything that's wrong with your baby, and some hospitals have better scanning equipment than others. The Royal College of Obstetricians and Gynaecologists (RCOG) is currently setting minimum standards for the anomaly scan and if a hospital cannot meet these, then it will not be allowed to offer the scan.

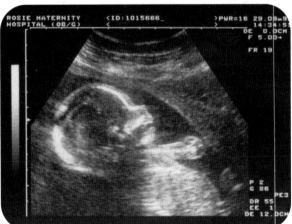

An anomaly scan *will be offered between 18 and 20 weeks of pregnancy. You can accept or refuse the offer.*

IMPORTANT ABNORMALITIES

There are two main types of abnormality: chromosomal and congenital.

Chromosomal abnormality

This type of abnormality is caused by a fault in the genetic information carried by the egg or the sperm that made your baby. It is built into a child's genetic make-up from the moment of conception and cannot be corrected. Down's syndrome is the most common chromosomal abnormality – these babies have an extra chromosome. People with Down's syndrome have a very distinctive appearance and learning disabilities. Often they will also have more health problems, including heart defects.

Congenital abnormalities

This abnormality occurs when something goes wrong while the baby is developing in the uterus. The congenital abnormalities looked for in screening tests are generally cardiac abnormalities or neural-tube defects. There are two types of neural-tube defects – spina bifida and anencephaly.

Spina bifida results when the baby's spine has not formed completely and this can cause physical disabilities that can range in severity, from weakness to paralysis in the legs with bowel and bladder problems.

Anencephaly is when the baby's brain has not formed and therefore, sadly, the baby cannot survive outside the uterus.

Screening tests

These are non-invasive tests that can estimate your risk of having a baby with a serious chromosomal abnormality such as Down's syndrome, or a congenital abnormality such as spina bifida. These tests are useful as they give an indication of risk without an increased risk of miscarriage.

Screening tests are not diagnostic so cannot tell you for certain whether your baby has a particular condition. However, they can identify those women where the risk of their baby having, for example, Down's syndrome is greater than one in 250. They do not, however, identify all women who have a baby with an abnormality.

A screening test for Down's syndrome (generally either a blood test, a nuchal-fold test, or combination of the two – see below and opposite) will be considered "positive" or "high risk" if your risk is higher than one in 250. However, a risk of one in 100 is very different from a risk of one in four, although both results would be described as "screen positive". A one in 100 risk means that you have only a one per cent chance of having a baby with Down's and a 99 per cent chance that your baby will be perfectly normal. A one in four risk means that there is a 25 per cent chance that your baby has Down's. If you receive a "high-risk" reading from a screening test you will be offered a diagnostic test to establish for certain whether your baby actually has the abnormality.

If your risk is less than one in 250 (for example, one in 750) your result will be described as "screen negative". This does not mean that your baby definitely does not have Down's syndrome or some other abnormality, but that the risk is so low that it is unlikely.

There are several types of screening tests offered, although all the tests are not available in every hospital.

Blood tests These are special blood tests that measure the amount of some substances that are found naturally in the mother's blood. These substances have passed to the mother from the baby.
A sample of the mother's blood is usually taken between 10 and 18 weeks. The timing of the test and details of the substances measured may vary slightly between different maternity units.

A computer programme then uses the results of the blood test, together with the mother's exact age, weight and stage of pregnancy (worked out from the dating scan) to work out the chance of the baby having Down's syndrome.

If you do get a "screen-positive" result, remember that this screening test is only an estimate of risk – you will be offered a further diagnostic test to establish whether your baby does have a particular problem. However, only about one in 60 women whose blood tests suggest there might be a problem actually have an affected pregnancy.

Nuchal-fold/translucency test In some areas, women are offered a nuchal translucency test about 11–13 weeks into pregnancy. This is sometimes combined with an early pregnancy scan. If it is not offered at your hospital it is often possible to have this test done privately.

This test is an ultrasound scan that carefully measures the pocket of fluid at the back of the baby's neck, known as the "nuchal translucency". An increased amount of fluid may mean that the baby has Down's syndrome. The measurement of fluid is combined with your age and the size of your baby to give an estimate of the chance of your baby having Down's syndrome. If the test shows a "high risk" (one in 250 or more) then you will be offered a further diagnostic test, such as chorionic villus sampling (CVS), see below.

Combined test This test, which is not available everywhere, is done at 11–14 weeks of pregnancy. It is a combination of the nuchal-fold test, a blood sample from you (to measure the concentration of the substance called pregnancy-associated plasma protein A, known as PAPP-A), and your age. It is used to estimate your chance of having a baby with Down's.

The integrated test This is a two-stage test and it is not available everywhere. In the first stage, at about ten weeks, you will have a nuchal scan and a blood test to measure the concentration of PAPP-A. In the second stage, at around 15 weeks, you will have another blood test that measures the concentration of four naturally occurring substances that have crossed into your blood from your baby. These four markers along with the results of the nuchal scan and first blood test are combined with your age to estimate the chance of your baby having a neural tube defect or Down's syndrome. If you have a risk greater than one in 100 you will be offered an amniocentesis, which is a diagnostic test.

What if screening gives a "high-risk" result?

If you are given a "high-risk" or "screen-positive" result for a screening blood test or scan, you will face more decisions. If you do get a high-risk result from a screening test, your midwife or doctor will give you the information and support you need:

- ask for counselling from medical staff straight away
- explore what you can learn from further diagnostic tests such as a more detailed ultrasound scan, CVS, or amniocentesis
- take time to talk things over thoroughly with a friend and/or partner and don't allow yourself to be pressurized into taking a hasty decision about diagnostic tests
- telephone the NCT Pregnancy and Birth Line 0870 444 8709 (see page 247) or Antenatal Results and Choices (ARC), (see Useful organizations page 245), for further information and guidance.

Diagnostic tests

Unlike screening tests, if you have a diagnostic test you will find out for sure whether your baby has an abnormality, but these are invasive tests

INHERITED GENETIC CONDITIONS

When both partners are carriers of a specific gene, but neither have the disease, there is a one in four chance of the condition being passed to their baby. If you think you may be affected by any of the conditions listed here, or any other inherited conditions, you can ask for counselling before you become pregnant or while you are pregnant.

Sickle-cell disease: One in ten black people in the UK carries the sickle-cell gene. Sickle cell anaemia is a life-threatening disease that cannot be cured. However, people with sickle cell anaemia can be given treatment for the tiredness, headaches, shortness of breath, and jaundice that it causes.

Thalassaemia: This condition affects families from the Mediterranean, Middle East, and South East Asia. Thalassaemia affects the red blood cells and cannot be cured. However, treatment can reduce the risk of serious illness such as jaundice, diabetes, and disease of the spleen, liver, and heart. All pregnant women are offered a blood test for thalassaemia.

Cystic fibrosis: This is the most common inherited disease among caucasian people. It causes serious, life-threatening lung infections that need to be treated with antibiotics and physiotherapy.

and they do carry a risk of miscarriage. There are two different tests available: chorionic villlus sampling and amniocentesis.

Chorionic villus sampling (CVS) This test can be done from 11–14 weeks of pregnancy. It is usually only offered in specialist centres. It involves taking a tiny tissue sample from the developing placenta to check the baby's chromosomes and test for Down's syndrome as well as certain inherited, or genetic, disorders. However, gene defects are not looked for as a matter of routine.

Using ultrasound as a guide, the tissue sample is taken either through the cervix or through the abdomen. (This test cannot diagnose spina bifida, which is most often diagnosed using ultrasound.)

Many women find the procedures uncomfortable but they should not be painful. You will be advised to take things easy for a couple of days. If possible, avoid activities that involve lifting, bending, or stretching. You may have some discomfort in your lower abdomen for a day or two after the procedure. It can take up to 18 days to get the results of diagnostic tests. The rate of miscarriage caused by CVS is one to two per cent, slightly higher than amniocentesis, but an advantage for some parents is that it allows an earlier diagnosis.

Amniocentesis This test can be carried out from 16 weeks of pregnancy. A tiny sample of the amniotic fluid that surrounds the baby in the uterus is taken using a needle guided by ultrasound. There is a one per cent risk of miscarriage as a result of the test. The results usually take about 18 days because cells from the sample have to be cultured so that all the baby's chromosomes can be checked.

Some hospitals now offer amnio-PCR or amnio-FISH. These are special molecular tests (so the cells don't have to be grown) that look at the sample from the amniocentesis and can check for the three most common chromosome abnormalities: Down's, Edwards', and Patau's syndromes. These tests provide some information within two to three days, but you will still have to wait up to 18 days for the full diagnostic result.

Cordocentesis/fetal blood sampling Cordocentesis is performed when amniocentesis, or CVS is unsuccessful or inconclusive in tracking fetal abnormalities. It is usually performed later in pregnancy, between 18 and 24 weeks, when the umbilical cord is sufficiently developed. A sample of the baby's blood is taken from the umbilical cord, or a vein. It is only offered in specialist centres. Results take three to four days. There is a one to two per cent risk of miscarriage with this test.

Do I have to accept the tests?

It's very common to feel unsure about which screening or diagnostic tests to accept, if any. You may find it helpful to talk it through with other parents, your midwife, or a counsellor. Think carefully about the advantages and disadvantages, your personal circumstances, and how you and your partner would feel about possible outcomes.

Questions to ask yourself If a screening test suggests that there is a high risk of your baby having a problem, will you go on to have a diagnostic test and run the small risk that it will cause a miscarriage and then confirm that nothing was wrong?

If a diagnostic test definitely shows that your baby has a problem, would you terminate your pregnancy? Or would you go ahead and have the baby? How would you feel? How would your partner feel?

Take your time You should be given time to think through your options. Go home and talk to the important people in your life. Don't be hurried into any decision. A few days will not make any difference. Remember, you can always call the NCT (see page 247) or Antenatal Results and Choices (ARC, see page 245).

see also

Pregnancy sickness	94–5
Discomforts in early pregnancy	96–9
Discomforts in late pregnancy	100–03
At risk pregnancies	104–07

ADVANTAGES AND DISADVANTAGES OF SCREENING AND DIAGNOSTIC TESTS

Test	Advantages	Disadvantages
Blood tests	• These tests may help you to decide whether to have a diagnostic test.	• If you get a high-risk result you will feel anxious. • The tests do not identify all affected babies.
Ultrasound scan	• You don't have to wait for information. • Detailed scans by experts give fairly accurate results. • Ultrasound is not painful. • There is no increased risk of miscarriage. • Scans can show if you have more than one baby.	• Sometimes ultrasound identifies conditions that are worrying but not significant such as a "low" placenta or cysts in the baby's brain. However, there are limitations to scans and many malformations will not be detected. • There is a risk of false-positive findings, that could lead to unnecessary anxiety and interventions.
Nuchal-translucency scan	• You find out early about the likelihood of your having a baby with Down's syndrome.	• If you get a high-risk result you will feel anxious about your pregnancy. • The test does not identify all babies affected by • Down's syndrome.
Chorionic villus (CVS) sampling and Amniocentesis	• These tests give accurate results about whether the baby is affected by a particular condition. • Chorionic villus sampling gives accurate information earlier in pregnancy than amniocentesis. • Ending a pregnancy before about 16 weeks does not involve an induced labour.	• The procedure can be worrying and you will have to wait 18 days for amniocentesis results. • You may find the procedures painful. • There is a risk of miscarriage with both tests – about one per cent for amniocentesis and two per cent for Chorionic villus sampling. • The test results may show that the baby is fine and you still miscarry.

Choosing where to have your baby

The decision of where to have your baby can be a difficult one, particularly if you are expecting your first baby and therefore have no experience of labour and birth. It's worth taking time to investigate all the options available, so that you can choose the place that will be right for you.

KNOWING WHAT'S BEST FOR YOU

Becoming pregnant for the first time means taking a one-way step into the unknown – something that is both exciting and risky. Many women will feel safer booking a hospital birth in an obstetric, or consultant, unit, knowing there will be high-tech equipment on hand should it be needed. However, a recent study of home births showed that having your baby at home was just as safe as in hospital for women with a normal, straightforward pregnancy (1).

If you are hoping for as straightforward a birth as possible, you may prefer to give birth at home or in a low-tech midwifery-led unit, or birth centre. With the continuous support and relaxed environment, this will give you the best chance of having a labour and birth without interventions. You may on the other hand feel that you would prefer to be in a hospital environment with epidural pain relief and other medical assistance readily available, should they be needed.

Arranging your care

The Government says that by the end of 2009 all women in England will be guaranteed options for place of birth. These are home birth, using a local midwifery unit or birth centre, or care from midwives and doctors in hospital. The place where you choose to give birth to your baby can have a profound affect on the birth itself. For this reason, it can be a good idea to think about what you really want and give yourself a lot of time before you make your decision. As long as yours is a normal pregnancy and there are no complications, you can leave the choice of where to have your baby until late in your pregnancy, and even then you can still change your mind.

Talk to your midwife or family doctor Your GP may be the first health professional you choose to see when you discover you are pregnant. However, you don't have to see your doctor in order to book your midwifery care; you can arrange it directly with local midwives.

If you do visit your doctor, he or she is likely to ask you where you want to have your baby so that a referral letter can be written. At this stage of pregnancy you probably won't have decided where you want to have your baby. Your midwife or GP should explain what your options are and give you sufficient information. You should then have time to consider your options before needing to make a decision later in pregnancy. If you are referred to a particular birth centre or hospital and later in pregnancy decide it is not where you want to give birth, you can change.

Main factors affecting your choices

When making birth choices, there are two important factors to consider:
- where you want to have your baby
- who will care for you during your pregnancy, the birth, and afterward.
These two factors are linked.

The place In most areas of the UK, there will be:
- at least one hospital maternity unit staffed by midwives and hospital doctors, or obstetricians (called a "consultant unit")
- the opportunity to choose a home birth
- a birth centre or local midwifery-led unit – either attached to a consultant unit ("alongside") or in a separate place ("stand alone").

"To me all births start at home – so why bother going anywhere else if you don't need to? Hospital can't 'do' the labour for you, you still have to do it."

Who will care for you? Wherever you choose to give birth, you will be looked after by midwives. If the midwives feel you or the baby need specialist care, then you will also be seen by a consultant obstetrician. Remember that for the vast majority of women, pregnancy and birth are normal, natural processes and your care should be given by midwives.

When choosing where to give birth, an important question to ask is "Will I receive continuity of care?" This means that the same midwife, or small team of midwives, will look after you during pregnancy, the birth, and after you have had your baby. Research has shown that this kind of care is beneficial to women (2). You are more likely to get this care if you plan to give birth at home or in a midwifery-led unit. Some hospital consultant units arrange for this type of team midwifery and you can try to request it.

Think over your options carefully

These are very personal decisions. The choices you make will depend on what is available in your area, the support you have from your partner, other family members, and friends, and your own hopes for the birth.

Home birth This choice should be available to everyone, regardless of age or whether it is a first baby. Your midwife will bring everything needed for the birth round to your house, including equipment for baby resuscitation. For pain relief, most women cope with "gas and air", a TENS machine, warm water, self-help techniques, and hands-on support from partners. Some women hire birth pools too. Pethidine is also available at a home birth.

Midwifery-led units These are also called birth centres, while in Scotland they are referred to as community midwifery units. These are informal "home from homes" run by community midwives with the same medical facilities that you'd get at a home birth (and often with a birth pool installed). They are either attached to hospitals or in a separate locality. If you need medical intervention, such as an epidural anaesthetic, you would have to leave the unit to transfer to hospital (just as with a home birth).

Hospital birth Many women give birth in hospital because they don't realize they have other options. Others specifically opt for it because they know that a hospital offers medical facilities. There is quite a lot of difference between hospitals regarding attitudes, facilities, intervention, and infection rates. It's worth asking your midwife what the local statistics are before you make your decision.

TIPS FOR LOOKING IN YOUR AREA

- For more information on your local options for giving birth, look at the www.birthchoiceuk.com website. This has been written by an NCT antenatal teacher who has compiled statistics from each maternity unit and can help guide you through the decision-making process.
- You could also contact a local NCT antenatal teacher to talk through your options.
- If you are thinking about a home birth, you could look at www.homebirth.org.uk, or there may be a local home birth support group in your area. Contact the NCT Enquiry Line for further details (see page 247).
- And if you are having problems finding the maternity care you want, you could contact Association for Improvements in the Maternity Services/AIMS (see Useful organizations page 245).

Home birth

The UK's National Perinatal Epidemiology Unit found that "there is no evidence to support the claim that the safest policy is for all women to give birth within hospital." There are huge advantages to giving birth at home. You are in your own familiar space, with people you have chosen to be with you, and in the care of a midwife who will stay with you throughout.

Getting continuity of care

Giving birth at home is the best way of getting continuity of care throughout labour, something that is known to make labour easier and shorter (1). Many women feel more in control in their own home surroundings. They may also wish to use warm water for pain relief and know that the availability of a birth pool cannot be guaranteed in hospital.

Giving birth at home is the norm in the developing world and in some European countries, the Netherlands for example, it is a lot more common than it is here, where hospital births account for the vast majority of births.

However, home birth is becoming more popular in the UK and one midwifery practice in Peckham, South London, based in a community centre , has a home birth rate of about 40 per cent.

"I loved the idea of labouring and delivering my baby in my own home, bathing in my own bath, then getting into my own bed with my new baby...."

AM I A SUITABLE CANDIDATE FOR A HOME BIRTH?

Most home births occur after a normal, healthy pregnancy, with one baby who is lying in the head-down position (see page 110). If you fall into a higher-risk category, see below, a home birth may still be an option, but seek specialist advice from your Supervisor of Midwives so that you can weigh up the pros and cons for your individual situation.

Higher-risk home-birth categories

In certain situations, some professionals will advise you to give birth in hospital, while others may be willing to support you at home. In order to reach a decision, you will need to understand the risks and benefits of giving birth at home in your specific circumstances. For example, many women in the following groups have made an informed choice to give birth at home, despite encountering varying degrees of opposition:
- moderately raised blood pressure

- anaemia (low iron count), see page 103
- previous difficult birth or heavy bleeding after the birth
- previous baby by Caesarean section
- fifth or subsequent baby
- over 42 weeks' gestation (you may be offered the choice of induction of labour, and if you accept, this can only be done in hospital).

Breech and twin births at home are rare, but they do happen – usually under the care of independent midwives who often specialize in such cases.

You are not suitable for home birth:

A home birth is not possible if:
- you have a full placenta praevia (placenta covering the cervix)
- your baby is in a transverse lie (lying sideways across your uterus), see page 113.

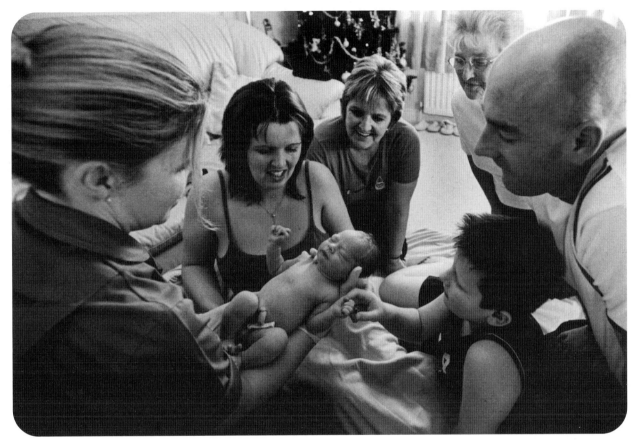

Giving birth at home *means staying in your own familiar surroundings. Your baby will be gently introduced to the sights and sounds of your home straightaway.*

How do I book a home birth?

You can book a home birth either directly through your local midwives or through your GP, although it's not necessary to involve your doctor if you do not wish to. To book direct with midwives, write to the Supervisor of Midwives at your local hospital, stating that you are expecting a baby, you are planning to have a home birth, you would like their support, and that you would like to book directly with the midwives and not through your GP's surgery.

If you would like some guidance on talking to your GP or midwives to help gain their support for your decision, contact your local NCT home birth support group. The NCT Enquiry Line (see page 247) will give you the relevant contact details for your area. You can also get in touch with the Association for Improvements in the Maternity Services (AIMS). You will find their details on page 245.

Is a home birth advisable with a first baby?

Some experts have said that the first labour is particularly suitable for a home birth because if anything goes wrong, it tends to do so very slowly, allowing plenty of time for transfer to hospital (2). In the UK, up to 40 per cent of first-time mothers who plan a home birth will eventually give birth

INDEPENDENT MIDWIFE HOME BIRTH

Independent midwives offer a private alternative for those who can afford their fees. They are fully qualified midwives who specialize in home births, and many women have found their support invaluable. They can accompany you to an NHS hospital if you need to transfer. Contact the Independent Midwives Association for more details (see page 245).

Your midwife will *bring entonox (known as gas and air) and pethidine to your home birth for pain relief.*

"It was lovely to be at home, the pain didn't seem to get out of control and I never felt any need for anything other than gas and air."

in hospital (1). Some women will switch to hospital care in late pregnancy (usually in order to have labour induced, or because of concerns about blood pressure). Others will transfer to hospital in labour because of slow progress, or to have epidural anaesthesia (2).

If you decide during your labour at home that you want an epidural, you can transfer to hospital if there is still time. Your midwife may phone ahead to try to arrange for this to be given soon after your arrival.

Pain relief options at home

Women who give birth at home consistently rate the experience as less painful than a hospital birth, perhaps because they are more relaxed and are more likely to feel uninhibited (3). However, midwives will bring entonox ("gas and air") and pethidine to a home birth, see pages 137–139. An epidural anaesthetic is not available as pain relief in a home situation because it has to be administered by a qualified anaesthetist – and monitored carefully once it is in place.

Other possible pain-relieving strategies at a home birth include massage, distraction techniques, moving around, "visualization", hypnosis, breathing, or singing/shouting through contractions. A TENS machine can be useful too, especially in the early stages.

Some women opt for self-help techniques alone, while others combine these with drugs supplied by their midwife. Many women find that a birth pool combined with lots of hands-on support from midwives and birth partners, plus entonox, (gas and air), is adequate to deal with the pain.

Is a home birth safe?

Research over the last couple of decades has found that home birth is a safe option for healthy women with normal pregnancies (4). Reviewing several studies, the British Medical Journal concluded that home birth was "safe for normal, low-risk women, with adequate infrastructure and support". The UK's National Perinatal Epidemiology Unit also found that there was no evidence to show that hospital birth was safer (5).

A study of nearly 6,000 women who planned home births in the UK noted the benefits of home birth (6). Each woman was matched for risk

PAIN-RELIEF DRUGS FOR HOME BIRTH
- Entonox (a mixture of nitrous oxide and oxygen known as "gas and air") that is inhaled through a mask or mouthpiece. Women often say that it "takes the edge off the contractions".
- Pethidine and other injected opiates – these relax your skeletal muscles and may make you feel sleepy, as if you were drunk, or confused. Some women love it, but others women find it does not relieve their pain, and can make them feel nauseous and helpless.

"Luckily I was already fully dilated so not many hours later gave birth in front of the fire in our living room, with the day gradually lightening outside and the Christmas tree lights twinkling in the window.... It was so nice to be in our own home afterwards."

level with a similar woman in the same area who planned a hospital birth. The study found that, compared to women planning a hospital birth, mothers in the home-birth group had:

- roughly half the risk of having a Caesarean section
- roughly half the risk of an instrumental delivery (forceps or ventouse)
- less risk of haemorrhage.

Babies in the home-birth group were:

- less likely to be in poor condition at birth
- less likely to have birth injuries
- less likely to need resuscitation.

Labours tend to progress well at home, where the mother is relaxed and free to move around as much as she wants. She will feel more comfortable and in control at home too and this can help to progress labour. She will also feel under less pressure to go through the stages of labour within the strict time limits that are set in some hospital consultant units. This means there is less need for medical intervention, for example, drugs to speed up labour or delivery with forceps or ventouse. These interventions carry risks as well as potential benefits and are more likely to be suggested for a hospital birth than a home birth. Finally, there is less risk of infection at home, for both mother and baby.

What if something goes wrong?

If there are complications with your labour, such as slow progress, concerns about your blood pressure or the baby's heart rate, you will usually be advised to transfer to hospital. You would travel either by car or by ambulance, depending on how advanced your labour is, but very few of these transfers are due to real emergencies(7).

Your midwife will monitor your baby's heart and your condition regularly through labour, and will advise that you transfer to hospital if she has any concerns about the health of either of you. The aim is to transfer well before the situation becomes an emergency.

If you need emergency treatment It is always possible that you may need emergency treatment, and it may take longer to get if you have to transfer from home to hospital. However, it is extremely rare for an intervention such as a Caesarean to suddenly become necessary with no earlier warning signs. If the midwife believes that you need a Caesarean then she will call

At a home birth, *your partner can often feel more involved in what's going on. He will be able to hold and cuddle your baby while your needs are being cared for by your midwife.*

ahead to have the operating theatre ready for your arrival. Even if you were labouring in hospital, there would normally be a wait of around half an hour while a surgical team was assembled. In a study of 29 midwifery practices in the United States, 8.3 per cent of women planning a home birth were transferred to hospital during labour and ten mothers (0.8 per cent) were transferred after delivery (1). In an earlier UK study of 285 women who booked home births, 9.4 per cent were transferred to hospital during labour (2). A large 1997 study showed a transfer rate of 16 per cent (3). According to these statistics, transfer rates actually in labour average out at about one in eight births.

Midwives are also trained to provide emergency treatment if there are complications after the birth. They carry resuscitation equipment to help babies who are slow to breathe, as well as drugs to treat heavy bleeding

"Afterwards, I asked Miles if it had stressed him out being at home, but he said that he much preferred it to being in hospital; he had a much more constructive role and felt more part of it all."

in the mother after birth. As facilities vary between areas, do discuss with your midwife what would happen in an emergency.

Occasionally, transfer to hospital occurs after the birth – perhaps because of problems with the delivery of the placenta, or because of concerns about the baby's breathing.

Although transferring from a planned home birth can be disappointing at the time, most women who have transferred say that they were glad to have spent time labouring at home, and would still plan a home birth for their next baby.

My partner is unsure about home birth
If your partner is worried about the safety of home birth, encourage him to talk to your midwife about it. You can also try contacting your local home birth support group to see if you can both talk to other couples about their experiences of it.

Many men who have been birth partners at home and in hospital say that they preferred the home birth experience, even if they had doubts initially. They are more likely to feel useful, and that they have a definite role. You may be relying on your partner to provide practical support to a greater extent than in hospital. After all, he, and not the midwife, will know where you keep the towels, baby clothes, and so on. If he is nervous about being with you, you could also invite a friend to help out as an additional birth partner.

Birth pool at home
Many people who opt for a home birth also hire a birth pool for use at home. In this case, it helps if your partner can take responsibility for assembling the birth pool, and maintaining the water at the correct temperature. However, a pool is by no means essential for a home birth. If you want the comfort of water you can always use the bath.

Is a home birth messy?
Most home births produce little mess. Any mess associated with the birth is easily contained with some forward planning. The midwives bring large absorbent, disposable pads to protect the surfaces you give birth on, and they will take away all the mess when they leave. Floors or beds can be covered with waterproof sheeting, a large waterproof tablecloth, or old sheets. Clearing up after a home birth is usually very straightforward.

Water birth

Water has been shown to help many women manage the pain of contractions during labour (1). Warm water can be relaxing, soothing, and calming – and some women have found that being in a birth pool, whether at home or in a hospital, gave them a sense of freedom and privacy that enabled them to follow their instincts and trust their own body during labour.

BENEFITS OF WATER BIRTH

For you: Research shows that the beneficial effects (of the use of immersion in water during labour) include maternal relaxation, less painful contractions, shorter labours, less need for augmentation, less need for pharmacological analgesics, more intact perinea, and fewer episiotomies (2).

For babies: In a UK observational study, fewer babies born in water were admitted to Special Care (3).

Water is comforting

Many women feel they have more control over their environment, even in a hospital setting, if they are in a birth pool. Being in water means you can create your own space, which can give a welcome sense of privacy. It also means you can use the buoyancy of the water to support your body as you move around.

If you hadn't intended to use water (and haven't already had pethidine or an epidural) and are able to gain access to a birth pool, you can just try it and see if it helps you. If you don't like the sensation of labouring in water you can always get out again.

Advantages of water birth for the mother

Some women find they don't like being in a birth pool, however, most women love the feeling of being in water during labour, and will stay in for the whole of their labour and the birth.

There has not been a lot of in-depth comparative research, although common strands in studies show that labouring in water has these advantages over "dry-land" labour:

- Women feel more in control during their labour and are more satisfied with their birth experience.
- Women feel more relaxed, their contractions are less painful, and they need fewer pain-killing drugs.
- It is easier for the mother to move around and change her position between contractions.
- Labours are slightly shorter and less likely to be speeded up with a drip of oxytocin.
- There are fewer episiotomies (see page 85) and fewer serious tears with births in water.
- In a birth pool, you can create a quiet space around yourself. This helps you to feel private and keeps interventions to a minimum.
- If you are a wheelchair-user, or find movement on dry land difficult, a birth pool can really help you change positions in labour.
- Unlike most pain-relief options, you can change your mind at any time about using water as a form of pain relief.

At a water birth, *babies must be brought gently to the surface of the pool, as soon as they are born.*

"As soon as the pain became too much I got into the pool and it was like being wrapped in a cosy blanket and my whole body breathed a sigh of relief. The contractions didn't slow down, in fact the opposite: the more I could let my body relax in between contractions, the faster they came."

Possible disadvantages for the mother

- Getting into a pool may slow down your labour, so it can work well to wait until the contractions are regular and strong and getting difficult to cope with before you get into the water, then the water can give relief. However, be prepared to get out for a while if contractions slow down.
- If you are asked to get out of the pool, you may suddenly feel the contractions more intensely.
- You can't use a pool if you have had pethidine or want an epidural.

Advantages of water birth for your baby

- Your baby will be under less stress and will get a better oxygen supply if you are more relaxed and warm water can help you relax. In a recent study of births in water, babies were less stressed at birth (4).

NEWBORN SAFETY

No one fully understands what stimulates newborn babies to take their first breath. If your labour progresses normally and the water temperature in the pool is around body heat (37°C) babies do not start to breathe while under the water (5).

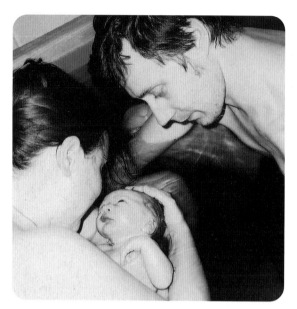

You can both *enjoy those first moments with your new baby in the pool.*

Possible disadvantages for your baby

- There is some suggestion that your baby may gasp for breath too soon if the water is too cold.
- In rare circumstances, a baby who is very stressed during labour may try to breathe under water.
- Your baby's heart rate may increase if the water is too hot. The Royal College of Obstetricians and Gynaecologists recommends that that women should be allowed to regulate the pool water temperature to their own comfort, although this should not be higher than 37°C (98.6°F) during the second stage of labour (1).

If your midwife has any concerns about your baby's condition during labour, she will advise you to leave the pool.

Do I have to book a water birth?

You can ask for a hospital water birth or you can hire a pool to assemble at home if you are having a home birth. Sometimes a hired pool can be taken to the hospital.

In hospital Many hospitals have birth pools and each hospital will have its own guidelines on pool use. Some require women to get out of the pool to actually give birth. The staff should provide written information as well as discussion on using water in labour and birth.

Usually hospital pools cannot be booked; they're available on a first come, first served basis. Tell your midwife you would like a water birth and discuss what will happen if another woman is using the pool when you go into labour. It is possible to hire a pool yourself, bring it into hospital with you, and set it up for your own use – but this would have to be agreed ahead of time with the midwives.

At home You can hire a pool to use in your own surroundings if you are planning to have your water birth at home. Ask to be looked after by a midwife with experience of water births. You may need to contact the Supervisor of Midwives at your local hospital for help in finding a midwife with suitable experience.

> "Everybody expected the baby to be late, but my instinct told me to get a birthing pool for the due date. I remember coaxing my husband into assembling it the night before. The next morning, I started to feel the contractions."

AM I A SUITABLE CANDIDATE FOR A WATER BIRTH?

Discuss your options with your carers – different health service areas follow different criteria. The Royal College of Midwives has recommended that a pool is suitable for women who have:

- enough information to make an informed choice
- a normal pregnancy that has reached at least 37 weeks
- one baby lying head down (cephalic presentation)
- not been given any drugs which cause sedation (such as pethidine)
- intact waters – or whose waters broke spontaneously within the last 24 hours.

Practical considerations when hiring a pool

First decide which room you want to put the birth pool in on the day.
You need to consider the following:

- Is the room is big enough? Birth pools vary in size but are generally about 1.5 x 1.2m (5 x 4ft). Smaller inflatable pools are also available from some hire companies.
- Is there enough space in the room for the midwife to sit beside the birth pool and enough floor space for you in case you decide to get out of the pool at any time?
- Is the floor strong enough? The large pools hold about 900 litres (200 gallons) of water, which weighs about a ton.
- Is there a convenient supply of water? How long will it take your own water system to fill the pool?
- Do you have a partner or friend who can set up the birth pool and keep the water warm for you?
- Is your hot-water system efficient enough to heat all that water? If you can afford it, would it be a better idea to hire a pool with its own thermostatically controlled heating system?

Hiring a birth pool

Birth pools come in various shapes and sizes (see left). Some are inflatable, others are more permanent structures that require assembly. Some pools have built-in heaters; others have to be filled with water from your own hot-water system. Do check that the pool is insured and meets the safety and hygiene requirements of the NHS if you are planning to take it to the hospital with you.

It's worth spending some time looking into all the options. Most of the pool-hire companies have websites or will be happy to give you lots of information by post or over the phone.

Using the pool on the day

Whatever the stage of your labour, you may find that when you get in the birth pool, you enjoy the sensation of the warm water and can find a comfortable position. Be guided by your own feelings and talk to your midwives, when the time comes. If you feel strongly that you want to get into the pool, you may well benefit. Equally if you feel you want to get out of the water, then you should do so.

If your labour is progressing slowly in the water, you might try moving into different positions in the water or getting out of the pool and walking around for a while; this often gets things moving. Squatting, kneeling on all-fours, or going up and down stairs can help move the baby into a good position for birth (see pages 130–33).

You are the best judge of the needs and comforts of your body while you are in labour. You may choose to stay in the pool to actually give birth, or you might find, as many women do, that dry land suits you better when this moment arrives.

OTHER WAYS OF USING WATER FOR PAIN RELIEF

If you are interested in the idea of using water but don't want to have a birth pool, relaxing in a bath or shower can provide some of the benefits.

- Blocking the overflow of your bath with plasticine or Blu-Tack™ will give a greater depth of water, although you can't move around in the bath.
- You can sit on an upturned plastic bucket or a sturdy plastic chair under the shower.
- Your partner could pour warm water over you using a jug.
- A strong shower jet directed against the small of your back can give wonderful relief.

Birth centre or midwifery unit

Although the majority of women in the UK go to a consultant unit in a hospital to have their baby, women who are hoping to have a straightforward birth with little or no intervention can also book into a midwifery-led unit alongside it, or into a separate birth centre.

Home from home

Midwives who work in a midwifery-led unit rather than a hospital consultant unit have the philosophy that pregnancy and childbirth are normal occurrences. For them, birth is not only seen as a physiological process, but one that involves psychological, social, cultural, and spiritual aspects as well. Care is based on the needs of individual women rather than being dictated by hospital policies and protocols. This freedom allows the midwives to be more flexible, which encourages normal labour and birth for you.

In the past, as childbirth moved from home into hospitals, maternity services were provided by small cottage hospitals and units run by GPs usually located within communities. Gradually maternity services became more centralized and became focused within district general hospitals. Women began to have their babies further out of their communities and except in a few rural areas, cottage hospitals and GP units closed down. The trend recently has been to amalgamate maternity services into larger and larger consultant units, and some of these big hospitals are now catering for more than 4,000 births a year.

With the emergence of the large consultant units, together with the ever-increasing rates of medical intervention, and the lack of provision for home birth, there has been a realization that many women simply do not need to be cared for by doctors in labour. Midwifery-led care has been recognized as a valid alternative and in some areas many of the remaining GP units have now become midwifery-led units. In addition, some new birth centres are opening up across the country. At the same time, in other parts of the country midwifery-led units are under threat of closure, often for financial reasons.

Types of midwifery-led unit

Midwifery-led units, often called "birth centres", or in Scotland, community midwifery units, offer a useful option as a place to give birth for women with uncomplicated pregnancies. These units may be totally separate and away from hospital (stand-alone units), or within the hospital grounds or simply in a separate part of a hospital building (alongside). They may be funded by the NHS or privately, but either way they aim to provide as close to a home-like environment as possible. There are generally more facilities

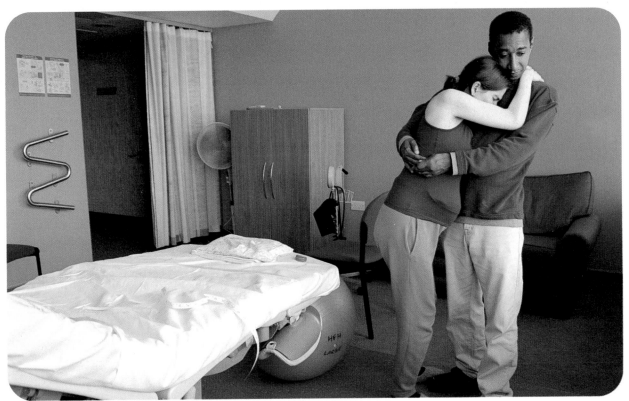

Midwifery-led units *are often much more "like home" than hospital labour wards.*

available to aid comfort in labour such as birth pools, and the midwives are experienced with water births. These units are usually small and family centred and the women are more likely to get continuity of care.

"Stand-alone" midwifery-led units Some of these midwifery-led units are situated in rural areas and provide a place where women can give birth without having to travel long distances to a hospital consultant unit during labour. However, if problems occur in pregnancy and labour, some women need access to the facilities of a consultant unit in a hospital, so there can be a strict set of rules as to which women can use this type of midwifery-led unit.

In some remote areas, there are facilities available for emergency operations. The local GP, for example, may be available to assist with forceps deliveries, and in some units, midwives have been trained to carry out ventouse deliveries. When these facilities are available, it can mean that greater numbers of women are able to give birth in the unit and don't have to be transferred to a consultant unit.

Other "stand-alone" midwifery-led units have been set up near hospitals so that women can easily be transferred if necessary. However, because there are usually no medical facilities available in these units, they are most suited to women with "low-risk" pregnancies, who are more likely to have a straightforward birth. This does include first-time mothers.

SAFETY AND BIRTHING CENTRES

Some birth centres have guidelines about who they can accept, although if you fall outside their specific criteria you may still be able to arrange care with them. Once you have booked with the birth centre, your care then rests in the hands of the midwives.

Having a baby at a midwifery-led unit is therefore generally equivalent to a birth at home as there are no doctors close at hand and limited drugs and technological equipment available. The midwives are experienced and competent to work in this type of environment, and have regular reviews of resuscitation and other emergency practices. There are usually excellent staffing levels and midwives can spend a lot of time with the women they are looking after, and have developed skills in supporting women who are labouring naturally.

With this level of attention, potential emergencies can mostly be detected long before they occur and the woman in question transferred to the nearest hospital if necessary, where the staff will have been pre-warned and will be waiting for the woman's arrival and ready to attend to her.

"Alongside" midwifery-led units These units are set up on the same hospital site as a consultant maternity unit, and are often adjacent to the main unit. It is hoped that women will experience the same type of "low-tech" environment and care that they would get at home or in a birth centre, but with the added convenience of being right next to medical facilities if they are required.

Although there has been little research in this area, it has been suggested that where a midwifery-led unit is built alongside a consultant unit, it is much harder for the midwives within that unit to retain a philosophy of normal birth.

The benefits of a midwifery-led unit

One of the great benefits of choosing to give birth in a midwifery-led unit is that you are likely to receive continuity of care throughout your pregnancy, labour, and birth. This will be provided by a small team of midwives who are dedicated to helping women give birth without medical intervention, and whom you will get to know as your pregnancy progresses.

"What we really appreciated was having our own space – comfortable, with all that we needed – and we knew the midwives were right there for when it all started happening."

Benefits supported by research Studies have shown that women who receive continuity of care from a team of midwives are less likely to have drugs for pain relief in labour, less likely to be admitted to hospital, and more likely to be pleased with their care than women who are not getting continuity of care (1). Further research shows that women who are supported throughout labour by an experienced female caregiver are less likely to need medical interventions (2).

This study was borne out in an evaluation of Edgware Birth Centre (3) – a stand-alone unit in North London – where it was found that there were significantly higher rates of normal vaginal births among women intending to have their baby at the birth centre when compared with a similar group of women planning to give birth in hospital. There were also lower rates of induction of labour, ventouse delivery, elective Caesareans, episiotomy, and fewer postnatal stays of more than three days. Another recent survey showed that women who had given birth at home, in a birth centre, or a midwifery-led unit, were more likely to believe they had been offered all the help, support, and information they required, compared to women who had their babies in hospital (4).

Relaxed environment At a birth centre, the emphasis is on supportive care and creating a relaxing environment in which you will be able to labour naturally and instinctively. Because the main hormone responsible for stimulating contractions during labour – oxytocin – is produced when you feel protected and nurtured, your labour progresses most easily if the surroundings are ones where you feel safe to let go and work with your body. Midwives experienced in normal birth will provide the environment you need and this works especially well if you are labouring with a midwife with whom you have been able to build up a relationship of trust during your pregnancy.

Emphasis on natural pain relief Because there is less access to medical pain relief at a birth centre, you are likely to be helped to cope with the pain of contractions in other ways. Many midwives at birth centres are experienced in water birth and often there are birth pools available for women who would like to use water for the birth, or just for pain relief.

Other helpful methods include using upright positions and movement; the use of equipment such as birth balls, birth mats, beanbags, or even bars and ropes to hold on to. You may also like to use TENS or entonox (gas and air) or even aromatherapy and music. In the supportive environment of a birth centre, most women find that their labour progresses well and they can manage the pain.

Unobtrusive monitoring You are also likely to be able to labour in a less rigid environment without reliance on strict rules, such as the need for vaginal examinations to assess the progress of labour, and the imposition of arbitrary time limits for labour. Monitoring the baby's heartbeat will also be carried out in a way that means you will not need to lie down strapped to a piece of machinery, and therefore does not interfere with your ability to move around and use positions that assist the natural process of labour.

Natural third stage Once your baby has been born you are more likely to have a natural third stage (delivery of the placenta) and there should also be the opportunity to have unhurried skin-to-skin contact with your baby.

Less interference throughout For women who want a birth in a more relaxed environment than a hospital where there will be less interference, and they can increase their chances of having a natural birth, a birth centre or midwifery-led unit is worth considering. You can find out more about your local midwifery-led units at the website www.birthchoiceuk.com.

Birth pools *and one-to-one care are more easily available at birth centres.*

Natural birth in hospital

It has been shown that you will recover from the birth more quickly, find it easier to bond with your baby, have a calmer, more settled baby, and you will establish breast-feeding more easily if you give birth without medical intervention when you are in hospital.

Medical intervention can be avoided

A hospital maternity unit can be a difficult setting for birth. To keep birth safe and efficient in this environment, many rules and guidelines have been put in place for managing maternity care. Some women will need to have medical interventions for the safety of themselves or their baby, and in these situations everyone is grateful for the technological advances that have been made in recent years.

However, the management of labour in hospital can change its natural path, making other interventions more likely. This has been described as "the cascade of intervention".

Even so, you may feel that you would be more comfortable in hospital. You may feel that you are happy to have medical interventions when offered. Alternatively, you may want a natural birth but do not want (or are not able) to give birth at home or in a birth centre. Whatever decision you have made should be respected by those around you.

If you intend to have your baby in hospital and want a natural birth without intervention, you may come across difficulties, especially if your labour doesn't fit into a standard model. Many hospital staff have little experience of labour without intervention and you may find you are working against the system. If you are hoping to have a natural birth in hospital, there are certain things you can do to help yourself.

> "I was lucky to have a room that was large enough for me to move around in, and my partner appreciated the opportunity of being able to stay overnight."

Preparation for labour

It is a good idea to prepare yourself as much as possible for the birth while you are pregnant. National Childbirth Trust (NCT) antenatal classes have a strong reputation for providing up-to-date, evidence-based information on your choices in maternity care. There is also lots of information available in books, the internet, and from other organizations campaigning for more awareness of natural birth (see Useful organizations, page 245). There are some important points to consider:

- Taking good care of yourself on all levels is paramount (see chapter 3), to ensure that your pregnancy is as trouble-free as possible.
- Be aware of your posture during pregnancy to help get your baby in the best position for birth.
- As the birth draws near it is helpful to arrange to have one or two people you trust and feel comfortable with to support you during labour.

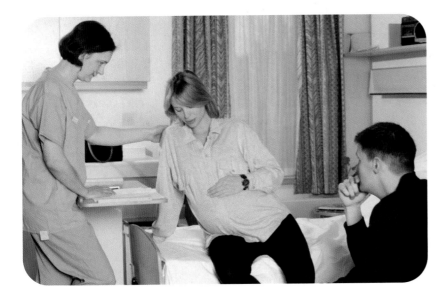

When you arrive *the midwife will ask you what has happened so far. She will feel your abdomen to establish how the baby is lying, as well check your pulse, blood pressure, and urine.*

- Pack everything you need to take to hospital well in advance of your due date so you aren't flustered trying to do this when labour begins.
- Having your labour induced (started off artificially) needs careful thought, as this can start the "cascade of intervention".

When your labour begins

Once you feel you might be in labour, it's wise to remain at home as long as you feel able to, to allow the hormones for labour to build up. You are more likely to get into established labour and things will progress more quickly if you're in an environment in which you feel familiar and at ease. Also if you are experiencing a false labour (one that fades away – which is very common when the body is preparing for birth) you are more likely to avoid going to hospital unnecessarily. Many women worry they won't be able to tell the difference between Braxton Hicks, or "practice", contractions and the real ones. It is quite rare for a woman to labour strongly without realizing it, and the hospital midwives are always happy to give advice over the phone. If at any time while you are labouring at home, you feel worried or uncertain, trust your instincts and ring the midwife for advice.

While you are at home (and later in hospital), when the contractions are becoming more intense, there are various things you can do to aid comfort and that act as natural forms of pain relief, for example, having a warm bath, using a TENS machine, a massage, and some complementary therapies.

Going to hospital

At some stage in labour a woman planning a hospital birth will decide the time is right to go to hospital. When you arrive, your midwife will check your notes for anything she needs to know about you and your pregnancy. You will be asked when and how things started and what is happening now. Your midwife will want to know the length and frequency of your

It's best not to lie back on a bed during labour: remaining upright and leaning forward helps labour to progress.

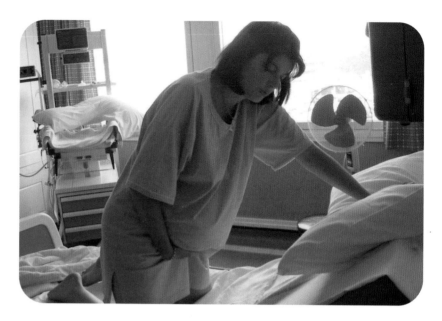

contractions, whether your waters have broken, if there has been a "show", and whether there has been any blood or fluid loss. She will also check your pulse, take your blood pressure, and test your urine. The midwife will also feel your abdomen to establish how the baby is lying.

Your baby's heart rate will be measured. Many hospitals still have in place the procedure of a "routine admission trace". This is where the baby is monitored for about 20 minutes using belts around your abdomen. These belts are connected by wires to a machine that prints out a trace of the baby's heartbeat and your contractions. The latest national guidelines do not support the use of this admission trace for women at low risk of complications and recommend that you are monitored intermittently using a small hand-held device instead (1). This enables you to move around freely, changing positions as you need to. (For more on monitoring, see chapter 5). If the hospital suggests a routine admission trace, find out why, and ask if you can have intermittent monitoring instead.

Keeping your birth natural

The hospital environment may not be an easy place to labour comfortably. Labour progresses best when you feel safe and relaxed, so it is worthwhile trying to turn the delivery room into your own space. You may find that moving the bed to one side gives you more room to move about. Keeping in upright positions and being able to move freely, rather than lying on your back, is important to help your labour progress well. If you want to use the bed, try to make sure that it is in its lowest position and try to keep upright on it using beanbags or pillows. Many women feel more stable if they are on the floor.

Remember that your baby will arrive in its own time and not to any agenda set by the health professionals around you. As long as you and the baby are coping well with labour there is no need to hurry it along to meet a fixed deadline. Two of the best ways to try and avoid unnecessary interventions are to trust that your body knows how to give birth, and to create the relaxing and safe environment in which it can do its job.

However, time can pass slowly when you are labouring in hospital, and you can feel impatient for your baby to be born. If you feel you are not making good progress, you may feel disheartened, and less able to cope with the pain of contractions. It is at this point that the right support is crucial. Hospital midwives vary in their experience of normal birth, and if they feel labour is not progressing, or that you are not coping with the pain, some may suggest various medical interventions. Other midwives may be more used to finding other ways of helping your labour to progress and helping you manage the pain. See chapter 5, which descibes medical interventions and how you can make decisions about them.

There are times when medical assistance is necessary for your or your baby's health. If you need it, try to stay positive and know that you are doing it because you feel it is the best thing for either yourself or your baby. When medical assistance is offered, it is not always possible to substitute a less invasive procedure, but consider the alternatives in the table below, and go through the "BRAIN" analysis outlined on page 153.

PROBLEMS, INTERVENTIONS, AND ALTERNATIVES TO TRY

Problem	Medical intervention	Alternative you can try	
Going past your due date	Hospital induction	Book an ultrasound scan to check your baby's well-being and ask for your baby's heartbeat to be monitored twice a week	See page 43
Labour is not progressing	Acceleration with drugs	Avoid going into hospital too early in labour. Wait at home for as long as feels comfortable, moving around and staying upright	See page 155
Concern that your baby is finding labour stressful	Continuous electronic fetal monitoring with belt monitor and/or fetal scalp electrode	Ask to be monitored with a hand-held device every 15 minutes in first-stage labour and every five minutes in second stage	See page 156
You're finding labour difficult to cope with and more painful than you expected	Epidural anaesthetic	Move around; get more hands-on support from your midwife and birth partner; use gas and air and a birth pool; visualize holding your newborn baby and breathe through the next five contractions before reconsidering	See page 158
You are having trouble pushing the baby out on your own	Ventouse, forceps, or Caesarean help to be born	Move your body; getting onto all-fours or lying on your side can help; push only when your body tells you to; gas and air can help you push with less pain	See page 161

Birth of a baby lying transverse at 39 weeks

"The baby is now breech, so spend morning on bed with bottom in the air. At lunchtime find that the baby is now transverse again."

A natural birth for a baby who can't make up his mind

"At 36 weeks, my baby is transverse, am not too bothered as the girls were lying that way until about 34–35 weeks. I trawl the internet for ways to make babies turn. Among the suggestions are: crawling around on all-fours, wearing tight cycling shorts, doing handstands in a swimming pool.

See consultant a week later, the baby is still transverse. I spend the week taking pulsatilla (homeopathic remedy), visiting osteopaths, and even doing handstands at the swimming pool! Have a scan at 38 weeks – baby is head-down at last. At 39 weeks I am examined and am shocked that the baby is now oblique (lying diagonally). The consultant says that he will do an external cephalic version (ECV) and induce me on Friday.

At 39 weeks, the baby is in the right position. Decide to be induced in case the baby starts moving again. I am taken to delivery the next morning and have Prostin gel inserted. Spend the next five hours wandering around to no avail. More Prostin at 3.45pm and off to stalk the corridors again. Onto the monitor and have to sit still – very uncomfortable. An internal is carried out but I am still not officially 'in labour'. I'm kept in anyway because of the baby's 'unstable lie'. Caesarean looks inevitable.

At 39 weeks and 3 days – books read: 2 ½. Decide to have a 'day off' to see if labour starts naturally. Nothing happens. At 39 weeks and 4 days – books read: 3. Have a show but sink into depression when midwife tells me the baby is transverse again. At 39 weeks and 5 days – books read: 3; distance walked round corridors: 7km (4⅓ miles). The baby is now breech, so spend morning on bed with bottom in the air. At lunchtime find that the baby is now transverse again. People are saying 'Still here?'. Doctor offers a Caesarean! I ask if the consultant would turn the baby using ECV and then induce me. Doctor returns to say they will try ECV tomorrow. I agree to stay in hospital because of the danger of cord prolapse should my waters break.

Final attempt to turn the baby

At 39 weeks and 6 days – the consultant arrives and scans to see what baby is doing. The ECV is uncomfortable (feels like the baby was got by the scruff of his neck and his bottom and edged round to the right position). Spend the next eight hours standing up or on the birthing ball but the contractions are painless. When examined, I am about 2cm (1in) dilated and I have my waters broken.

The contractions get painful and within an hour I'm on entonox. At ten to midnight, I wanted to push. I was told that the baby had dark hair and within a few minutes Joseph Frederick arrived! I could not hold him as I was shaking – partly because I had had nothing to eat for 24 hours but also through exhilaration that I had done it without a Caesarean! I stare at my son (who spends the next eight hours fast asleep and motionless, no doubt worn out by his acrobatics of the previous week)."

Home birth with an independent midwife

"When I started my NCT classes, I became aware of my options and decided to give birth at the Edgware Birth Centre. However, my baby was breech and the centre only handles low-risk births. They assured me that I could give birth there if the position changed, but if not – what then?

At the Royal Free Hospital, doctors tried to convince me to have a Caesarean. When I refused, wanting a vaginal birth, they said they were "too dangerous". Without my antenatal teacher and yoga teacher at the Active Birth Centre, I would have given up.

I encouraged the baby to turn using homeopathy, reflexology, acupuncture, and spending 20 minutes each day hanging head-down from the sofa – nothing worked. I went to St John's and Elizabeth's Birth Unit to try to turn the baby by external cephalic version (ECV); this was a failure, too.

I then asked St John's and Elizabeth's Hospital whether I could have a vaginal breech birth there. They took time to think about it, and then offered me an elective Caesarean.

My husband searched for information on breech births and it emerged that they are something of a lost art. We found an article on the website of the Association for Improvements in the Maternity Services (AIMS). It said a breech is best delivered by a non-interventionist approach. I cried with relief, there was hope! AIMS put me in touch with an independent midwife called Jane Evans who said she'd be delighted to deliver the baby. Jane shared my care with Brenda, another independent midwife. We agreed that, if necessary, I would transfer to the hospital and they'd stay with me for a Caesarean.

The day arrived

I started to feel the contractions in the morning and pottered around totally relaxed. By lunchtime, the pressure in my pelvis meant that I could not sit and I called the midwives. Jane and Brenda arrived and helped me find comfortable positions while my husband filled the pool. I coped with contractions until they felt unbearable and then descended into the pool.

In four hours I was 8cm (3 ¹/sin) dilated and then half an hour later, the urge to push became uncontrollable. I knelt in front of a bed and Jonas was born within 45 minutes. He was stuck at the perineum, but after a few contractions his legs flopped out, followed by the arms and face. Brenda guided the back of his head – no medical intervention was needed. The fetal heartbeat was monitored so unobtrusively that I wasn't aware of it. It was better than I could have dreamt.

The birth of my son was a rite of passage. I hope my account will encourage women also to trust their instincts and fight for the birth experience they want."

Normal birth of breech baby

"I encouraged the baby to turn using homeopathy, reflexology, acupuncture and spending 20 minutes each day hanging head-down from the sofa – nothing worked."

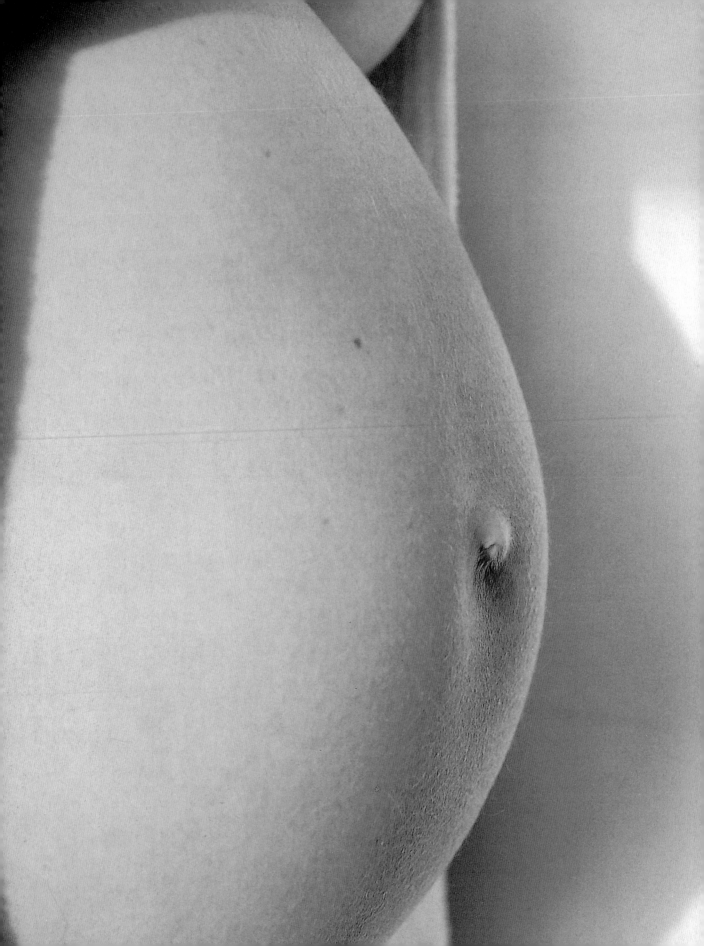

3

Self-care during pregnancy

Changes in body and mind

Over the next nine months, more or less everything about your body – from the size of your breasts and your belly, to the rate that your heart beats – is going to change as your baby grows.

Help your newly pregnant body by caring for it: protect it, feed it well, keep it fit, and give it plenty of time to relax and rest. This won't just be good for you, it will be good for your baby as well. By looking after your body well now, you are looking after your baby too, and helping him to grow healthy and strong.

Just as your body will be changing during your pregnancy, so your mind will be changing too. Your thoughts and interests will alter as you focus on the life growing inside you. Your feelings toward everything will change as your baby becomes your new priority. If you have a job outside the home, you may find that the world of work becomes less appealing. You will also find that your priorities change significantly as you nurture your growing baby inside you.

your birth year

	make an appointment to see your dentist – treatment is free on the NHS from now until your baby is a year old			inform your employer that you intend to take maternity leave at least 15 weeks before your expected week of childbirth		
FIRST TRIMESTER			**SECOND TRIMESTER**			
1 2 3 4 6 7 8 9 10 11 12	13 14 15 16 17 18 19 20 21 22 23 24 25 26					
If you're not already taking folic acid, start now (400mcg)	pregnancy nausea may mean you have to eat little and often, keep up fluid intake too	If at work, check your rights to maternity leave and maternity pay	if employed get MAT B1 form from your doctor or midwife; if you don't qualify for maternity pay, ask benefits agency for MA1 to apply for maternity allowance			

These changes are all part of the process of adjusting and adapting to impending motherhood. As you adjust to the changes going on in your body and to feeling your baby growing inside you, so are you also adjusting to your new mental state, the new life that lies ahead of you, and the new person that you're becoming. For most women this is a time of ups and downs and emotional mood swings; a heady mixture of happiness and tears. Care for your mental well-being too, by sharing any concerns with the people closest to you. Because women experience the physical changes of pregnancy, they tend to think of themselves as being a mother even before their baby is born. However, men, probably because they don't have this experience, tend to think of themselves as a father only after their baby has arrived.

Our frantic modern world often doesn't allow pregnant women the space or time to nurture themselves. Busy jobs, demanding work schedules, and increasing stress levels abound as we all struggle to balance home, work, and family. So don't feel guilty about taking as much maternity leave as possible after your baby is born.

Right now your body is doing the most important work possible: making a new human being. The following pages will give you lots of ideas on how best to care for yourself and your growing baby. It's time to celebrate your new body and the new you.

---

most airlines won't allow
you to fly after 36 weeks

keep up exercise – swimming is
especially good in late pregnancy

THIRD TRIMESTER

BIRTH AND FIRST 3 MONTHS

| 27 | 28 | 29 | 30 | 31 | 32 | 33 | 34 | 35 | 36 | 37 | 38 | 39 | 40 | 41 | 42 | 43 | 44 | 45 | 46 | 47 | 48 | 49 | 50 | 51 | 52 |

you may now require
a doctor's certificate
to travel by air

make sure your home delivery
pack is prepared, or pack your
hospital bag

Early signs of pregnancy

The beginning of your pregnancy is the beginning of a new life, not only your baby's, but yours as well. At this point, your baby's birth probably seems a long way off, but that's good. You've got nine months to get used to the idea of becoming a mother.

PREGNANCY TESTS

Most women find out for sure that they're pregnant by doing a home pregnancy test. These test for the presence, in your urine, of the hormone human chorionic gonadotropin (hCG), which is only produced in pregnancy. Many of these tests will produce a positive result if you test on the first day of your missed period.

If your period is late but the pregnancy test is not positive, you may have tested too soon, or your urine may have been too dilute at the time of the test (the tests work best on urine that has been in the bladder for at least four hours). You may get a different result if you test again in a few days on an early morning urine sample.

First signs of pregnancy

Becoming pregnant is the start of a big process of change, not just in your body, but in your heart and mind as well, as you adjust to new feelings and a different sense of what matters. Some women have a strong sense of having conceived straight away, but for most women, the first obvious sign is a missed period.

Even before you realize your period is "late", there are other signs of pregnancy that you might notice. About a week before your period is due, your breasts might start to feel tender. You might also experience pains a bit like period pains or even have some bleeding (these things occur when the cluster of cells that will develop into your baby is attaching to the wall of your uterus).

As you get to the time of your period being due, you may be starting to feel distinctly different. You may have a feeling of heaviness in your lower abdomen, and possibly some mild cramps that come and go. As time goes by, you may notice an odd, metallic taste in your mouth and go off things, like coffee or alcohol or fried foods. You'll probably find that you're unbelievably tired, almost as if you've been drugged, and you may start to feel – or be – sick. You may need to go to the loo more often too.

Doing the maths

Pregnancy is generally regarded as lasting for 40 weeks. The 40 weeks is counted from the first day of your last period, as this is usually easier to pinpoint than the day you conceived.

The formula that is usually used to work out your due date involves adding nine calendar months and seven days to the first day of your last period. This is based on your menstrual cycle being 28 days, though, so if your cycle is longer or shorter than that, you need to add or subtract the difference (for example, if you have a 35-day cycle, add seven days to the final total). Sometimes your due date is calculated by counting forward 40 weeks from the first day of your last period. This will produce a slightly different result.

Dating ultrasound scan Early ultrasound scans also provide estimates of due dates and you will probably be offered one at your first midwife appointment. These are considered to be accurate to within a few days

CALCULATING YOUR DUE DATE

Write down the first day of your last period (for example, 3 July). Then, add nine months (which brings you to 3 April) and seven days (which makes it 10 April). The average menstrual cycle is 28 days, but yours might normally be longer (or shorter) than that. If your average cycle is 33 days, then you need to add another five days to your due date (33 minus 28 equals 5). This will make your due date 15 April.

Exercising gently *in the fresh air can help you stay both physically and mentally fit during pregnancy.*

if the scan is done in the first three months of pregnancy. This is because babies seem to grow at a similar rate in the early months, so measuring your baby gives a good indication of how many weeks pregnant you are.

Due dates are estimates It's worth remembering that your due date is an estimate. A normal pregnancy can last anywhere between 37 and 42 weeks, and only about five per cent of babies are actually born on their due date. Although it can be hard to resist the idea of a due date, it might be more realistic to think in terms of a due fortnight. So for example your baby might be due "in the middle of April" rather than on 15 April. This may help your peace of mind as you get to the end of your pregnancy.

How pregnancy affects your body

Hormones have been called "chemical messengers". They are produced in one part of the body and pass into the bloodstream, which in turn carries them to distant organs or tissues so they can modify the structure or function of those organs. Pregnancy is a hormone-driven event, steered by your pituitary gland.

CHANGES TO YOUR SKIN

Melanocyte-stimulating hormone causes increased skin pigmentation, which is why your nipples darken. A dark line develops from the navel to the pubis in some women known as the linea nigra. A few women also develop a "butterfly mask" or chloasma, a mottled pigmentation in the shape of a butterfly around the eyes and forehead. Freckles and scars may darken and you tan more deeply in pregnancy.

Changes triggered by hormones

The hormones of pregnancy are triggered by activity in the pituitary gland, which sits just under the centre of your brain. Changes in hormone levels during pregnancy have a profound effect on every part of your body, not just your reproductive organs.

Breasts Hormones trigger an increased blood supply to your breasts, making them tingle and look marbled with veins. Your breasts will get larger and your nipples darken. From halfway through pregnancy, your breasts may leak colostrum, the early "milk" your breasts produce.

Cervix Your cervix increases in width during pregnancy and the tissue becomes softer. Glands in the cervix secrete a thick mucus that forms a plug-like barrier protecting against bacteria until the start of labour.

Digestive system You may feel nauseous in the early months, and again later, as the uterus pushes upward on your intestines and stomach. Your taste buds change in pregnancy and two-thirds of women have cravings (often for fruit and highly flavoured salty food) or aversions to other foods.
  You may experience heartburn because the hormone progesterone affects the muscle that closes off your stomach, which means stomach acid can be regurgitated. Also, food doesn't pass through your stomach as quickly, and not as much gastric juice is secreted to digest it, which can result in nausea. Progesterone also causes increased water absorption in the large intestine, which may lead to constipation, and as your uterus enlarges and presses on the large intestine, increased flatulence.

Gums The hormone oestrogen may cause your gums to become swollen and bleed easily.

Hearing and smell Your nasal passages become congested, which causes stuffiness and blocked ears. You may become very sensitive to smell and may find particular smells make you feel, or even be, sick.

Heart, circulation, and blood clotting The volume of blood in your body increases by 30 to 50 per cent during pregnancy, more if you are expecting twins, and new vessels are formed to deal with this extra flow. However, blood pressure tends to fall before the volume of blood increases, which may explain why women feel faint in early pregnancy. Later on in pregnancy, lying flat on your back is uncomfortable and not advised, because the uterus's pressure affects your heart output. Swelling of your feet and ankles can be caused by relaxation of veins and your heavy uterus impeding, or slowing down, blood from returning to the heart. There is also an increased tendency to varicose veins and haemorrhoids (piles). Your bleeding time in pregnancy decreases by about one-third due to an increase in clotting factors in the blood, in preparation for labour when the placenta will separate from the uterus.

Bones and joints In the final ten weeks of pregnancy your baby takes the equivalent of 80 per cent of your dietary calcium. However, if your calcium intake is adequate, this will not affect your bones.

Hormones also soften the connective tissue that attaches muscles to bones and your ligaments that support your joints in preparation for labour. The pelvis also becomes wider. A combination of the weight of your uterus and the tissue-relaxing hormones cause the curve at the base of your back to curve inward more, with your shoulders thrown back to counterbalance the weight in front. Backache is very common in late pregnancy and there are things you can do to help (see page 83). Pressure from your uterus on nerves and blood vessels may result in numbness and tingling in your legs. Symphysis pubis dysfunction (SPD) and pain in the joints of the pelvis can also be a problem.

Kidneys and bladder Your kidneys increase excretion of waste products as more are now produced by you and your developing baby. The tubes from the kidney to the bladder elongate so they can take an increased volume of urine. This is, however, linked with increased risk of infection. You may find that the urge to urinate increases early in pregnancy as the growing uterus puts pressure on your bladder. Later, the bladder is pushed upward so you won't feel the need to empty it so often, but the lax walls of the bladder may mean you don't empty it completely, which also increases possible urinary infections.

Lungs and breathing Early in pregnancy your diaphragm (the muscle beneath the lungs) shifts upward, your chest broadens, and ribs flare so there is more room for your lungs to expand and diaphragm to rise. Progesterone also makes you breathe more deeply, taking in more oxygen.

Sight In the third trimester slight swelling of the cornea is common and this can distort light rays going into your eye, blurring vision.

Vagina Due to an increased blood supply caused by oestrogen, your vagina becomes softer and more stretchy, ready for the passage of the baby.

CHANGES IN YOUR UTERUS

The uterus is composed of involuntary muscle, which contracts slightly throughout pregnancy. This causes Braxton Hicks contractions – painless, irregular contractions that are measurable from the first trimester, although not all women feel them. They are often called practice contractions. You also may be aware of them after orgasm, or during sex. These contractions don't actually dilate the cervix but do help with blood circulation.

About two to three weeks before the birth, your baby may drop down into the pelvic brim as a result of the lower part of the uterus softening. This means the top of the uterus sinks away from the diaphragm, which will also ease your breathing.

Relationship changes

Finding out you're pregnant for the first time starts a chain of events that will change your life forever. It's no wonder you feel a little uncertain about what you've taken on. Fortunately, you're not alone. You will find information, support, and lots of friendly interest from other pregnant women.

HORMONES AFFECT EMOTIONS

During your birth year, your feelings will go through changes, many of which are caused by increasing levels of the hormones *progesterone* and *oestrogen*. You will probably find your emotions fluctuate, especially at the beginning, but by the middle of pregnancy you may experience a sense of self-absorbed well-being. Toward the end, you may be looking forward to meeting your baby and may be anxious about what is to come. In the days before going into labour you'll probably be restless and feel energetic as you physically, and psychologically, prepare for the birth.

A mixture of excitement and anxiety

Discovering that you're pregnant can unleash a host of different feelings. You may be excited and thrilled, but will probably also be anxious and apprehensive – about miscarrying, whether the baby will be all right, about giving birth, or about whether you'll be a good enough parent. Pregnancy can also make you feel vulnerable and scared about the way you live, whether what you're doing, eating, or taking, or how you're feeling, might be affecting your baby.

Pregnancy involves huge changes in your body and your contours. Some women love their growing breasts and belly and feel proud of this new shape, but others are concerned about gaining weight and getting bigger. Some women really enjoy the attention that their pregnancy receives from other people, while other women feel embarrassed about their bodies being "on show".

Even if your pregnancy is much wanted, you may still have a feeling of "Oh no, what have I done?" By becoming pregnant, you've shifted the focus of your life from yourself and you've set out on the journey to becoming someone's mother. This is exciting, but it can be alarming too, as you begin to realize what a big responsibility you're taking on. Some women feel trapped by this responsibility and worry about the impact the baby will have on their lives. Many women find that their priorities change significantly when they become pregnant – things that were once important to them now take second place to the baby they are nurturing inside. It has been said that a woman develops a fundamentally different mindset when she embarks on motherhood. Gradually, she begins to put the needs of her baby first.

Pregnancy can affect your moods

With so many mixed emotions and concerns going through your head, and such big physical changes going on in your body, to say nothing of the effects of pregnancy hormones, it's not surprising that many pregnant women find that their moods are up and down. Mood swings are quite normal, but if you feel persistently down or anxious, you may be suffering from antenatal depression (it's estimated that ten per cent of women experience this). Talk through your concerns with your midwife or doctor if you think this might be the case. They will be able to help.

Relationship with your partner

Just as you are now having to adjust to a new life, so your partner is having to adjust too, and his feelings about the pregnancy may also be mixed. He may feel proud and excited, but also anxious about becoming a father. Some men feel particularly protective toward their pregnant partners – others feel shut out by their partner's involvement in her pregnancy. Make time to talk about how you're both feeling, share your worries, reassure each other of your love, and plan together for the arrival of your baby.

Sex during pregnancy

Some couples find that sex is more enjoyable than ever: they love the woman's new, fuller shape and their sex drive seems to increase. Others feel differently: they're tired and uncomfortable and are put off by the presence of the baby.

Some couples worry that making love will harm the baby. This is rarely the case (your midwife will advise you if there's any need to avoid sex in your particular circumstances). Some find it difficult to find comfortable positions, especially in later pregnancy. Some women may find their attitude to sex changes if there have been concerns about this pregnancy or the baby's health. A lot of screening tests, or frequent internal examinations at the beginning of pregnancy can interfere with a woman's libido. But if for whatever reason you don't want to have intercourse, don't forget that there are other enjoyable ways of being intimate.

Orgasm stimulates the production of the hormone oxytocin, which stimulates contractions. If you feel contractions in your uterus after making love, don't worry – these are just Braxton Hicks, or "practice contractions" (see box, page 77) and they will settle down again.

Telling other people the news

The right time to break the news of your pregnancy is when it feels right for you. Some women want to tell the world straight away, while others prefer to wait until the risk of miscarriage has lessened (after around 12 weeks) before they let anyone know. There may be some people that it's hard to break the news to – someone you know who has recently lost a baby, for example, or someone who has been trying for a long time to conceive. Tell them with sensitivity – they will feel even worse if they find out the news from someone else.

Telling your employer If you are working, it's up to you to decide when to tell your employer, as long as you notify him or her that you intend to take maternity leave at least 15 weeks before your expected week of childbirth (sometimes written on your notes as EWC). You will need to show your MAT B1 form (proof of pregnancy that you get from your midwife or GP after 20 weeks). If your work involves anything that might put you or your baby at risk, you may want to tell your employer sooner. You will need to tell him or her in order to get time off for your antenatal appointments.

MATERNITY RIGHTS

If you are employed, you are entitled to 26 weeks ordinary maternity leave (OLM) regardless of how long you have worked for your employer. When you go back to work, you have the right to return to your old job. You can also have an additional 26 weeks maternity leave (AML). At the end of your AML you have the right to return to your old job or, if that is not reasonably practical, to one on the same terms and conditions. If you wish to take just part of your maternity leave (ordinary or additional) then you need to give your employer eight weeks' notice of your plan to return to work.

Your employer will usually pay you Statutory Maternity Pay (SMP) for 39 weeks – you'll receive 90 per cent of your average pay for the first six weeks and £108.85 per week for the remainder. If you earn less than £120.95 per week then you'll receive 90 per cent of your average earnings for the 39 weeks. Some employers have more generous allowances.

The earliest you can start maternity leave is 11 weeks before your expected week of childbirth and SMP starts as soon as you stop work. If your baby is premature, SMP starts immediately.

If you are not employed or you are self-employed, you may be eligible for Maternity Allowance.

Fathers who have been working for their employer for 26 weeks continuous employment by the end of the 15th week before your due date, can take two weeks paternity leave after the birth, paid at £108.85 a week.

Caring for your body

Growing a baby makes big demands on your body: your blood supply can increase by as much as 50 per cent, your kidneys work harder, and your need for oxygen increases. Look after yourself – you need to be fit and relaxed for labour and birth and your life as a new mother.

TAKE IT SLOWLY

If you're new to exercise, take things gently and build up slowly. Regardless of how experienced you are, though, there are a few precautions that it's wise to take:

- Avoid jerky movements, twisting, or movements that strain your joints.
- Invest in a good pair of training shoes and a good sports bra.
- As your baby grows, your centre of gravity changes, which can affect balance, so move around with care to avoid falls.
- Eat regularly and make sure you drink plenty of water.
- In the second half of pregnancy, avoid exercising while lying flat on your back.
- Consult your midwife and/or GP before exercising if you've had any bleeding, if you have high blood pressure, if your placenta is low-lying, if there are any problems with the growth of your baby, or if you're carrying more than one baby.
- If you've had two or more miscarriages, talk to your midwife or GP about whether exercise is safe in the early weeks.

Rest and exercise are important

If you go out to work every day, see if you can re-negotiate your hours for a while. If your journey is difficult it may help if you can miss the rush hour and start work later, or leave work earlier too. Try to go to bed early: have a warm (not hot) bath first and you'll find you sleep better. Think, too, about trying to follow a gentle fitness programme that will help strengthen your changing body.

Good forms of exercise to do in pregnancy are Pilates for pregnancy, modified yoga, swimming, and walking. Types of exercise that it's best to avoid include contact sports, competitive team sports, skiing, climbing, scuba diving, trampolining, and gymnastics.

Walking

This helps to improve your strength and stamina, without putting much strain on your joints. Walking is also good for your heart and lungs. Try to go out for a walk in the fresh air every day: it will also help you to relax and give you the chance to think about and connect with your baby.

Start slowly – build up to at walking for a minimum of 30 minutes at least four times a week. You should be doing enough to make you feel a little out of breath.

Pilates

This is a form of exercise that uses your deep abdominal and pelvic floor muscles. It improves your posture, stability, balance, joint alignment, and strength. Pilates is ideal if you are suffering from any back or pelvic pain during pregnancy.

Pilates is based on several key principles, one of which is developing strength in your core postural muscles (abdominal, back, and pelvic floor). This helps your body to support the growing weight of your baby and your abdomen, and protects your joints. Pilates exercises reduce tension in your muscles as well as helping you to relax mentally. In addition, because the exercises require concentration, they also help to relieve stress.

You can find a qualified Pilates for pregnancy teacher by contacting the Pilates Foundation, The Pilates Institute, or the Body Control Pilates Association or the Guild of Pregnancy and Postnatal Exercise instructors (see Useful organizations, page 245).

Try to give yourself *some time every day to sit quietly in your own space, using controlled breathing exercises and careful stretches to release accumulated tension from your body.*

Yoga

This is an ancient Indian philosophy and a discipline through asana (posture) and pranayama (regulation of breathing). The word yoga means "union", and the main principle of yoga is that it involves body and mind working together, the one influencing the other, in order to promote the well-being of both.

Certain yoga postures are ideal for pregnancy. Physically, the movements help to strengthen your body, and improve your flexibility and stamina. Mentally, they require you to breathe in a conscious way, and this helps to relax your mind, and to reduce tension and stress. Yoga helps you develop an awareness of your body and what's going on inside it, which in turn helps you to connect with your baby, and to get to know him.

Swimming is a wonderful *way for you to exercise when pregnant. The water bears your weight, while also offering good resistance, ensuring that your muscles are strengthened. It provides cardiovascular benefits and allows you to feel supported and weightless, despite your extra pounds.*

Many of the yoga positions are also positions that are good to adopt in labour. The breathing techniques involved in yoga are helpful in labour too, as they help you to stay calm, and keep you and your baby well supplied with oxygen.

To find your nearest yoga teacher, contact the British Wheel of Yoga, or the Active Birth Centre (see Useful organizations, page 245).

Swimming and aquarobics

This is an excellent form of exercise for pregnancy because the water supports your weight and there's little strain on your body. It's beneficial for your heart and lungs, strengthens your muscles, and helps to improve your stamina and flexibility.

If you're suffering from pain in your pelvis, it's best to avoid breaststroke leg actions when you are swimming, as this stretches the joint at the front of your pelvis, increasing the strain on the joint. Try not to hold your head up out of the water either, as this can put a strain on your back. If you wear ear plugs and goggles, you won't have to hold your head up. If there's a jacuzzi at your pool, don't use it, as very hot water can overheat your baby.

Aquarobics or aquanatal classes for pregnant women are ideal. They involve gentle aerobic exercise and held in a swimming pool – often in the shallow end, so you don't even have to be able to swim. The classes involve gentle stretches, as well as moving in the water, to tone your muscles. Many classes include a floating session (with floating aids) to allow you to relax. They are often run by midwives. Ask your midwife about classes in your area, or contact The Aquanatal Register (see page 245).

Relaxation

The more relaxed you are, the easier it is to cope with the demands of daily life. Relaxing your mind and body (rather than just slumping in front of the TV) has physical benefits too, as well as helping you to sleep better. It also ensures a good supply of oxygen to your baby.

Using complementary therapies for relaxation Aromatherapy massage and reflexology are excellent ways of relaxing. Always make sure your practitioner knows that you are pregnant.

Learning how to relax

Help yourself to relax by practising one or more of the following relaxation exercises for ten minutes to half an hour a day. It may help if you get someone to read out the instructions to you.

Breathing deeply Sit in an upright dining chair, with a cushion behind you to support your lower back or sit with your back straight, cross-legged on the floor. Rest your hands loosely in your lap. Close your eyes. Breathe in, then breathe out slowly, dropping your shoulders and feeling your body relax as you breathe out. Keep breathing deeply and evenly, in through your nose and out through your mouth, concentrating on your out-breath. Part your lips as you breathe out. Rest your hands on your belly, feeling, thinking about, and connecting with your baby.

Note that because you'll be taking in lots of oxygen when you breathe in this way, your baby may well start to move about.

Relaxing your body Lie on your left side with your right leg bent, and a cushion or pillow between your legs to support your bent knee. Rest your head on a cushion. Close your eyes and focus on your breathing and your body. With each out-breath, allow your body to become heavy and sink down into the surface you're lying on. Concentrate on each part of your body in turn, allowing it to relax more deeply. Relax your face and neck. Let your shoulders drop toward your feet. Let your arms, hands, and fingers flop. Feel your chest and abdomen sinking down into the floor. Relax your hips and pelvis. Let your legs, feet, and toes flop. Your whole body is now deeply relaxed.

Visualization You can practise this technique either sitting or lying down. Start by focusing on your breathing, concentrating on your out-breath, and letting your body relax. Then imagine that you're in a place you know where you feel particularly at peace. Everyone will have their own special place – it might be a cosy room, a garden, a beach, a mountainside, or a warm bath. Think about what you can see in this place, what you can hear, smell, and touch. Think about how you feel being there. If you find that other thoughts come into your mind, acknowledge them, and let them go. Just enjoy being calm and peaceful in your special place.

TAKING CARE OF YOUR BACK

Back pain is a common pregnancy complaint, because pregnancy hormones soften all your ligaments, making the joints in your spine looser. Also, the weight of your abdomen tends to pull your lower spine forward, putting a strain on your lower back.

Protect your back:
- Pay attention to your posture. Straighten your lower back and gently draw your bump in. Visualize your baby as being tucked into the pelvis, close to your centre of gravity. You may find that just thinking about your baby this way will help you stand more upright and hold a better posture. Open your shoulder blades to relieve upper back pain.
- Be careful about lifting any objects, particularly heavy things (avoid these if you can). Always bend your knees when you pick something up, especially something heavy.
- Wear flat or low-heeled shoes.

Here are some ideas for treating your back pain:
- Wear a maternity support belt.
- Ask your GP to refer you to a physiotherapist.
- Some women find reflexology or acupuncture helpful.
- See an osteopath or chiropractor.
- Ask your partner or a friend to give you a back massage.
- Join a Pilates for pregnancy class.

Caring for your pelvic floor

During pregnancy, a hormone called relaxin softens the ligaments of your pelvic floor, allowing them to become more elastic. However, your pelvic muscles also need to support the weight of your growing baby and help you during the birth, so it's important to keep them toned and in good condition.

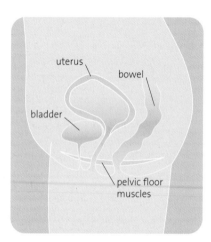

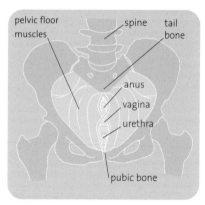

Your pelvic floor muscles *support the weight of your internal organs. They need to be strengthened during pregnancy with specific, repeated exercises.*

Important muscles and ligaments

The pelvic floor is a hammock of muscle at the base of your pelvis. The deepest layer of muscle is attached to the pubic bone at the front of your pelvis, and to your tail bone, or coccyx, at the back. Another layer forms a swirling "S" around the three female openings, the urinary outlet and the vagina at the front, and the back passage and anus at the back. The thick wedge of tissue between the back of your vagina and your back passage, known as the perineum, is also part of your pelvic floor.

To find out where your pelvic floor muscles are, imagine that you need to go to the toilet. The muscles that you hold tight to prevent passing urine or wind are your pelvic floor muscles.

The pelvic floor muscles need to be strengthened during and after pregnancy because they support everything that is in your pelvis and they can be weakened by childbirth:

- the bladder and its outlet (urethra)
- your uterus and your baby
- the vagina
- the back passage and the anus.

Toward the end of pregnancy, the weight of your baby is considerable. During labour, your pelvic floor muscles help your baby's head to turn into the best position to be born. Damage to the pelvic floor is possible during childbirth when the muscles are stretched as your baby's head comes down the vagina. Exercising the muscles during pregnancy and especially afterward helps keep them in good condition so that you don't leak urine when you cough or sneeze, and you don't have problems with bowel control. Well-toned pelvic floor muscles also make sex more satisfying.

Exercising the pelvic floor muscles

There are two kinds of muscle fibre in your pelvic floor and you need to exercise both. There are the slow fibres that control the strength of the pelvic floor, and the fast fibres that help you tighten everything quickly when you cough or sneeze.

Do your pelvic floor muscle exercises whenever you're sitting on the toilet, after you've emptied your bladder. Do five drawbridge exercises and relax. Then ten of the quick tightenings (see opposite). Spend a few extra minutes on the toilet each time you go so that you can do your exercises.

Strengthening exercises: Find a comfortable position, sitting down or lying with your knees a little apart. Tighten the muscles around your back passage, then around the front passage. Hold tight for a count of five. Make sure that you keep breathing while you are counting. Check by putting a hand on your abdomen. Now relax. Concentrate. Tighten the muscles from the back to the front again; hold for a count of five (keep breathing). Relax. Start by repeating this exercise five times and then, day by day, build up until you are doing ten repeats.

Drawbridge exercises: Imagine that your pelvic floor is like a drawbridge. Tighten the muscles around your back passage and then the front, just a little, and then a little bit more as if you're gradually raising the drawbridge. Now tighten them as hard as you can as if the drawbridge is closing. Keep breathing. Start to let the drawbridge down, relaxing the muscles a little, then a little more, and then let them relax fully.

Quick-tightening exercises: To exercise the fast twitch muscle fibres, tighten your pelvic floor muscles as quickly and as tightly as you can. Relax them. Then immediately tighten them again, and relax them. Repeat five times. Finally – relax.

Avoiding tears and episiotomy during labour

The strategies listed below and opposite may help you avoid cuts (episiotomy) or tears in the perineal area during the birth.

- Do perineal massage 3 to 4 times a week for 3 to 4 minutes (see box).
- Try to avoid having an epidural as you are more likely to need forceps or ventouse for the birth. An episiotomy is essential if you have forceps and possible if you have a ventouse.
- Don't push too hard in the second stage of labour.
- When you're ready to give birth, go onto all-fours or into an upright kneeling position. Let your pelvic floor muscles bulge between your legs. Familiarize yourself with this sensation in pregnancy by pushing the muscles out as well as tightening them. Always return the muscles to their normal relaxed position.
- Consider a water birth. There's some evidence that being in water when your baby is born prevents tearing, and that the water helps make the tissues more soft and stretchy (1).

Recovering from a tear or episiotomy

If you do have a tear or cut (episiotomy) during the birth, doing your pelvic floor exercises as soon as possible after childbirth will increase the flow of blood to your pelvis and will certainly help your perineum to heal more quickly. So start practising your pelvic floor exercises as soon as you can after the birth. Continue to do them for the rest of your life to keep your pelvic floor muscles strong.

HOW TO DO PERINEAL MASSAGE

There is some research to show that massaging your perineum from about six weeks before the birth can help prevent tearing (2). Do the massage after you've had a bath or shower, when the the tissues are soft and supple.

Lubricate your thumb with a little olive or grapeseed oil. Put your thumb about 5cm (2in) inside your vagina and sweep it gently from side to side, in a 180° arc. Press gently downward at the same time. If you find this uncomfortable, take a deep breath in and then start massaging as you breathe out, letting all your muscles relax. Stop massaging, take another deep breath in, and then start to massage again while breathing out and letting go of any tension. Continue for about three minutes.

Then, with your thumb still inside your vagina, move two fingers gently down the perineum toward your back passage. If you feel a stinging sensation, massage as you breathe out. This sensation is very similar to what you will feel as your baby's head is about to be born.

see also

Birthing your baby	140–41
Changes in your body	180–83
The end of your birth year	198–9

Healthy eating

A nutritious, balanced diet is important during pregnancy. With fresh food plentiful all year round, eating well has never been easier. This is good because it's one of the best things you can do for the future health of your baby as well as yourself.

IRON LEVELS IN PREGNANCY

Iron is needed by you and your baby, who builds up a supply in his liver to last until after birth. Iron is contained in haemoglobin which is found in red blood cells, and carries oxygen around your body. During pregnancy, your fluid levels increase, which "dilutes" the red blood cells. In the past, this was seen as iron deficiency.

However, research shows that the increase in red blood cells generally meets a mother and baby's increased need for oxygen. So there is therefore no need for routine iron supplements in pregnancy if you are not anaemic and if you have a good intake of iron-rich foods, such as red meat, sardines, wholemeal bread, baked beans, and green, leafy vegetables (see opposite).

Eat a balanced diet

Think carefully about what you eat during your pregnancy, because your baby is reliant on you, and what you eat is an important part of this. A healthy diet is made up of starchy carbohydrates, fruit and vegetables, protein foods, dairy foods, and only small amounts of fats and sugar. By eating different combinations of foods each day, you'll ensure that you get all the nutrients you and your developing baby need.

Carbohydrates Starchy carbohydrates are things like cereals, bread, potatoes, pasta, and rice. They give you energy, as well as vitamins, minerals, protein, and fibre. They're filling and inexpensive. Aim for five or six servings of carbohydrates a day (a serving is a bowl of cereal, two slices of bread, a couple of potatoes, or three tablespoons of cooked rice or pasta).

Fruit and vegetables All of us, pregnant or not, should have a minimum of five portions of fruit and vegetables every day. However, this is particularly important in pregnancy. Fruit and vegetables contain essential vitamins and minerals, as well as carbohydrates and fibre.

Vegetables *are very good sources of fibre, antioxidants and many contain a variety of vitamins minerals including folate.*

VITAMINS AND MINERALS FOR PREGNANCY

Vitamins and minerals are needed for your own health as well as for your baby's healthy growth and development.

Vitamin/mineral	What it's needed for	Where it's found
Calcium	Development of your baby's bones and teeth	Dairy products, tinned salmon and sardines, fortified soya products, spinach, spring greens, pulses such as chickpeas and kidney beans, sesame seeds, almonds, brazil nuts, and white flour products
Iron	Healthy blood for you and your baby, and your baby's growth and development	Red meat, sardines, breakfast cereals, wholemeal bread, green leafy vegetables, pulses, dried fruit, and nuts (Eating foods with Vitamin C helps iron absorption, whereas tea or coffee, taken at the same time, or just after meals, impairs iron absorption.)
Folate (Folic acid is the manufactured form of this vitamin)	Development of your baby's nervous system; and for healthy blood	Green leafy vegetables, other vegetables (green beans, cauliflower, potatoes), fortified breakfast cereals and bread, pulses, baked beans, citrus fruits (Folate is destroyed by cooking, so eat some raw, and steam rather than boil vegetables.)
Vitamin C	Helps your body to absorb iron and keeps your immune system healthy	Most fruits and vegetables, especially citrus fruits, kiwi fruit, and blackcurrants (Prolonged cooking and storing destroys vitamin C, so eat fruit and vegetables raw or steamed and as fresh as possible.)
Vitamin B12	For cell growth, especially blood cells, and nervous system	Meat, fish, eggs, milk, fortified breakfast cereals, and yeast extracts
Vitamin D	Helps your body to absorb calcium for strong bones and teeth	Sunshine. Oily fish, fish oil, fortified margarine, whole milk, eggs, and fortified cereals
Omega-3 essential fatty acids	Development of your baby's brain and nervous system	Oily fish, fish oil, flaxseed, walnuts, and eggs

Fruit *can provide a refreshing as well as nutritious snack.*

Your fluid needs *are increased during pregnancy, so you should try and drink at least 2 litres (3 ½ pints) of fluid a day. Water is best. You can also drink fruit juice – though remember that this also contains sugar. It's best to limit the amount of cola-type drinks you have, especially if these contain caffeine.*

Protein This is needed to maintain your body and for the growth of new cells. Your baby needs protein in order to grow and develop. Protein is found in meat, fish, pulses (dried beans, lentils, chickpeas), eggs, nuts, and seeds. These foods also contain certain vitamins and minerals. During pregnancy, you need two or three servings of protein foods a day (a serving would be a couple of slices of lean meat, a small chop, a piece of fish, two eggs, or three or four tablespoons of cooked pulses).

Dairy foods (milk, cheese, yoghurt) These are another source of protein and are high in calcium, the mineral needed for the growth of your baby's bones and teeth. Dairy foods also contain useful vitamins. Aim to have two or three servings of dairy foods a day (for example, a glass of milk or a small yoghurt). Low-fat dairy foods provide just as much calcium and protein as higher-fat versions. (See page 90 for dairy products to avoid.)

Fats These occur in a lot of foods, such as meat, oily fish, dairy foods, nuts, and vegetable oils, and contain important nutrients. However, it's best not to eat too much fat. You can reduce the amount of fat in your diet by cutting the fat off meat and the skin off poultry, grilling rather than frying, making sandwiches without butter or margarine, and cutting down on foods like pies, sausages, cakes and biscuits, and crisps.

Sugar Although this is a source of energy, unlike other energy sources, such as starchy food or fruit, it doesn't provide vitamins or minerals, so is of little nutritional value and leads to tooth decay and weight gain. This doesn't mean that you need to avoid all sweet foods, but it's best not to be eating them frequently or in large amounts. Processed foods (for example canned and packet foods) tend to be high in sugar, so it's best to eat fresh instead.

Are vitamin and mineral supplements safe?

The only officially recommended vitamin supplement that you should take during pregnancy are folic acid (synthetic folate) and vitamin D. All women are advised to take 400mcg of folic acid a day while trying to conceive and also for the first 12 weeks of pregnancy. Folic acid is important for the development of your baby's nervous system, and taking a supplement in this way has been shown to protect against neural tube defects.

A balanced diet, as described above, will meet all of your nutritional needs and your baby's. However, while this is the ideal, sometimes it's not possible to eat as healthily as you would like – if you're suffering from nausea or heartburn, for example, or are otherwise unwell, or you simply don't like certain foods that contain important nutrients. In this situation, taking a special pregnancy multivitamin might be helpful. If you're concerned that your diet might not be adequate, ask your midwife or GP about whether he or she recommends a supplement.

Eating a lot of fresh fruit *and vegetables is important because these foods are full of vitamins and minerals as well as antioxidants – chemicals that protect your body from heart disease, cancer, and the effects of pollution.*

Eating safely

While you're pregnant, your immune system functions at a slightly lower level, which means that you may be more vulnerable to food-borne infections, which can affect you or your baby. There are also certain foods that can be harmful to your baby in other ways.

Infection risks from food The two main food-borne infections that pose a risk in pregnancy are listeriosis and toxoplasmosis. Listeriosis, caused by the listeria bacteria, causes a mild flu-like illness in the mother, but can lead to miscarriage or stillbirth, or to a baby being severely ill at birth. Toxoplasmosis is caused by the toxoplasma parasite. It can also cause mild flu-like symptoms in the mother, though it may cause no symptoms at all, but it can cause serious problems for the baby, especially if the mother develops it during the first six months of pregnancy. Both listeriosis and toxoplasmosis are very rare, however. See page 90 for how to avoid them.

Another infection that you may be vulnerable to during pregnancy is salmonella, which causes food poisoning. This doesn't affect the baby, but can make you quite unwell.

Other food-related risks

In very rare instances, high intakes of the animal form of vitamin A (retinol) have been found to be associated with birth defects in the baby. It's therefore best to avoid foods containing large amounts of this, particularly

WHEN TO AVOID PEANUTS

If you or your partner's family has a history of asthma, eczema, hayfever, or other allergies, then the UK Government recommends that you avoid eating peanuts or peanut products during pregnancy (and while breast-feeding). It's thought that this may help to reduce the risk of your baby developing allergies. This advice doesn't extend to other types of nuts.

FOODS YOU CAN EAT AND FOODS YOU SHOULD AVOID

It's OK to eat	It's best to avoid	Why avoid it
Hard cheeses, such as cheddar, parmesan, mozzarella, Gruyere (even if these are made from unpasteurized milk), and soft processed cheeses, like cottage cheese, cream cheese, and cheese spread	Ripened soft cheeses, such as Brie and Camembert, and blue-veined cheeses (even if they're made with pasteurized milk); cheese from unpasteurized sheep or goat's milk – they can be eaten if they've been thoroughly cooked, though	Risk of listeria
Yoghurt, fromage frais (including bio products)		
Pasteurized, sterilized, and UHT milk	"Green top" cow's milk and unpasteurized sheep and goat's milk, unless it's been boiled for at least two minutes	Risk of listeria or contamination with toxoplasma parasite
Ice cream in cartons	Home-made ice cream or soft whipped ice cream from machines	Risk of listeria
Meat and poultry that have been thoroughly cooked all the way through	Raw or undercooked meat	Risk of toxoplasmosis or salmonella
	Ready-cooked poultry unless thoroughly reheated	Risk of listeria
Cooked ham	Raw cured meat (for example, Parma ham, salami)	Risk of toxoplasmosis
	Paté (meat, fish, or vegetable) unless it's tinned or marked pasteurized	Risk of listeria, plus high levels of vitamin A
	Liver and liver products	High levels of vitamin A
White fish, such as cod, plaice, haddock Oily fish like salmon and mackerel	Shark, swordfish, and marlin. Limit your consumption of tuna to one fresh steak or two cans a week	High levels of mercury
Cooked shellfish	Raw or undercooked shellfish	Risk of bacteria that can cause food poisoning
Eggs cooked so that the white and yolk are solid Commercially prepared mayonnaise and salad cream	Raw, or undercooked (runny) eggs Foods such as mousses, mayonnaise, icing made with raw egg.	Risk of salmonella
Washed salads	Packaged salads unless you wash them first. Bought, dressed salads such as coleslaw or potato salad	Risk of toxoplasmosis Risk of listeria
Cooked-chilled foods that have been thoroughly heated through	Unheated cooked-chilled foods	Risk of listeria

liver and liver products. There are no risks associated with eating the plant form of vitamin A (betacarotene), which is found in carrots and other orange or red vegetables and fruit.

Taking in high levels of mercury can affect the development of the baby's nervous system. High levels of mercury are found in certain fish, and it's advised that you avoid these during pregnancy (see table opposite).

Harmful substances to avoid

If drinking and smoking were part of your lifestyle before pregnancy, you should reconsider now, as both alcohol and nicotine cross the placenta and as a result may affect you baby.

Alcohol There are differences of opinion among experts on how much, if any alcohol, it's "safe" to drink during pregnancy. The consensus among medical professionals and organizations is that you shouldn't drink more than one or two units once or twice a week (1). A "unit" of alcohol is 280ml (1/2 pint) of ordinary strength beer or cider, a 25ml pub measure of spirits, or a small 125ml (4 floz) glass of wine. However, there have not been enough in-depth studies to be conclusive about the effects of alcohol. As it does cross the placenta, some women choose to avoid it completely as it's the only way of being certain that their baby is safe from its effects. The risks associated with alcohol are increased if you smoke, or if your diet is poor. Also if you're small, a unit of alcohol is likely to have more effect on you and your baby than a larger woman.

Smoking This is known to be potentially harmful to unborn babies. It can affect their growth, make their heart beat faster, and put them at risk of being born prematurely or affected by cot death after they're born. If you're a smoker, stopping is one of the best things you can do for your baby and yourself. If you're finding it difficult to stop, speak to your midwife or GP about the support available to help you give up.

Caffeine Another substance that can affect your baby is caffeine. Too much may be associated with an increased risk of miscarriage, as well as of the baby not growing properly. The government advises that you limit your intake to no more than 300mg a day (2). A cup of instant coffee contains 75mg, a cup of brewed coffee 100mg, a cup of tea 50mg, a can of cola 40mg, a can of "energy" drink up to 80mg. You may not know that a 50g (2oz) bar of chocolate contains up to 50mg caffeine.

Recreational drugs Unborn babies can also be affected if their mothers use recreational drugs, such as cannabis, cocaine, or heroin, during pregnancy. If you're a user of these drugs, you may find it hard to stop and also hard to talk about, but your midwife won't be judgmental, so do tell her. She'll be able to put you in touch with specialist help to give up.

Travel in pregnancy

Being pregnant doesn't mean that you need to avoid travelling, unless your midwife or doctor advises you otherwise. There there are some precautions that it's best to take to protect yourself and your baby, however, whether you are travelling abroad or in the UK.

**DON'T FORGET
YOUR NOTES!**

Wherever you're travelling to, whether it's in the UK or overseas, don't forget to take your maternity notes with you.

Best time to travel

For most women, the middle three months of pregnancy are when they feel at their best, so this may be the best time for travelling if you have a choice. But this doesn't mean that you can't travel at other stages if you want or have to.

Travelling by car

To make sure that both you and your baby are as safe as possible when you're in a car, position your seatbelt so that the lap belt goes under your bump, across your pelvis, and the shoulder belt over the top of your bump, between your breasts (see below). Don't wear it across your bump. If you are a passenger, have your seat as far back as possible. It's OK to drive, or be a passenger in, a car with airbags, but if you're driving, sit so that your breastbone is at least 25cm (10in) away from the centre of the steering wheel.

If you're making a long car journey, stop every hour or two to get out and stretch your legs. If you're not driving, do foot and ankle exercises in your seat – point your toes up and down, circle your ankles and wiggle your toes. This can help stop your feet and ankles swelling. Make sure you drink plenty of water too. This can also help prevent swelling.

Three-point seat belts *should be worn whenever you are in a car. Place the lap strap as low as possible beneath your bump, across your thighs, and the diagonal shoulder strap above the bump, lying between your breasts. The belt should be adjusted to fit as snugly as possible.*

TIPS FOR TRAVELLING OVERSEAS

- If you're travelling abroad, check your insurance to see what cover it provides for pregnancy-related incidents. If you're going to a country within the EU, make sure you take your European Health Insurance Card (EHIC) with you to access the same level of medical care that is given to citizens of the country you're visiting.
- Follow the usual precautions about food and drink. Drink bottled water if you're unsure about the quality of the tapwater in the area you're visiting and avoid ice in your drinks. Make sure you drink lots of water if you're going somewhere hot.
- Check if any vaccinations are required for the area you're going to. Not all vaccinations can be given during pregnancy. The practice nurse at your GP's surgery will be able to give you information about this. It's best to avoid going to an area where malaria is a problem, as pregnant women are especially vulnerable to malaria and catching this disease in pregnancy can have serious consequences. If you are travelling somewhere where there is malaria, check with your GP's practice nurse which prophylaxis tablets are advised for that area and whether they are safe to take while pregnant – not all can be taken during pregnancy.
- Take a first aid kit with you, remembering to include any remedies you're taking for any pregnancy complaints.

Travelling by air

Commercial air travel is generally regarded as being safe in pregnancy, but if you have any complications such as high blood pressure, diabetes, or severe anaemia, or have had problems with bleeding, check with your midwife or GP before you make your trip (1). If you're planning to fly (or fly back from a trip) after 28 weeks of pregnancy, find out from your airline what their policy is on carrying pregnant passengers. Some airlines require a letter from your doctor certifying that you are fit to fly after 28 weeks and most will not carry you after 36 weeks (or 32 weeks if you're pregnant with more than one baby).

Pregnancy puts you at an increased risk of deep vein thrombosis (DVT), so during your flight, get up and move around the cabin every hour or so, and do foot and ankle exercises while you're seated. If you are seated in an aisle or bulkhead seat, you'll be able to stretch your legs. Drink plenty of water and avoid coffee or alcohol. You'll be more comfortable wearing loose clothing, and, if possible, slip-on shoes. If you're travelling long-haul (a flight of more than three hours), wear compression flight socks (2). Put them on as soon as you get up on the day you're travelling and keep them on until you go to bed. If there's any history of DVT, or other clotting problems in your family, see your midwife or doctor before making a long-haul flight. You might be able to get a prescription for free compression stockings from your midwife. Ask your health professionals whether they recommend taking a paediatric aspirin (75mg) before a flight. As in a car, wear your seatbelt under your bump, not across it.

see also

The role of your midwife	30–3
Caring for your body	80–3
Caring for your pelvic floor	84–5
Healthy eating	86–91

Pregnancy sickness

One of the earliest signs of pregnancy can be an odd, metallic taste in your mouth and sometimes a sudden aversion to tea and coffee. Nausea and, perhaps, vomiting tend to start in the second month, but most women feel a lot better after about 12 weeks.

Sickness is very common

As many as 70 to 80 per cent of pregnant women experience sickness of some kind in the early weeks of pregnancy. This ranges from feeling slightly nauseous to vomiting several times a day. Pregnancy sickness can start even before you miss a period, though it's more common for it to begin in the second month. It usually passes after around three months, but for some women it lasts into the fourth and fifth month, and for an unfortunate few it persists throughout pregnancy. Some women find that although sickness passes after the first three months, it returns toward the end of pregnancy. Pregnancy sickness is often referred to as "morning sickness", but in fact it can occur at any time of the day.

What causes it?

The cause of pregnancy sickness isn't yet fully understood. It may be due to a combination of factors. In part, it may be a reaction to the hormone human chorionic gonadotrophin (hCG) circulating in your body in early pregnancy. Levels of this hormone start to tail off at around 12 weeks, which may be why nausea often improves after then. Sickness may also be a reaction to increasing levels of another hormone, oestrogen, which continue to rise throughout pregnancy. Tiredness, which is very common in pregnancy, especially in the early weeks, may contribute to sickness too, as may low blood sugar and low blood pressure. Some experts think that pregnancy sickness may also be associated with stress and/or anxiety.

Although it's unpleasant, there's a theory that nausea is a way of protecting your baby from harmful substances, and some research has also suggested that it's linked to a lower risk of miscarriage (1). In fact there is an association between

> "First time around I was nauseous and very sensitive to smells, and ginger worked like a charm. Second-time around I was sick until 28 weeks and couldn't stand the sight of ginger – nothing worked."

TIPS ON EATING WITH MORNING SICKNESS

- Try frequent small snacks every two or three hours, or more often if it helps.
- Avoid rich, fatty, or spicy foods.
- Eat bland foods, like crackers, bread, cereals, home-made popcorn.
- Eat or drink things made from ginger, such as ginger biscuits, crystallized ginger, or ginger ale.
- Eat lots of fruit.
- Suck or sniff a cut lemon.
- Suck peppermints.
- Drink plenty of water or fruit juice.
- Drink herbal tea, such as lemon and ginger or peppermint.
- If you feel sick first thing in the morning, try having a dry biscuit or cracker, and a cup of tea, before you get up.
- Eat foods that contain vitamin B6 such as bananas, potatoes, avocados, brown rice, whole grains, nuts, fish, lean meat, and poultry.

COMPLEMENTARY THERAPIES THAT MAY HELP

- There is some evidence that ginger extract or B6 supplements can help. Ask your midwife or GP about taking a supplement.
- Wear sea sickness bands.
- Listen to the "Morning well" audio tape that is thought to interrupt the signals between the gut and the brain that lead to sickness (available from NCT Sales – see page 247).
- Rest as much as possible – try relaxation.
- Acupuncture or acupressure helps some women.
- Reflexologists offer treatment for sickness.
- There are homeopathic remedies for sickness; consult a homeopath to find out which would be the most suitable for you.
- Herbal remedies, such as slippery elm, help some women, but it's best to consult a herbalist about these.
- Some women find hypnotherapy helpful.

Experiment with herbal teas – *anise, fennel, meadowsweet, spearmint, or peppermint teas have all been recommended for pregnancy sickness.*

nausea and vomiting in early pregnancy and favourable birth outcome. The research also indicates that there is a link with increased placental weight to support this theory (2).

Not all women experience sickness in pregnancy, though, and if you don't, it's unlikely to mean that there's any problem with your pregnancy. It's also possible for sickness to fluctuate, being worse some days than others. The main thing you need to remember is that normal pregnancy sickness will not harm your baby. Even if you are eating very little, drinking only water, and vomiting several times a day, your baby will still continue to develop and grow.

Strategies that might help

There are various strategies different women have found to help with pregnancy sickness (see opposite and above). There have been few in-depth studies however, so the research evidence on their effectiveness is limited.

If you're feeling sick, it can sometimes be difficult to eat even small amounts. Or it may be that the only thing you can stomach is something that's not "healthy". Some women worry that if they're not eating well, this will be harmful for their baby. However, while it's always best to eat a good, balanced diet during pregnancy, if you can't do this in the early weeks because of sickness, don't worry. Babies are very good at ensuring that their needs are met and your body will have stores of nutrients that your baby can draw on if necessary.

If you're being so sick that you're finding it impossible to keep anything down, though, do see your doctor. Severe sickness (or hyperemesis gravidarum) affects about one per cent of women, and if not treated can lead to dehydration and malnourishment. Contact the Hyperemesis Gravidarum Support Group for support and information on this condition (see Useful organizations, page 245).

see also

The role of your midwife	30–3
Healthy eating	86–91
Discomforts in early pregnancy	96–9

Discomforts in early pregnancy

Growing a baby involves your whole body and it's hardly surprising that the changes that occur in early pregnancy can result in a range of minor physical discomforts. But there are things that you can do to help ease them and reduce their effects.

HORMONES IN EARLY PREGNANCY

The initial classic signs of pregnancy such as a missed period and sensitive breasts are caused by alterations in hormone secretion. One hormone involved is human chorionic gonadotrophin (hCG), which may be partly responsible for the nausea and vomiting many women experience in the first few months because it affects appetite and the laying down of fat. It also affects thirst and promotes the growth of the muscle layer of your uterus. In addition, it suppresses your immune system so that your body will not reject your baby. Human chorionic gonadotrophin reaches a maximum level by around 12 weeks of pregnancy and then drops for the rest of pregnancy, which may be why many women feel less sick after this time.

Why do discomforts occur?

When you are pregnant, all the systems in your body are working harder than usual to meet your and your baby's needs. The hormones that you produce during pregnancy circulate all over your body and affect how it works as a whole. This can lead to various minor discomforts and ailments. They're minor in the sense that they don't – mostly – put you or your baby at any risk, though they may not feel minor in terms of how uncomfortable they can make you feel.

Breast tenderness

This can be one of the first symptoms , especially if you're pregnant for the first time, and can occur before you've missed your period. Your breasts become enlarged and may even throb and feel painful. This is because the hormones oestrogen and progesterone preparing them for breast-feeding – blood flow is increasing and milk-producing cells are growing.

What you can do Wearing a good supporting bra should help to make you feel more comfortable. Make sure that your bras fit you properly and aren't too tight. Your bra size may go up several times. If your breasts feel hot, put a cold flannel on them. Massaging your breasts gently can also help. Some women find that avoiding caffeine (found in coffee, tea, cola, and so-called "energy" drinks) helps too.

Tiredness

This is a very common experience in early pregnancy. It's thought to be partly due to the sedative effects of pregnancy hormones, but it also occurs because your body is working very hard to support your developing baby.

What you can do There isn't a great deal that you can do about tiredness, other than resting as much as possible, which isn't always easy. Eating frequent small meals may help to keep your energy levels up. Extreme tiredness does usually pass after the first three months.

Constipation and bloating

One of the effects of the pregnancy hormones is to soften all your muscles, including those of your bowels. This can make your bowels sluggish, leading to constipation, bloating, and wind, which can be uncomfortable. If you're prescribed an iron supplement at any point in your pregnancy, this can also cause constipation.

What you can do To help with constipation, eat lots of fibre, fruit, and vegetables – though note that cabbage-type vegetables, as well as beans, lentils, and eggs, sometimes make bloating and wind worse. Try sprinkling linseed, available from health-food shops, on your breakfast cereal or drink a teaspoon of olive oil. Drink plenty of water, fruit juice (especially orange or prune juice), or herbal tea (normal tea sometimes makes constipation worse). Take regular exercise (for example, walking, swimming). Some yoga positions can also help with constipation. Get someone to massage your tummy in a clockwise direction from your belly button. And when you are opening your bowels, relax and avoid straining.

Headaches

These can be caused by a widening of the blood vessels in your brain, under the influence of pregnancy hormones, and by the extra blood that you have in your circulation putting pressure on blood vessels. Other possible causes are your low blood sugar levels, not drinking enough fluids, and swelling in your sinuses. Anxiety and tension can lead to headaches too.

What you can do You may be able to help prevent headaches by drinking lots of water and avoiding caffeine, and by not going too long without eating. Make time to relax each day too. If you have a headache, massaging your scalp with your fingers (as if you were washing your hair), or getting someone to massage your shoulders, can help, as can getting fresh air.

WEIGHT GAIN IN PREGNANCY

The amount of weight gained in pregnancy varies from woman to woman. It averages around 11–15kg (24–33lb), but women with normal pregnancies can put on a lot more or less than this. If you are overweight at the beginning of your pregnancy try not to gain more than about 10kg (22lb). If you are underweight, you should aim for weight gain at the upper end of the range. Many midwives and doctors feel that there is nothing to be gained from routinely weighing women.

In the early weeks your baby weighs very little, but you may put on weight as your body starts to lay down fat, your breasts get bigger, your blood supply increases, and you retain fluid (after the birth, your most rapid weight loss occurs as you lose the extra 2–8 litres/3 $\frac{1}{2}$–14 pints of water that you're carrying in your urine). As pregnancy progresses, the placenta and amniotic fluid contribute to weight gain.

On the other hand, you may find that in the first three months you actually lose some – perhaps due to sickness, or because you've started eating more healthily and are consuming fewer "empty" calories, or your metabolism has speeded up. If this happens, it won't harm your baby – he'll still be getting what he needs from you.

Bleeding gums

The softening effects of pregnancy hormones and the increased blood volume that you have can combine to make your gums soft and spongy, and more prone to bleeding. Because of this sponginess, bits of food may become trapped in your gums, which can cause infection to develop. Severe gum infection may cause problems as infection can travel around your body to your baby.

What you can do Brush your teeth gently twice a day with a soft toothbrush, paying particular attention to your gum line, and floss every day. Eat plenty of fruit and vegetables (for their vitamin C content) and avoid sugary foods. Make sure you visit your dentist if you are worried about your teeth or gums. You qualify for free dental care on the NHS during pregnancy and for the first year after the birth.

Stuffy or bleeding nose

The softening effects of pregnancy hormones and your increased blood volume can also make the lining of your nose and your sinuses soft and spongy. This can make your nose feel blocked up, or cause nosebleeds. The increased blood supply to your nose can also lead to you producing more mucus, which can make your nose run.

What you can do Be gentle with your nose, and don't blow it too hard. If your nose is stuffy, try steam inhalation. Don't take any decongestants without medical advice. If you have a nosebleed, pinch the sides of your nose together gently and lean forward slightly.

Dizziness

It's quite common to have dizzy spells in pregnancy. There are two main causes of this. One is that your blood pressure may be low. This happens because pregnancy hormones make your blood vessels dilate, which can slow the flow of blood to your brain. It can occur particularly if you stand for too long, but also if you get up too quickly. The other cause of feeling faint, especially if it comes on more gradually, is that your blood sugar levels may be too low.

What you can do To try and prevent dizziness, avoid standing still for long periods of time, and get up slowly if you've been sitting or lying down. Eat small regular snacks (not sugary though) to keep your blood sugar levels up. If you feel faint, sit down, put your head between your knees, and breathe deeply.

Thrush

This is yeast infection that often causes a thick white vaginal discharge, redness, and itching around the vagina. The organism normally lives in the vagina without producing any symptoms. During pregnancy, however, the acid–alkali balance of the vagina changes, creating conditions that make it possible for the yeast to overgrow, leading to thrush.

What you can do Eating live yoghurt can also help as this contains organisms that compete with thrush. The condition flourishes in a warm, moist environment, so wear loose cotton knickers and avoid wearing anything that's tight around your crotch. Use a clean towel every day and wash your genital area with your hand rather than a flannel to prevent thrush from spreading. Contact your GP if symptoms persist and he or she may prescribe an antifungal pessary for you and a cream for your partner.

Urinary complaints

Needing to urinate frequently is common in the first three months of pregnancy. This is due to pressure on your bladder as your uterus starts to enlarge. Also, the increased blood supply to your pelvic area can make your bladder feel full so that you need to empty it more frequently.

Another urinary complaint that pregnant women are susceptible to is cystitis (a urine infection). Pregnancy hormones make your bladder softer, so it may not empty so efficiently, and if the bladder isn't emptied properly, bacteria in the urine that's left behind can multiply, causing infection. Symptoms of cystitis include wanting to pass urine frequently (but you only produce a small amount), and burning or stinging when you urinate.

What you can do Drinking lots of water and cranberry juice can help to flush bacteria out of your system, but if your symptoms persist, contact your GP. For information on bleeding and abdominal pain in early pregnancy, see page 105.

Allergies

If you suffer from allergic reactions, you may find that they get worse while you're pregnant. Some women even find that they develop allergies for the first time during pregnancy. This is because your body's immune system has to get weaker so that it doesn't reject your baby, since half the baby's genetic make up is the father's, not yours.

What you can do If you're already taking medication for an allergy, check with your midwife or doctor that it's safe to use in pregnancy.

Cravings

The desire to eat certain foods can strike early in pregnancy. Strong dislikes or cravings for specific tastes may be the first clue that you're pregnant.

What you can do You can probably expect to go off drinks containing caffeine. If weight is a problem, try to fight that longing for ice cream or chips. "Pica" – strong cravings for unlikely things like soap or coal – should probably be mentioned to your midwife, but they are rarely a problem.

COMPLEMENTARY THERAPIES THAT MAY HELP

If you want to try complementary therapies to help with pregnancy discomforts, consult a qualified practitioner as some treatments are not advisable during pregnancy.

- Acupuncturists offer treatment for constipation, headaches, and cystitis.
- There are homeopathic remedies for constipation, headaches, bleeding gums, thrush, and cystitis.
- Herbal remedies exist for constipation, headaches, thrush, and cystitis.
- Aromatherapists use essential oils to treat constipation, headaches, stuffy nose, thrush, and cystitis although some advise against using them in the first three months of pregnancy.
- Reflexologists treat constipation, headaches, stuffy nose, and cystitis. However, some reflexologists will not offer treatment in the first 12 weeks of pregnancy, especially if you've had a previous miscarriage.
- Osteopathy provides treatment that may help constipation, headaches, and back pain.

Discomforts in later pregnancy

By the time you reach the second trimester, some – though not all – of the complaints you may have had in the early months will have disappeared. However, from the second half of pregnancy, you may develop some new discomforts as your body continues to change to meet your baby's needs,

Discomforts change as your baby grows

After the first months of pregnancy, your uterus rises up out of your pelvis into your abdomen where, as it gets bigger, it'll take up space previously occupied by other organs. As your baby grows and your body grows to accommodate him, you may develop other discomforts. By the time the due date approaches, you'll feel more than ready for your baby to arrive.

Heartburn

The symptoms of heartburn are a burning feeling in your chest and throat, sometimes accompanied by nausea. It happens because pregnancy hormones relax the muscle at the entrance to your stomach, allowing stomach juices to back up into your gullet. During the last ten weeks or so, pressure on your stomach from your growing uterus contributes to it too. Heartburn tends to be worst when you're sitting or lying down.

What you can do Eating little and often, and avoiding rich, spicy, or greasy foods, can help relieve heartburn. Some women find drinking milk, fizzy water, or peppermint or fennel tea helps. Allow at least two hours after eating before you go to bed and sleep slightly propped up. Some yoga positions may help alleviate heartburn.

"I remember the cramp in the middle of the night – it was excruciating – give me labour any day!"

Varicose veins

Pregnancy hormones soften the walls and valves of your veins, which can result in blood pooling in your legs. This can lead to swollen, itchy, and painful varicose veins in your legs.

What you can do Keep your circulation moving by not standing for long periods of time, and exercise regularly (yoga is good for your circulation and may help). Don't cross your legs when you're sitting down. Put your feet up whenever you can. Raising the foot of your bed 10cm (4in) or so might help. Don't wear tight clothing tight around your knees or crotch. Wearing compression stockings helps to prevent your blood from pooling (you may be able to get a prescription for these). Using the shower, spray your legs alternately with hot and cold water, or put your feet alternately into buckets of hot and cold water, to relieve the discomfort of varicose veins. The symptoms should disappear once you've had your baby.

Some women find *that drinking fizzy water can help to relieve heartburn. It's always a good idea to drink water because it is important to keep your body hydrated.*

Piles

These are varicose veins in your back passage and if you have them they tend to worsen as pregnancy progresses. Symptoms include itching, soreness, pain when you open your bowels and sometimes a small amount of bleeding afterward.

What you can do Doing pelvic floor exercises can help to keep blood flowing through the area. Putting a cold compress or a sanitary towel soaked in witch hazel against your back passage may help to shrink the piles. You can also buy gel-filled pads that you cool in the fridge to use in the same way (also available from NCT Sales, see page 247), you can buy over-the-counter remedies from the chemist too. Minimize the risk constipation by eating plenty of fibre and drinking lots of water.

Itchy skin

Hormonal changes and your skin stretching can lead to your skin being itchy, especially on your belly.

What you can do Wearing loose cotton clothing can help to reduce itching. Moisturizing your skin or applying calamine cream or lotion may help too. You can also try putting a cup of bicarbonate of soda in your bath, tying a handful of oatmeal in a muslin square and letting the water run through it as you fill the bath, or washing yourself with it. See page 107 for circumstances in which itching may be a sign of something more serious.

Cramp

Many women experience painful cramps in their legs in the last ten weeks of pregnancy, especially at night. What causes this isn't really known, although there are various theories about it. Cramps haven't been shown to be connected with any deficiencies.

What you can do Doing foot and leg exercises for ten minutes or so before you go to bed (rotate your ankles and legs, and point your toes upward) may help to prevent cramps occurring.

If you get cramp, flex your foot upward, or lean forwards against a wall with the cramped leg stretched out behind you and your foot flat on the floor. Relaxing may help the cramp to pass more quickly.

The pain associated with cramp usually passes within a few minutes. If you have longer lasting pain in either of your calves, especially if there's also any redness or swelling, see your doctor as soon as you can. Leg pain can be associated with a blood clot having developed in one of your veins.

Swelling

Your body retains extra fluid during pregnancy to soften your joints so that they can make space for your baby. Some of this fluid may collect in your feet and hands, causing swelling. This tends to be worse if you've been standing for a long time, or if the weather is hot.

What you can do Avoid standing for long periods, especially when it's hot, and rest with your feet up as much as you can. Don't wear clothes that are tight around your ankles or wrists. Wearing support tights or stockings can help reduce swelling. If your feet are swollen, massage your legs firmly upward from your ankles, using both hands. Spraying your legs alternately with hot and cold water, or putting your feet alternately into buckets of hot and cold water, might help reduce swelling too. Drink plenty of fluids (some women find nettle tea helpful). There are also some yoga positions that can help with swelling.

See pages 104–7 for circumstances in which swelling could be a cause for concern.

Carpal-tunnel syndrome

If fluid collects in your hands, this can put pressure on the median nerve, the nerve that passes between the bones of your wrist, the "carpal tunnel", causing carpal-tunnel syndrome. The symptoms of this are numbness, tingling and pain in your hands, thumb, and first three fingers, and occasionally your arm, which sometimes makes it difficult even to do simple things like holding a pen.

What you can do Tell your midwife. She should be able to get you a special wrist support to keep it straight. Or you can try the following exercises. Hold your fingers stretched out, then relax them. Make a fist, then straighten out your fingers. Or, move your hands up and down, from side to side and round and round (you can do this in cold water). Flick your wrists. Press your hands down on a flat surface, then turn them over so that the backs of your hands are pressing down. You can also try putting your hands alternately in bowls of cold and warm water. Keep your hands raised as much as possible – put them up on a pillow when you're resting.

Symphysis pubis dysfunction (SPD)

SPD is a loosening of the joints of the pelvis. The symphysis pubic joint is low down at the front where the two bones meet, and the two sacro-iliac joints are at the back, where the pelvis joins the spine. SPD causes pain in your pelvis, sometimes severe, particularly at the front. If you are experiencing pain in the pelvis, tell your midwife. Pain tends to be worse when you do anything that involves the two sides of your pelvis moving against each other, such as going up and down stairs or getting in and out of bed. In severe cases, crutches, even a wheelchair, might be needed.

What you can do Minimize pain by keeping your knees as close together as possible. Walk with small steps, go up stairs one at a time, and when you get into bed, a car, or the bath, sit with your knees together and swing your legs round. Avoid standing still for too long and rest as much as possible. Place a cold pack (wrapped in a towel) over your pubic joint. Make an appointment to see your midwife or doctor: wearing a special pelvic support often helps and your midwife or GP can provide you with one.

Anaemia

Your baby's need for iron increase in later pregnancy, and this can lead to you becoming anaemic. Symptoms of anaemia are looking pale, feeling tired, and sometimes feeling dizzy and breathless.

What you can do You can boost your iron intake through your diet (sources of iron include red meat, dark chicken or turkey meat, fortified breakfast cereals, sardines, wholemeal bread, pulses, egg yolks, green leafy vegetables, cashews, or dried apricots) or by taking a liquid iron supplement, available at health-food shops. Discuss your symptoms with your midwife or GP who can do a blood test to check for anaemia.

Stress incontinence

This is the technical term for the leaking of urine that can happen when you do something like cough or sneeze or lift something. It happens as a result of pressure on your pelvic floor from the weight of your baby and your enlarged uterus.

What you can do To prevent this – or reduce it – do your pelvic floor exercises. Emptying your bladder frequently so that there's less urine to leak out can help, too.

COMPLEMENTARY THERAPIES THAT MAY HELP

If you want to try complementary therapies to help with pregnancy discomforts, consult a qualified practitioner as some treatments are not advisable during pregnancy.

- Acupuncturists offer treatment for heartburn, varicose veins, piles, swelling, carpal-tunnel syndrome, SPD, and anaemia.
- There are homeopathic remedies for heartburn, varicose veins, piles, cramp, fluid retention, and anaemia.
- Herbal remedies exist for heartburn, varicose veins, piles, and anaemia.
- Aromatherapists use essential oils to treat heartburn, varicose veins, piles, and swelling.
- Osteopaths and chiropractors manipulate your joints to help ease SPD. Osteopaths also treat heartburn, swelling, and carpal-tunnel syndrome.
- Reflexologists treat heartburn, varicose veins, piles, and swelling.

At risk pregnancies

The vast majority of pregnancies are completely straightforward. Yet many women will find that something happens during the nine months that causes them anxiety. While it's really important to enjoy your pregnancy as much as you can, it's also a good idea to know the warning signs that mean you need to consult your midwife or doctor.

ECTOPIC PREGNANCY

Also known as a tubal pregnancy, this occurs when the fertilized egg implants somewhere other than in the uterus – most commonly in the Fallopian tube. If the egg implants in the Fallopian tube, the tube will be stretched as the embryo grows, which can cause severe pain on one side of the abdomen and shoulder pain is also common. Serious internal bleeding takes place if the tube bursts and the situation then becomes a medical emergency.

If you think you have signs of an ectopic pregnancy, consult your midwife or GP straight away. Don't hesitate. The pregnancy needs to be removed surgically and possibly the Fallopian tube.

An ectopic pregnancy is very frightening, and you may worry about your chances of having another baby, especially if you have lost a tube. Get as much information as you can from the hospital, and find someone to support you. The Ectopic Pregnancy Trust and The Miscarriage Association help women who have had ectopic pregnancies (see page 245 for their details). Your local NCT teacher may know of someone in your area who will be very happy to talk to you.

Miscarriage

It's quite common to lose some stale brown blood or even a little bright red blood in the first 14 weeks of pregnancy. You can consult your midwife or GP about it, but provided you have no other symptoms, you will probably be reassured that, in all likelihood, the bleeding will stop quickly and there will be no more. A heavy loss of blood, particularly if you are passing clots and have low backache, could mean a miscarriage. Sadly, about one quarter of confirmed pregnancies end this way. Often the miscarriage is because there is something wrong with the baby. Some women want to consult their midwife if they think they are having a miscarriage, and others prefer to cope on their own.

Occasionally, the baby dies in the uterus, but isn't expelled from the body. You may know that "something isn't right" and feel "less pregnant" than you did before. This is called a missed miscarriage and can only be confirmed on a scan. You may prefer to wait for the miscarriage to complete itself, or choose to have a minor operation to empty your uterus.

Following a miscarriage, your body will probably return to normal in four to six weeks, but emotions may take much longer to heal. Some women take miscarriage in their stride while for others, it is a bereavement that stays with them for a long time. If you are having difficulty dealing with your loss, find someone to talk to who will understand, perhaps a friend who has experienced miscarriage, or contact the Miscarriage Association or the NCT (see pages 245 and 247 for their numbers).

Placenta praevia

This is the medical term for a placenta that has implanted low down in the uterus so that it partly or completely covers the cervix. In the first half of pregnancy, before the uterus has become very large, it is quite usual for the placenta to be close to or over the cervix. However, by about 32 weeks of pregnancy, most placentas have moved well away from the cervix as the uterus has stretched, and only a tiny percentage still cause a problem.

How will my care be affected? A minor degree of placenta praevia, when the placenta is just at the edge of the cervix, is unlikely to cause any problems. However, you will be offered regular scans to ensure that all is well. If the

WARNING SIGNS TO WATCH FOR

Symptom	Description	What you should do
Bleeding before 20 weeks	• Small amount • Heavy loss or passing clots • Dark brown, watery bleeding	• Probably OK, mention it your midwife • Could be miscarriage, consult your midwife or doctor • CALL MIDWIFE OR DOCTOR NOW; it could be ectopic pregnancy
Bleeding after 20 weeks	• Slight bleeding at the end of pregnancy • Any other bleeding	• May indicate that labour is starting • Should be reported to your midwife
Pain	• Period-like pain • Cramps • Vague aches and pains in the pelvis • Sharp pain in the groin, especially when you cough or sneeze • Severe pain in the abdomen and especially if it radiates to your shoulder • Severe pain, especially at the top of your abdomen on the right-hand side • Severe headache • Sudden agonizing pain in your abdomen with bleeding, faintness, and shock	• Quite common in early pregnancy • Also common, generally due to wind or constipation, however, both period-like pain and cramps might indicate a miscarriage, talk to midwife or doctor • These are common. Talk to your midwife if concerned • Probably due to stretching of the ligaments that support your uterus • CALL MIDWIFE OR DOCTOR NOW; it could be ectopic pregnancy • CALL MIDWIFE TODAY, it may indicate pre-eclampsia • CALL MIDWIFE TODAY, it may indicate pre-eclampsia • May mean a placental abruption, see overleaf. CALL AN AMBULANCE
Itching	• Itching over your abdomen • Itching in the area of surgical scars • Relentless, generalized itching • Itching on the palms of your hands and soles of your feet	• Itching as skin stretches in late pregnancy is common • This is also common and caused by stretching • CALL MIDWIFE NOW, it could be obstetric cholestasis, see overleaf • CALL MIDWIFE NOW This could indicate the possibility of obstetric cholestasis, see overleaf.

placenta covers the cervix, this can lead to serious bleeding during pregnancy and the baby will need to be delivered by Caesarean. The bleeding associated with placenta praevia is bright red and painless, and can be very heavy. It generally stops and then starts again, perhaps heavier than before. If you have a bleed, you might be admitted to hospital for the rest of your pregnancy, or you might be able to go home if you live near the hospital. You will have to take it very easy and avoid sex.

Pre-eclampsia

This is a potentially life-threatening condition that can develop in pregnancy. Pre-eclampsia is symptomless in the early stage and is only detectable by regular antenatal checks on the mother's blood pressure

GESTATIONAL DIABETES

The way in which your body produces insulin changes during pregnancy, and in some women this can lead to the development of gestational diabetes.

The condition doesn't usually produce any symptoms, though it may be suspected if high levels of sugar are found in your urine or blood, or if you have an unusually large bump. Gestational diabetes is diagnosed by a blood test (a glucose-tolerance test). Following diagnosis, it can usually be controlled through diet, though occasionally insulin needs to be given. Gestational diabetes needs to be well controlled because if not, it can lead to the baby becoming big, which can cause complications with the birth, and/or to him having low blood sugar after birth.

After your baby is born, the condition disappears, though women who have had it are at increased risk of subsequently developing Type 2 diabetes (non-insulin-dependent diabetes) later in life.

and urine. It is thought that this disease starts right at the very beginning of pregnancy when the placenta is in the early stages of development. However, it's unusual for signs or symptoms to appear before 30 weeks. The main symptom is high blood pressure, accompanied by protein in the urine and, sometimes, swelling of the face, hands, or feet. About five to eight per cent of all pregnant women develop pre-eclampsia. It sometimes runs in families.

Having very high blood pressure can cause difficulties for both you and your baby, which is why your midwife checks your blood pressure at every antenatal appointment. You will be offered regular checks if you have any symptoms of pre-eclampsia. The circulation of blood through the placenta may be affected so that your baby does not grow properly, and, in extreme cases, you may have problems with blood clots, and even have fits, or seizures. This is why your midwife checks your blood pressure at every antenatal appointment.

Your kidneys do not normally allow protein to pass into your urine. However, if your blood pressure is too high, protein will be squeezed out, which is why protein in the urine is another sign of pre-eclampsia. The amount of protein in the urine is shown as +, ++, +++, ++++, see page 32.

If your blood pressure creeps up from week to week, and there is an increasing amount of protein in your urine, your doctor may advise you to have an induction at around 37 weeks of pregnancy.

Sudden onset pre-eclampsia Sometimes, pre-eclampsia develops very suddenly. Your blood pressure may have been fine at your last clinic visit, but, out of the blue, you may become very swollen, you may have bad headaches, and your vision may be blurred. You must act on these signs immediately, and contact your midwife or doctor. Your baby may need to be born very quickly.

Placental abruption

Occasionally, the placenta starts to peel away from the wall of the uterus during pregnancy. It's a very uncommon occurrence, except in cases of severe placenta praevia. A placental abruption could be brought on by a serious car accident or a blow to your abdomen, or by very high blood pressure (see pre-eclampsia), or sometimes through smoking or taking street drugs such as cocaine.

How will my care be affected? If the placenta only separates a little from the wall of the uterus, there will be some bleeding and pain, but things should settle down again, although you may be offered regular scans for the rest of your pregnancy. In the case of a serious abruption, the symptoms are heavy dark bleeding and severe abdominal pain. Your tummy feels rigid and your uterus may start to contract strongly. This is a medical emergency and you and your baby need immediate attention. You will probably be offered a Caesarean section.

If your baby is born as an emergency following a serious bleed, he may need to go to the Special Care Baby Unit for a while. And you will need a blood transfusion and specialist nursing.

A birth like this can leave you feeling emotionally battered. Before you leave the hospital, make sure that you understand exactly what happened and what treatment you and your baby received. Find out if there are any long-term implications and whether the same thing is likely to happen in another pregnancy.

Obstetric cholestasis (OC)

Sometimes called "cholestasis of pregnancy", obstetric cholestasis is caused by a problem with your liver. Bile is produced in the liver and normally travels down bile ducts into the intestines where it helps digestion. For some reason that no one quite understands, the flow of bile can be obstructed in pregnancy, which results in bile salts accumulating in the mother's blood. The main symptom is unbearable itching all over the body, generally from about 30 weeks of pregnancy. The itching is worst on the palms of the hands and the soles of the feet, and at night. Therefore if you have severe itching at any time during your pregnancy, consult your midwife or doctor straightaway.

The percentage of women who have obstetric cholestasis varies from country to country. For some reason, Chile has the highest rate in the world; in Europe, only about one per cent of women develop obstetric cholestasis. You're more likely to develop it if someone else in your family has had it or if you're expecting twins.

Bile is needed for the absorption of vitamin K from the gut. If no bile is reaches the gut, vitamin K can't be absorbed from the food. Vitamin K is one of the factors that makes the blood clot. Women affected by obstetric cholestasis can have develop problems with bleeding during or after the birth. In addition, babies are at increased risk of being stillborn at 36 to 40 weeks of pregnancy.

How will my care be affected? If you develop obstetric cholestasis, you may be given extra vitamin K during pregnancy to help your blood clot, and your doctor may advise inducing labour at around 37 weeks. Some women may be advised to take a specific drug for the condition.

After the birth, your baby will need an injection of vitamin K, but otherwise he shouldn't have any problems. Your liver will return to normal. However, you need to bear in mind that you are very likely to get obstetric cholestasis again if you decide to have another pregnancy.

To cope with the itching, try calamine lotion and creams containing chamomile. Have a look at your diet. You may need to reduce your intake of fatty foods. Some women may find that an aqueous cream or calamine lotion could help soother the itching. Contact the Obstetric Cholestasis Support Group (see Useful organizations, page 245) who will also be able to help you.

BABY "SMALL FOR DATES"

An ultrasound scan might show that your baby is not growing well in the uterus, usually as a result of not enough blood flowing to and from the placenta (called placental insufficiency). This can result in your baby either not growing properly (known as intrauterine growth retardation) or not getting enough oxygen.

There are various factors that can cause placental insufficiency, including problems with the development of the placenta or its blood supply, high blood pressure, smoking, certain medical conditions, and some infections.

Signs of placental insufficiency include the baby being small, or having a slow heartbeat, or his movements being reduced. It's generally diagnosed through a doppler ultrasound scan, which measures blood flow through the placenta. If the condition is found, the baby is usually then carefully monitored. It may be necessary for him to be delivered early.

Getting ready for the birth

You may be feeling a mixture of anxiety, elation, perhaps even sadness that your pregnancy will soon be over, but most of all, you'll be impatient to see your baby at last. These last few weeks are the time for final preparations and making sure you have everything you need.

WHAT YOU'LL NEED FOR THE BIRTH

Whether you are having your baby at home, in a birth centre, or hospital you will need certain basics ready.

For you:
- Comfortable cotton clothing such as T-shirt to wear during labour
- Old (or cheap new), paper, or mesh knickers (mesh knickers are available from the NCT, see contact details on page 247)
- Maternity sanitary towels
- Nursing bra and breast pads

For your baby:
- Clothes, nappy, and cotton wool
- Towel.

Remember that people are likely to give you gifts of baby clothes so may not wish to buy too many yourself before your baby is born.

Pack ahead of your due date

As your baby will be mature enough to be born from 37 weeks, it's a good idea to have everything you need for his birth organized by then.

In the final days before the birth, it can be a good idea to get your hair cut into a fuss-free style, fill your freezer with meals you've prepared earlier, and buy two of everything when you go shopping for basics. Visit a friend with a new baby, if you can, and ask her advice on what to organize ahead of time. Make sure your birth partner knows where you have put your labour bag, the hospital emergency bag, and the baby's clothes.

If you are having your baby at home

Your midwife will probably visit you at around 37 weeks to drop off a pack containing the things she will need for the birth. She will bring the entonox (gas and air) and pethidine on the day. You might also like to have the following to hand:
- Some plastic sheeting, a plastic shower curtain, or some old newspapers to protect your floor and furniture, and a protective covering for your bed, if you plan to use it
- Birthing ball (available through NCT Sales, see page 247)
- Plasticine or Blu-Tack™ to block the overflow if you want to use your bath for pain relief
- Snacks for you to eat, and drinks with bendy straws
- Food and drink for your midwives that your partner or birth supporter can leave out
- Large towel to put round you and your baby after he's born
- Bowl or bucket to put the placenta in
- Bin bags for clearing up
- Emergency bag in case you need to transfer to hospital (see opposite).

Water birth

If you're having a water birth, there are different pools that you can hire, and the costs vary (see page 59). Things to consider when choosing a pool include your height, whether you want your birth partner to be in it with you, the size of the room in which you'll be using the pool and the strength of the floor, how quickly the pool can be filled, whether the hose supplied is long enough to reach your taps, and whether the hose adaptor will fit your taps. Check with the pool-hire company what the fee covers, as well as the hire period (and what happens if you go over it).

If you're hoping to have a birth centre or hospital water birth, ask your midwife what you will need to bring with you on the day. If you want to take a pool with you to the hospital this needs to be agreed in advance.

You will also need to prepare your home birth pack or hospital bag. Extras that you might want for a water birth include:

- Some plastic sheeting to put under the pool
- Water thermometer (this may be supplied by the pool-hire company)
- Inflatable pillow for your head and/or swimming floats so that you can rest your arms
- A piece of sponge or a folded towel to kneel on in the water and something similar for your midwife to kneel on beside the pool
- Plastic sieve or fish net and a bucket
- Lots of towels and a thick, warm dressing gown
- Small stool or chair to sit on or use to get in and out of the pool
- T-shirt to wear in the pool if you want
- Swimming trunks for partner if he's going to join you in the pool.

Having your baby in hospital

Different women find different things useful during labour so think about what would make you most comfortable. Pack a separate bag for a hospital stay after the birth (see box right). These are some suggestions for essential items that you will need.

- Your maternity notes and your birth plan
- Comfortable cotton clothing such as a baggy T-shirt to wear in labour
- Water spray, baby wipes, or flannel, to freshen your face, or a new natural sponge, to freshen your face or dip in cold water to suck
- Plenty of drinks as the hospital environment can be drying
- Change for the phone, or a card, as you may not be able to use a mobile
- Toiletries, including toothbrush and toothpaste or mouthwash
- Food and drink and a change of clothes for your birth partner
- Maternity sanitary towels and knickers for after the birth
- Nightie or pyjamas and a dressing gown, or change of clothes
- Clothes and a nappy for your baby.
  The following items may be nice to have with you but are not essential:
- Warm socks or slippers
- Hair ties or clips to keep your hair off your face
- Lipsalve
- Oil and/or wooden roller for massage
- hot water bottle, or ice pack in case of backache
- Ice cubes in a thermos (to suck or put in drinks)
- Music and player (and batteries)
- Notebook and pen for recording your labour
- Camera and film or spare card (and battery or charger)
- Large towel.

IF YOU'RE STAYING IN HOSPITAL

For you:
- Nightie or pyjamas, light dressing gown, and slip-on slippers
- Old (or cheap new), paper, or mesh knickers (mesh knickers are available from NCT Sales, see page 247)
- Maternity sanitary towels
- Nursing bra and breast pads
- Toiletries and a towel
- Ear plugs and/or sleep mask
- Change for the phone, or a phonecard
- Books/magazines
- Day clothes for going home

For your baby:
- Nappies and cotton wool
- Clothes
- Towel

Don't forget that if you're going home by car, you'll also need a car seat for your baby.

Best baby positions for birth

The way in which your baby lies in your pelvis is important: it can affect how smoothly your labour progresses. In the last few weeks of your pregnancy, it's a good idea to stand and sit as much as possible in ways that will encourage your baby into the best position, prior to birth.

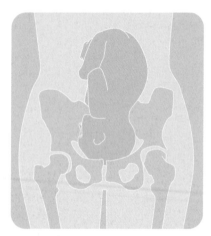

When your baby *lies "left occiput anterior" with spine facing outward, his head will press neatly on your cervix, helping it to open up.*

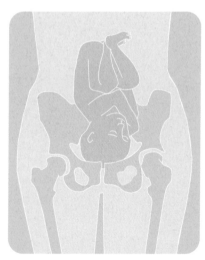

If your baby lies *the other way round "right occiput posterior", this can slow down the first stage of labour because his head does not press so effectively on the cervix.*

Why it makes a difference

The best position for your baby to be in for birth is head down, with his back against your belly, facing your back. This way, he can fit through your pelvis as easily as possible. He can "flex" his head and neck, tucking his chin into his chest, so that the narrowest part of his head (the back) is pressing on your cervix, helping it to dilate. The flexible joints in the baby's skull allow the head to change shape and negotiate the birth canal during birth.

This position is known as "occiput anterior" (OA), meaning that the back of the baby's head, or "occiput", is at the front, or "anterior". The majority of babies lie this way and it may be written in your notes as LOA ("left occiput anterior") if the baby is lying to your left or, less commonly, ROA ("right occiput anterior") if he is lying to your right.

Back-to-back babies Some babies lie with their back against their mother's back, which is known as an "occiput posterior" (OP) position. Labour tends to take longer if the baby is in this position because he can't tuck in his chin very well and getting through the pelvis is more awkward. If a baby is lying OP, this often causes backache during labour.

Certain aspects of our modern lives, such as lounging on sofas and sitting in cars, may make babies more likely to lie in a posterior position. Because the back of your baby's body is heavier than the front, his back will tend to roll toward the direction you're leaning in. So if you're leaning backward or reclining (as on a sofa), his back may roll toward your back – so he will be in a posterior position.

If you're leaning forward, however, his back may roll toward your front – an anterior position. Leaning forward is therefore better than leaning backward. Also, if you're in a position in which your knees are below your hips, this creates more space for the baby's head to lie in the front of your pelvis. Some babies, however, will not shift their position.

Back or front facing – can you tell? It's not always easy for you to know which way round your baby is lying, but your midwife should be able to tell you. There are also some signs that you can look for. If your baby is lying OP or "back to your back", your bump may feel squashy and you may feel (and see) kicks in the middle of your belly. Another particular tell-tale sign of the baby facing forward is a dip around your belly button.

Helping your baby into a good position

To help your baby to get into a good position, spend as much time as you can in positions in which you can lean forward and where your hips are above your knees, particularly from 34 weeks onward if it's your first baby, or 37 weeks if it isn't. Evidence that "re-positioning" your baby works, however, is mainly anecdotal (1).

Positions you can try

- Sit the wrong way round on an upright chair and lean over the back.
- Sit on an upright chair, with your feet flat on the floor, and lean forward with your elbows resting on a table.
- Sit on the edge of a chair or sofa with your feet apart and lean forward so that your belly hangs between your knees.
- Sit on a birthing ball.
- If you sit a lot at work, take regular breaks to stand up and move around. If necessary, sit on a couple of cushions to keep your hips raised up above your knees.
- Kneel forward over a pile of pillows, a beanbag, or a birthing ball, with your knees apart and your bottom down; watch TV in this position.
- Get onto all-fours and move around.
- Put a cushion under your bottom if you're travelling by car.
- Lie on your left side, with your right leg over and in front of your left leg (with a cushion or pillow between your knees).
- Swim or float on your front (avoid breast-stroke leg actions if you have any pelvic pain).

Positions to avoid

- Sitting leaning back on a squashy sofa or chair.
- Sitting with your legs crossed.
- Squatting deeply.

Breech babies

Although most babies turn head-down toward the end of pregnancy, about three to four per cent of babies will be breech at full term. This means the baby's head stays uppermost in the womb with his bottom or feet positioned to come out first. It's perfectly possible for a breech baby to be born naturally, although a head-first position makes the birth easier.

Can a breech baby be turned? If your baby is breech before 34 weeks into your pregnancy, it's quite likely that he will turn head down by himself.

If he's still breech after 34 weeks, you can try to encourage him to turn by using "bottom-in-the-air" positions. Either kneel with your forearms on the floor, your head down, and your bottom up, or lie on your back with your feet on the floor, your knees bent up, and three or four pillows under your bottom, for 10–15 minutes two or three times a day. There is currently insufficient research evidence to say how effective these positions are.

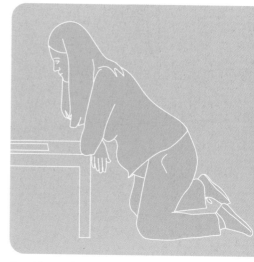

Kneel forward *against a low table or stool with your knees apart to help your baby into a forward position.*

Toward the end *of pregnancy, it can be good to spend some time each day in upright, forward-leaning positions. Leaning over the back of a chair is a good comfortable forward position that will encourage your baby to settle into lying "occiput anterior".*

EXTERNAL CEPHALIC VERSION

If he won't move by himself, an experienced midwife or obstetrician may be able to turn your baby manually – a process known as external cephalic version (ECV). If this is carried out after 37 weeks of pregnancy, research has shown a 58 per cent success rate, with a 48 per cent reduction in the risk of a Caesarean (4).

If your baby is still breech at 37 weeks and your pregnancy is otherwise straightforward your midwife or doctor should offer you the opportunity to have external cephalic version, see left. Some complementary therapies also offer ways of turning a breech baby. The acupuncture technique of moxibustion, which involves burning a small stick of the herb mugwort on your little toe, has been found to have a success rate of as high as 70 per cent in a small study (1). Reflexologists also have techniques for trying to turn breech babies, and there is a homeopathic remedy for this too. Consult a qualified homeopath.

Why are some babies breech? Most babies are breech for no obvious reason. Premature babies are often breech and in about 40 per cent of twin pregnancies, one baby is in the breech position. Other possible conditions that make it difficult for the baby to settle head down include:

- A uterus that has a divider, or "septum", running down the middle
- A tumour or fibroid low in the pelvis
- Placenta praevia (placenta in the lower half of the uterus, instead of the upper, see page 104)
- Too much amniotic fluid.

Birthing a breech baby

Results of an international trial of over 2,000 women around the world giving birth to babies in breech positions, were published in 2000 (2). Conclusions drawn in the study were that it is best for a breech baby to be born by Caesarean section as the risk to the baby was higher with a vaginal birth. However, the trial methodology has been criticized (3). The balance of benefits and risks is uncertain, particularly for women who may have

BREECH PRESENTATIONS

- Extended, or frank, is the most common breech presentation in first babies: the baby's legs are straight with toes by his ears.
- Complete is the next most common breech presentation where the baby's knees are bent.
- Footling breeches, where a foot comes first, and "knee breeches" are very rare and more complicated. With a smaller presenting part (such as a foot or knees rather than a bottom) there is a greater risk of the cord coming down and getting squashed, cutting off the baby's oxygen supply.

Extended, or frank, breech.

Complete breech.

another pregnancy. There are, for example, more obstetric complications in future pregnancies following surgery, and a small increased risk of reduced fertility and stillbirth.

Mothers who plan to give birth vaginally to their breech baby will need to make sure they receive care from a midwife experienced in natural breech births. Ask to talk to the consultant midwife or a supervisor of midwives at your local hospital or discuss with an independent midwife. You will find details on page 245.

Transverse and oblique positions

Nobody knows what influences a baby to move into the best position for birth, or why some babies are more contrary than others and don't. But when a baby is lying awkwardly, the natural process of labour cannot work so efficiently.

About one in 200 babies lies "transverse", or across the uterus, and about one baby in 75 may lie "oblique", or diagonally across the uterus. Babies who are lying in the oblique position usually straighten up before birth. If your baby is lying transverse and stays that way, then he will need to be delivered by Caesarean.

Twin presentations

Your twins may be both head down (also known as "cephalic" or "vertex") – the presentation likely to be the easiest – or both breech (feet or bottom down) or one head down and one breech. Sometimes, when the first twin has been born, the second twin turns around spontaneously, as a result of the extra space in the uterus.

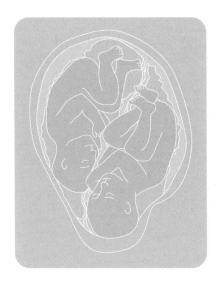

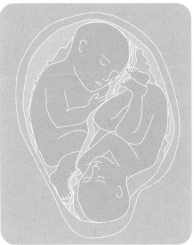

Twins are usually *lying either both head down (top) or one head up, one head down and one head up, or breech. Sometimes both babies may be breech or one may lie across your uterus in the tranverse position.*

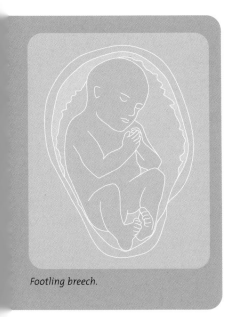

Footling breech.

Twin birth

It is very unusual for a twin pregnancy to last more than 40 weeks (in fact term for twins is usually considered to be 37 weeks rather than 40) and many obstetricians advise induction of labour at 38 weeks.

The birth will be influenced by the way the twins are lying in the uterus. If the first twin is in a cephalic presentation (head down) labour is usually able to continue to a normal birth, but if the first twin is presenting in any other way, an elective Caesarean is usually recommended. Discuss the options fully with your midwife and obstetrician.

Going past your due date

Most people tend to think of babies as being "due" on a specific date, and of pregnancy as lasting 40 weeks, but exactly what triggers labour is still not known. Only a small percentage of babies – about five per cent – are born on their "due" date.

YOUR DUE DATE

Calculating your due date is not an exact process because it depends on factors that it's difficult to be certain about. The first of these is when your baby was conceived. The formulas used for calculating due dates on the basis of your last period make certain assumptions, while estimates based on a scan always have a margin of error.

The second area of uncertainty is how long the average pregnancy actually lasts. In the UK, it's calculated at 40 weeks, but there's debate about this, backed up by research evidence. In France for example, it's regarded as lasting 41 weeks.

Why are some babies "late"?

It can be frustrating to sit through your "expected day of delivery" with no baby yet in your arms. Most babies (around 80 per cent) are born at "term" – between 38 and 42 weeks. Babies born before 37 completed weeks are therefore considered to be "preterm", or premature, while those born after 42 weeks are "post-term". In most cases, it isn't known why babies arrive when they do. However, your baby's position may affect the start of labour. Also your emotional state influences when your baby is born; if you're anxious, your body may "hang on" to the baby.

Trying to start labour yourself

If you're feeling fed up and uncomfortable, and are desperate to meet your baby, or if you want to avoid a medical induction, you might be tempted to try and start labour off yourself. There are many different ways that women have used over the years to do this, including sex, or arousal, and nipple stimulation, drinking castor oil, or eating curry. But there are few, if any, studies of these measures, so effectiveness hasn't been established. It could be just coincidence that some women will find that they will go into labour after trying one of them. Acupuncture, reflexology, homeopathy, herbalism, and aromatherapy all offer methods of encouraging labour to start, but again, research into effectiveness has not been established.

Your body produces labour hormones more readily if you're relaxed, and one way of helping labour to start might be to try some relaxation exercises, and perhaps to spend time thinking about your baby.

Sweeping your membranes

If you've gone past your due date, your midwife may offer to "sweep" your membranes. This involves her inserting a finger gently into your cervix and running it between the top of the cervix and the bag of waters. This has been shown to increase the likelihood of labour starting in the next few days, and to decrease the need for induction, but it isn't always effective.

Avoiding medical induction

Once you've gone a few days past your due date (usually between seven and 14), the issue of starting labour artificially will probably be raised by your carers. If you have had an uncomplicated pregnancy you should be

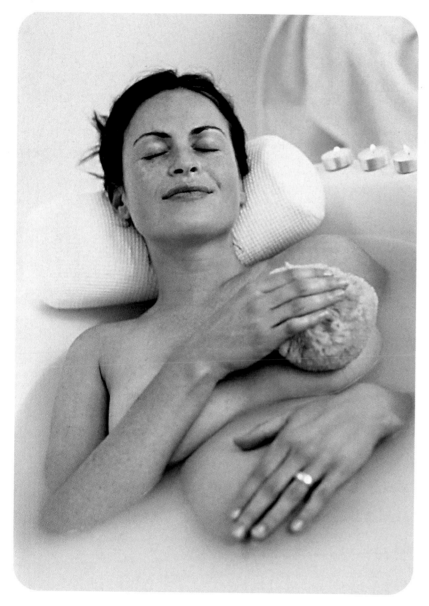

GUIDELINES ON INDUCTION

Clinical guidelines have been drawn up to help guide decision making in situations such as this one where choices need to be made. When induction of labour is being considered, it is essential that your obstetrician discusses all your options with you before any decision is reached.

Even if you have had a healthy, trouble-free pregnancy, you should be offered induction of labour after 41 weeks because from this stage the risk of your baby developing health problems increases(1).

Your body produces *labour hormones more readily if you are relaxed. Relaxing baths can be enjoyed throughout pregnancy, but make sure the water is not too hot – around blood heat (37°C/98.6°F) is fine.*

offered induction after 41 weeks. If you decline, then you should be offered extra monitoring – a twice weekly fetal heart-rate check (known as CTG) and ultrasound examination to check the volume of amniotic fluid.

Induction can be done through use of a prostaglandin pessary or with an oxytocin drip. Prostaglandins should be offered if your membranes are still intact. With the drip, labour is likely to start more abruptly with strong powerful contractions. Continuous electronic monitoring is usual to ensure that the drug to stimulate the contractions is not putting the baby under stress. You are likely to be less mobile and you won't be able to use a pool. Because of the strength of contractions, women are more likely to opt for an epidural if their induction of labour is done with an oxytocin drip.

An unplanned Caesarean birth

"When the registrar said we would reconsider the options, she meant we were running out of options fast!"

A fortunate outcome from a frightening situation

"The day after my due date, I started having contractions that continued all day without increasing in intensity or frequency. I went to bed, but was awake at 1.30am since the contractions started to become more intense. By 10am the contractions were five to six minutes apart. I phoned the hospital and they asked me to come in. After being examined I was told I was about 1cm (½in) dilated. We were admitted and I was told to walk around. At about 4pm, Michael went home to have some sleep to conserve energy for what was ahead. At this point, my contractions were every five minutes and the pain was manageable, so I was given some sleeping tablets and painkillers and left to sleep. The following morning the contractions had decreased to every 15 minutes so I was allowed home.

By 5pm the contractions had started increasing again, so I was back on the TENS machine, and by 7pm, they were quite intense. I needed something more, so we went to the hospital, having phoned our friend Rachel, who we had invited to be present at the birth. After being monitored at the hospital, I was given gas and air (entonox).

The midwife examined me and pronounced me 5cm (2in) dilated, so the baby was on its way, but the initial period of monitoring indicated that the baby's heartbeat was fast. The midwife called the registrar who decided that I needed to be monitored for longer. At 11.30pm the registrar examined me to find I was still 5cm (2in) dilated. She broke my waters, which were stained with meconium. The midwife was worried about the baby's oxygen supply so in between contractions I was given an oxygen mask to wear.

Caesarean was suggested

The registrar decided to put in a drip to speed up the contractions and asked whether I wanted an epidural. This was put in, and the drip was started. Although Rachel was reassuring me her face looked scared. The baby's heartbeat was dropping and was now half its previous rate. When the registrar said we would reconsider the options, she meant we were running out of options fast! This is when a Caesarean was advised.

I was whisked down the corridor to the theatre and the epidural was topped up to make me free from pain, though aware of movement. Michael was brought in wearing hospital greens. The operation was very quick. The anaesthetist checked the epidural and minutes later we heard the first cry, with the doctor pronouncing "What a whopper!" Michael and the baby were taken off so that the baby could be weighed and after half an hour I was wheeled through to the recovery room. I held my baby Matthew for a proper cuddle and after 20 minutes he had his first feed."

After a first bad experience, a joyous home birth helps to heal the wounds

"When I realized I was pregnant again, one of my first thoughts was, 'Oh no! That means I've got to give birth!' I spent the first few months planning to use all the drugs this time and make it easy on myself – no heroics.

My partner encouraged this; he really didn't want to see me in that sort of pain again. But something about this made me feel uneasy. What did I really want this birth to be like? In my heart of hearts, what I really wanted was to be at home with no drugs, in a birthing pool. But this seemed to me the kind of thing that other women did – Mother-Earth types, yoga fanatics – stronger women than me.

As the baby grew inside me, I felt a powerful urge to own the whole experience. I didn't want to put it all in someone else's hands at the end of nine months. I wanted to be that stronger woman who just did it.

The possibility thrilled me and I decided to go for it. I ordered the pool, asked my mum if I could borrow her back room (nice view of the garden) and planned my joyful birth experience. To put my mind at rest (and the minds of those who love me) I asked for the hospital notes of my last labour and discussed with a consultant if there was any reason why I shouldn't have the baby at home. There are many scaremongers around this issue but basically the odds are that it will be fine. You just have to trust your instincts. My midwife gave me all the support I needed.

Like a true pro

When the day came and my labour began, I did not for one second regret my choice. It was just as I had hoped it would be. No drugs; feeling the pain, but controlling it; breathing through the contractions. I was doing it like a true pro! When it was all over and I sat there with my new baby, I was struck by the enormity and the simplicity of what had just happened. Women do have babies all the time and you do have to literally push them out – simple. But isn't it just the most full-on amazing thing? And I had done it! To have had a bad birth experience, but then to trust myself to do it right the second time, and succeed, was liberating.

I had exorcized the horrors of my first labour and become that strong woman I had dreamed of being. Does that sound over the top? Try it and see for yourself!"

A second-time-round home water birth

"In my heart of hearts, what I really wanted was to be at home with no drugs, in a birthing pool!"

4

The birth

Trust the process

Women have been giving birth since time began. All around the world they are doing so right now, as you read this book, so trust your body.

Your body is designed to give birth, thanks to profound physical changes that take place during late pregnancy and labour, which enable your uterus to open up and let the baby out. Once labour has really started, the process is unstoppable. You need to trust in the process and go with it. Giving birth is an overwhelming experience and can be frightening, but it can also leave you with a feeling of exhilaration that is unmatched by any other.

This is how it works. During the last few weeks of pregnancy your body starts to produce its own natural pain-relieving chemicals called endorphins. These circulate in the body making you feel a bit "out of it", rather dreamy and forgetful. There are different theories about what actually triggers labour to start, but it seems that the baby sends out a chemical message to its mother signalling readiness to be born. If the mother

the birth year

	tell your doctor or midwife you are pregnant	think through all options for your care – your choice can affect your birth experience		keep up your pelvic floor exercises	think about hiri a pool now if yo want a water bi
FIRST TRIMESTER		**SECOND TRIMESTER**			
1 2 3 4 5 6	7 8 9 10 11 12	13 14 15 16 17 18 19 20	21 22 23	24 25 26	
	pregnancy test shows you're pregnant. Growth at this stage is rapid	take plenty of exercise, but don't start anything new without talking to your midwife	think about possible birth partners to have with you at the birth		

is also physically and psychologically ready, a biochemical switch is triggered. The hormone oxytocin pulses through your body, the great muscles of your uterus begin to contract, and the cervix, or exit, to the uterus gradually widens. Your contractions get more intense and frequent and your body releases more and more endorphins, which bring about a dream-like state, enabling you to "let go". Gradually the exit to your uterus opens more and more to allow the passage of the baby. Once the cervix is fully open, you are ready to work with your contractions to push your baby out into the world.

Certain elements may get in the way of this magnificent process: if you are tense, anxious, don't feel confident in your surroundings, or you are without the right support, the pain-relieving endorphins may not be so effective.

Just remember:
• You have nothing to fear: your body has been designed to give birth, thanks to millions of years of evolution.

• The intellectual part of you has to let go. The sooner you are able to let go, the quicker your labour will be.
• Take as much time as you need to choose the right place to have your baby and the right people to be with you during your labour — it's much easier to let go when you feel safe.
• Having a baby isn't just a physical experience: it affects your whole self.

you may start to feel your practice, Braxton Hicks, contractions now

your baby's head may well "engage", or drop down in your pelvis

THIRD TRIMESTER

BIRTH AND FIRST 3 MONTHS

| 27 | 28 | 29 | 30 | 31 | 32 | 33 | 34 | 35 | 36 | 37 | 38 | 39 | 40 | 41 | 42 | 43 | 44 | 45 | 46 | 47 | 48 | 49 | 50 | 51 | 52 |

write a birth plan and put it with your notes

hire a TENS machine now if you're planning to use one for pain relief

make sure your home birth pack is ready, or your hospital bag is packed

keep important phone numbers handy and make sure you know how to contact your midwife

The role of hormones in labour

It is not known exactly what triggers labour to start, but it's thought to be the baby. The hormone oxytocin is transferred across the placenta to the mother's bloodstream, which suggests that both the starting and continuation of the birth process are influenced by the amount of oxytocin produced by the baby.

Importance of oxytocin

In a normal labour, the amount of the hormone oxytocin that is secreted into your body is the same as the level of syntocinon (artificial oxytocin) that's used by doctors when they induce contractions, that is, bring them on by artificial means. Oxytocin, also known as the "feel-good hormone" is released into your bloodstream in labour. The French obstetrician Michel Odent has suggested that natural birth releases a "cocktail of love hormones" (1). These hormones stimulate contractions, breast-feeding, the bonding between you and your baby, and in addition they can take the edge off your pain in labour.

Hormone production is controlled by your brain

Different parts of the brain each govern different activities and functions in your body. The cerebral cortex acts as a processor of input from your senses, it interprets and makes decisions, regulates your voluntary muscle activity, and is concerned with memory, learning, and reasoning. The thalamus under the brain, passes sensory information on to your cerebral cortex. An archaic region of the brain called the hypothalamus, co-ordinates the action of your endocrine glands (those that produce hormones) and your autonomic nervous systems (see box opposite). It is also the control centre for food intake and water balance. Another gland, the pituitary gland, controls and integrates your hormonal activity.

Your labour is controlled by your brain through the hormone system, which in turn affects how you feel. In order for you to give birth instinctively, you must feel secure and comfortable in your birth environment. Different hormones released during the birth process – oxytocin, endorphins, prolactin, adrenocorticotrophic hormone (ACTH) – originate in the hypothalamus and the pituitary gland. In other words the most active component of your body in labour is also the primitive part of your brain. Essentially, you do not think rationally during labour and birth; you must act instinctively.

Adrenaline and noradrenaline When the natural flow of labour is disturbed, adrenaline is released and this has the effect of delaying the birth, which is nature's way of protecting your baby. (If you don't feel that you are in a safe place, then it may not be safe for your baby to be born.)

The natural flow of labour can easily be disturbed by all kinds of unnecessary stimulation, such as:

- Bright lights and loud noises
- Being asked questions and being expected to respond
- Feeling observed by others
- Feeling unsafe or under threat
- Invasive procedures
- Too many strangers
- Not enough reassurance.

Adrenaline and noradrenaline are hormones that make your heart beat faster, constrict small blood vessels, and increase your metabolic rate. A surge of adrenaline sends blood rushing to your brain and muscles to enable you to fight or run away, the so-called "fight or flight" mechanism. The blood going to the brain and muscles is diverted from the digestive tract, the uterus and other internal organ functions.

Adrenaline can make you panicky and raise your blood pressure. Your contractions will then slow down because it inhibits oxytocin production. Your body's natural response to what is seen as a threatening situation may then be diagnosed by medical staff as failure to progress. Pain-killing drugs might then be given and a synthetic oxytocin drip set up, when in fact simple steps like dimming the lights and providing privacy, quiet, and an empathic carer and birth partner could get the labour on course once more just as effectively.

However, the hormones adrenaline and noradrenaline do play some positive part in the interaction between you and your baby immediately after birth. During the very last contractions of a natural birth, the levels of these hormones peak. One of the effects of this hormone surge is that the you are alert when your baby is born. The baby releases his own hormones and so is also alert, with wide-open eyes and dilated pupils.

Ocytocin helps you bond Gazing into each other's eyes is an important feature of the beginning of the mother and baby relationship, just as it is when two adults fall in love. The hormone oxytocin is also necessary for the natural delivery of the placenta, because it causes the uterus to contract. Oxytocin is also released into your bloodstream when you put your child to the breast for the first time after birth.

Other hormones involved in birth

A number of other hormones are released during labour. Oestrogen prepares your uterine muscles for contracting by causing a dramatic increase in the number of "oxytocin receptors" in the uterine muscle toward the end of your pregnancy.

Cortisol is produced by your adrenal glands. This releases fats and amino acids into your body to help you deal with the stress of labour. The surge of cortisol produced by labour also releases extra lung surfactant, which in turn helps your baby to breathe at birth.

THE NERVOUS SYSTEM

This system is divided into the "somatic" and "autonomic" nervous systems. The somatic nervous system controls the voluntary or skeletal muscles that you use to smile or walk; the ones you have control over.

In contrast, smooth muscle and cardiac muscle, as well as the muscle of your uterus, is controlled involuntarily by the autonomic nervous system, which works automatically. This system also controls body functions such as circulation and digestion. The autonomic system is divided into the "sympathetic" and "parasympathetic" systems, which balance each other out. The sympathetic system produces the "fight or flight" reaction in response to stress or excitement. The parasympathetic system works to counteract this, and it is this system that dominates the body during sleep.

Going into labour

As you approach your approximate date of birth, you'll start to get restless; eager to meet your baby yet increasingly anxious about labour. Try to relax. Remember that for most women giving birth for the first time, the move from pregnancy into labour is a slow process, and it's often spread over several days.

YOUR BABY'S MOVEMENTS

It's not true that babies move much less, or even stop moving, before labour starts. Your baby's movements may gradually change over the last few weeks because she has less space – but she should still be moving. If you think your baby is moving less, make sure you contact your midwife or labour ward the same day.

CONTRACTIONS: REAL OR PRACTICE

"Practice" or Braxton Hicks contractions (named after the obstetrician who first described them) are different from real contractions.

- Real contractions become gradually stronger, longer, and closer together as time passes.
- The upper part of the uterus moves forward perceptibly during real contractions – you should be able to feel this movement if you put your hand on your bump.
- Each real contraction builds up to a peak of intensity in the middle and then dies away again.

Waiting for labour to begin

Increasingly in modern life we expect to know exactly when things will happen so that we can put a date in the diary, plan, and be in control. Birth, however, is an event that is to some extent out of our hands.

To help you track the journey through birth, labour is officially divided into three stages. The first stage is when the cervix, or exit from the uterus, unplugs and opens up, or dilates, wide enough to let your baby through. The second stage is the "pushing" part, when you literally push your baby out into the world. The third stage is when the placenta is expelled. These three stages form one smooth, unstoppable process, but can be further divided into:

First stage: pre-labour (or the "latent" phase); early labour (until the cervix is 3–4cm/1¼–1½in dilated); and active or strong labour (4cm/1½in to 10cm/4in)

Transition Preparing to push

Second stage Pushing and the birth

Third stage Delivery of the placenta.

Pre-labour

The countdown before true labour starts is known as "pre-labour". It can last for more than a day. You may notice a gradual increase in practice, or Braxton Hicks, contractions, especially at night. These contractions should not be painful – but they can be uncomfortable and stop you sleeping.

Many women also start getting low tummy pains: colic-like discomfort that comes and goes at odd intervals. The most likely cause of these pains is your cervix softening and relaxing ready for action. The midwifery term for this is "ripening". You may also notice an increased flow of mucus from your vagina around this time, too.

Other signs that your cervix is becoming more active include having a "show" (when the mucus plug sealing the neck of the uterus during pregnancy comes away, sometimes with a little blood) and loose bowel motions. On its own, a show is not a reliable sign of imminent labour. Some women have repeated shows over a week (the mucus keeps being produced); others never have one. Similarly, if you get a touch of diarrhoea, it could be a sign that the cervix is waking up and tickling the nerves shared with the lower bowel – or it may be nothing to do with labour at all.

Before your cervix can begin to open, it has to change from a firm, tight tube 2–3cm (1–1¼in) long, that is designed to keep your baby in your uterus, to a soft, stretchy disc that's ready to open up and let her out. Midwives call this process "effacement".

During the pre-labour phase, your contractions may be uncomfortable enough to stop you sleeping. However, unlike in "real" labour, these contractions never seem to get stronger, longer, or closer together. If your midwife were to examine your cervix at this time, it would probably be closed or only 1cm (½in) dilated.

Early labour

Eventually, your contractions start to increase until they are coming about every 20 to 30 minutes and lasting 10 to 40 seconds. If you are planning to have your baby in a birth centre or hospital, there is no need to go in during early labour, unless you are worried or your midwife suggests this course of action. Swapping the comfort, privacy, and intimacy of your home for a clinical, noisy, bustling hospital environment may make it harder to cope and accepting strong pain relief in the early phase of labour may also increase the risk of your baby being born by Caesarean section (1).

If you're in bed, *stay there. You need your rest. If this is labour, it will keep going. If it's not labour, at least you're resting.*

Tips for coping with early labour

- If you're in bed, stay there. You need your rest.
- If it's daytime, carry on as usual. Send your partner off to work. Potter about, go for a walk, chat to a friend.
- Keep eating and drinking.
- Try simple remedies for the pain: a warm bath, a hot-water bottle, or a gentle massage.
- Be careful who you tell; other people may start to worry unnecessarily.
- Be positive. Think of this as a special time of gentle, private preparation.
- Ask for help if you need it. Phone your midwife or labour ward; your midwife may be able to visit you at home, or she may suggest you visit the labour ward for some professional reassurance.

"I had been 'niggling', as one of the midwives called it, for about ten days before actual labour. Contractions started around 3.30pm, and I soon knew they were different to the 'niggles' I'd been having previously."

HOW A BIRTH PARTNER CAN HELP

- Be interested – but don't fuss. Give your partner time and space to get used to what is happening. She will involve you when she needs to.
- Look after her. Make tea, prepare food, run a bath, find clean clothes.
- Get ready and carry out normal tasks in preparation. If you are planning to have the baby in a birth centre or hospital then make some sandwiches, fill a thermos flask, put bags in the car. If you are planning a water birth at home, check you have everything ready, but don't fill the pool just yet.
- Conserve your strength. In 24 hours' time, you will probably be more tired than you ever thought possible.

see also

Dealing with the pain	134–39
Your feelings after birth	178–79
Changes in your body	180–83

Established labour

The phase of labour when the cervix is dilating from about 4–10cm (2½–4in) is known as strong or "active" labour. You will know when you are moving into this stage because the contractions will get stronger and closer together and the pain will become more intense.

When active labour begins

Sooner or later, your labour really gets going. Your contractions will get longer, stronger, and more frequent, until they are coming every five minutes, and lasting well over a minute. You won't be able to talk during contractions. You may start to withdraw into yourself, become less aware of your surroundings or time passing. You're now moving into established labour. It's time to call your midwife or to think about going to hospital.

Why does labour hurt?

Contractions are like waves: they build up slowly, gaining in strength until they reach a peak, then fade away, losing power before the next wave starts. They start as small waves and get bigger and faster as labour progresses. In active labour, contractions can come every two to three minutes.

Hormones are released The pain of contractions seems to play a part in stimulating the release of the hormones necessary for the smooth progress of normal labour (1). The increasing intensity of labour pain also makes a vital contribution to the way in which mother and newborn respond to

"The quiet reassurance and comforting I received from Karen, my husband and the midwife was first-class, just enough and not too much to distract me."

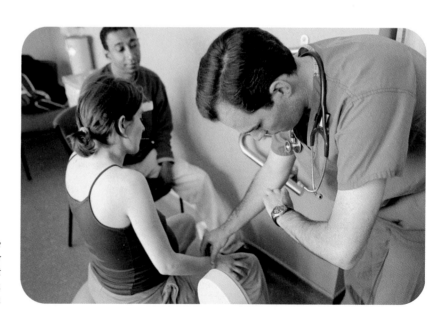

Your pulse and blood pressure will be checked throughout labour. Your midwife will monitor you to ensure that your labour is progressing normally, both for you and your baby.

each other when they meet (2). By the end of a straightforward labour, both mother and baby are buzzing with nature's opiates, endorphins. Shortly before the birth and fuelled by the expulsive contractions, both of you experience a surge of adrenaline. You'll be bursting with protective energy, while your baby is born alert, eyes wide open, ready to meet your gaze.

Productive pain The pain of labour will probably be greater than anything you have ever experienced. But, unlike the pain of disease or trauma, labour pain is positive and productive. It also comes with built-in pain relief. When pushed to the limit, your body produces endorphins (natural morphine-like hormones), which ease pain, change your perception of time, and make you feel good, giving you the will and energy to go on longer than you would have thought possible. Working with labour is all about using the power of endorphins – and letting your body get on with the job it is designed to do.

Occasionally, labour may not be straightforward. Things may not go as planned and the pain may just be too intense. If this is happening, be kind to yourself. Accept the help that modern drugs and medical advice can provide. What matters ultimately is that you do what's right for you.

Continuous care is important

Although it is policy that a midwife should be with you at all times, about half of the women who give birth in hospital are on their own for parts of their labour. It's invaluable to have a companion with you to give you support and to get assistance when you need it. You can't be guaranteed the same midwife throughout labour, as shifts may change, but the support will remain. Apart from regular observations pertaining to the well-being of you and your baby, your midwife will be watching to make sure that labour is progressing normally. She will keep you and your partner informed of what is happening, encourage you when the going gets tough, and help you make decisions regarding pain relief or other interventions. Your midwife is there to keep you safe and protected, so you can work with your labour freely and intuitively.

GROUP B STREPTOCOCCUS INFECTION

Many people carry group B streptococcus bacteria (known as group B strep) in their bodes without ever developing infection or illness. However, the bacteria can be deadly to people with weak immune systems and to newborn babies.

It's possible for a pregnant woman to transmit this infection to her baby during the birth. Infection passed from mother to baby at the time of delivery can be very serious. However, as most babies born to mothers who carry the bacterium do not become infected, there is no routine screening for this infection for pregnant women.

The majority of group B strep infections can be prevented by administering penicillin at the onset of labour in those cases where the risk of infection is highest. In practice, this means giving intravenous antibiotics to any woman with a raised temperature, prolonged rupture of the membranes, preterm labour, an episode of group B streptococcus bladder infection during pregnancy, or a history of a previous child with the infection.

HOW A BIRTH PARTNER CAN HELP

- Be aware of what's happening. Your confidence in the birth process will make an enormous difference.
- Accept her pain. Seeing somebody you love in pain is very difficult and it is natural to want to stop the pain. Try to understand that in labour this response is not necessarily appropriate or even possible.
- Respect her. Tell her what's going on and if something is not going as planned, explain clearly what the staff recommend to sort it out. Remember that your partner's consent is needed for every aspect of her care and treatment.
- Look after yourself. Take a short break every hour.

Working with your labour

If you can help your body through this process, working with it, the pain of contractions can feel less intense. Move your body into positions that feel comfortable and right to you; concentrate on your breathing to stay calm, and create the space you need for this birth.

The support *of a strong and reliable birth partner can help you withstand the pain of contractions.*

Comfort is paramount

Left to follow their instincts, all creatures seek out a safe and private place in which to give birth. If you're having a home birth, it's easy to create the space you need. It may not be so easy to do this if you are in a hospital. At the very least, however, all staff should knock and wait to be invited before entering your birthing room.

When you are in your labour room, adjust the furniture to suit yourself. Close the curtains and turn down the lights. Consider using a birthing pool or bath. Water "holds" you, surrounds, and separates you. Many women find this helpful in labour. Spend time in the bathroom or toilet – people tend to respect the privacy of a bathroom.

Stay upright

If your body is upright and leaning slightly forward during labour, your uterus forms an efficient column of contracting muscle. Your baby's head is pressed down centrally on your cervix so it opens evenly. As you approach the second stage of labour, your lower spine and sacrum are free to move back to give your baby room to descend. Staying upright also means you are free to move instinctively in response to the changing sensations. This means any position in which your upper body is upright with your weight is off your bottom, be it standing, kneeling, all-fours, or sitting leaning forward.

The best upright position for labour is one that leaves your lower body free to move during contractions, but which supports you so you can rest in between them.

Fetal monitoring If you arrive at hospital and continuous electronic fetal monitoring (EFM) is advised, ask your carers why they have decided that it is necessary. "Any interference with the natural process of pregnancy and childbirth should be shown to do more good than harm" (1). Continuous EFM restricts your freedom of movement in labour and may demand you assume certain positions (such as lying down). If you agree to continuous monitoring, ask if this can be done while you remain upright. Better still, ask if the unit has a "telemetric", or remote, fetal monitor, which uses radio waves to transmit ultrasound signals of your baby's heart to a base unit.

Try to breathe through contractions

Breathing in a relaxed, measured way throughout your labour can really help you stay calm, as well as increase oxygen levels.

Holding your breath is a natural response to sudden pain – natural, but not helpful, especially in labour. If you hold your breath, your body tenses, and adrenaline levels rise. One of the effects of adrenaline is to divert blood from the uterus (and other internal organs) to prepare for "fight or flight". The muscle of the uterus therefore becomes short of oxygen, and contractions become more painful. Adrenaline may also upset the co-ordinated action of the uterus, adding to the pain.

Take time during pregnancy to become more aware of your breathing. So with luck, when you start having strong contractions, it will feel natural to respond by breathing and relaxing rather than tensing up. Always breathe in through your nose and then out through your mouth, concentrating on your out-breath.

As labour progresses, there will come a time when you can no longer breathe smoothly through contractions. Don't panic and don't hold your breath. Just let your breathing naturally speed up – just as it does when you run upstairs or dash for a bus. Don't think about it; just let it happen.

If you breathe in this sped-up way for more than a minute or so, you may feel an odd tingling sensation in your fingers and around your lips. This is caused by "over breathing", which results in a temporary imbalance in the two gases involved in respiration – oxygen and carbon dioxide. The cure is very simple – just cup your two hands around your mouth and nose and breathe steadily for five breaths. This helps balance up the gases.

HOW A BIRTH PARTNER CAN HELP

- During pregnancy, think about whether you need to take any extra equipment into hospital for her – beanbag, extra pillows, small sturdy stool?
- Don't talk too much at this stage of labour. She needs to focus. Rational brain activity can interrupt the flow of her endorphins.
- Care for her. She is working harder than she has ever done in her life before.
- Protect her. Help your midwife choose the best moment to speak with your partner. Keep your voice low so others will follow your example.
- Understand the importance of keeping upright during labour.
- Hold her while she leans against you.
- Be practical. Is she really comfortable? How about a pillow under her head/thighs/feet/bump/knees? Can she reach her water bottle?
- Be prepared to rub her back for hours on end. Couples labouring in upright positions generally work up a wonderful rhythm of hip-wriggling and massaging.
- Tell her how well she's doing. Loving encouragement is what she needs now.

Good positions for labour

To help your uterus contract most effectively, try to stay upright and lean forward slightly. This will enable your baby's head to press firmly on your cervix and ensure that gravity is on your side. You'll probably find that it just feels "right" to adopt some of the positions shown here.

"I'd say to any woman, move around and change your position as often as you want – it is up to you. Rocking on my birthing ball in the early stages was really comforting, and I found that squatting on all fours helped me when things were more pressing! Do whatever feels right at the time."

SUPPORTED ON CUSHIONS

Sitting the wrong way round *on a chair, or even on a toilet, supported with cushions can help move the baby into a good position.*

A pile of firm pillows *can provide support while your birth partner massages your lower back.*

STAY AS UPRIGHT AS POSSIBLE

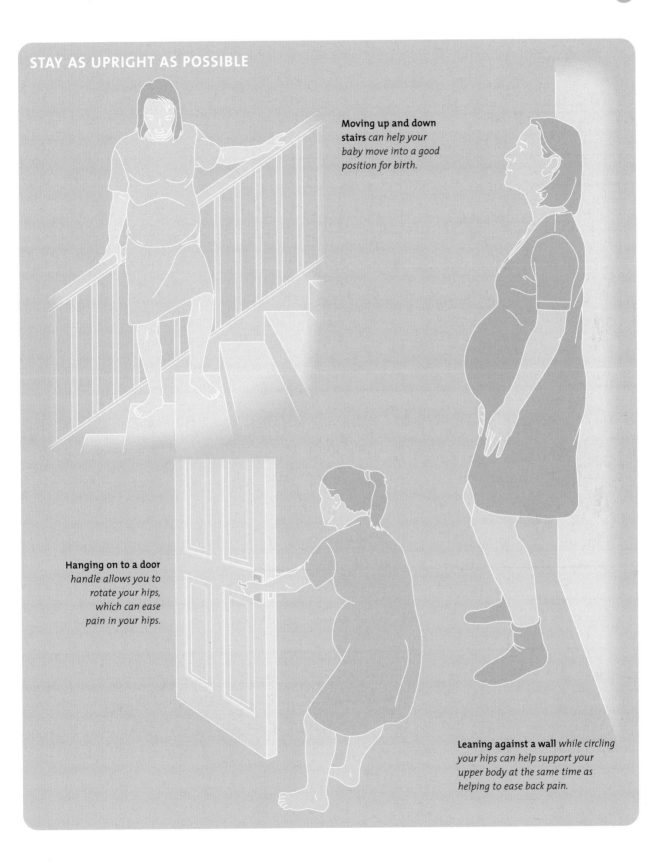

Moving up and down stairs *can help your baby move into a good position for birth.*

Hanging on to a door *handle allows you to rotate your hips, which can ease pain in your hips.*

Leaning against a wall *while circling your hips can help support your upper body at the same time as helping to ease back pain.*

BACK MASSAGE HELPS PAIN

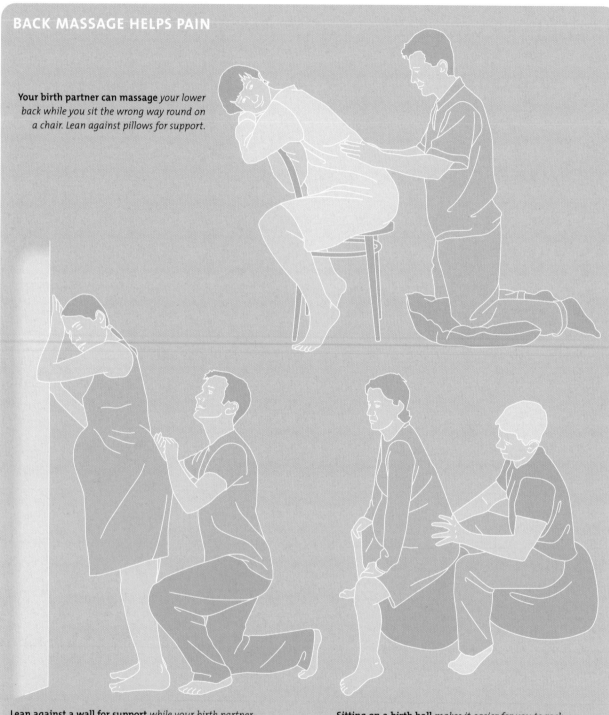

Your birth partner can massage *your lower back while you sit the wrong way round on a chair. Lean against pillows for support.*

Lean against a wall for support *while your birth partner massages your lower back firmly during your contractions.*

Sitting on a birth ball *makes it easier for you to rock your pelvis back and forth, or circle your hips gently during contractions. Your partner can massage your back at the same time.*

YOUR BIRTH PARTNER CAN SUPPORT YOU

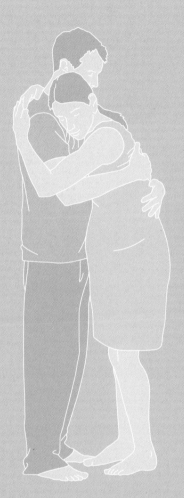

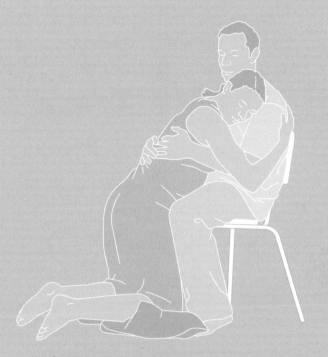

Kneeling upright *helps keep your baby in the right position. Instead of cushions, lean against your partner; he can physically support you and talk you through your contractions.*

Lean against your partner *for extra support. It keeps you upright, encouraging the baby into a good position for the birth.*

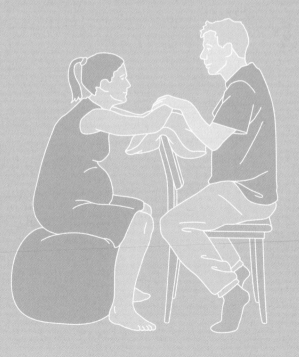

When you're tired *sit on a birth ball and keep moving your hips. Your birth partner can sit at the same level to encourage you .*

Dealing with the pain

Endorphins, the body's natural pain-relieving hormones, rise during labour and peak at the point of transition between first and second stage, when contractions can be at their most powerful. Instinctively, you'll also find other ways to deal with the pain. Your midwives will be there too, giving support.

Make as much noise as you like

Many women find they get quite noisy during strong labour. Don't hold back. Making a noise can be really helpful, especially if you fit it in with the rhythm of your breathing.

Using a TENS machine for pain relief

TENS stands for Transcutaneous Electrical Nerve Stimulation. This is a machine that consists of four electrodes, attached to rubber pads, which are taped to your back. The electrodes are connected by long wires to a base unit, which contains the small batteries needed to power the equipment, plus control knobs. When activated, TENS administers a mild electrical impulse to the area covered by the electrodes. The theory is that this impulse "occupies" the nerve fibres serving the lower back, thus "blocking" the transmission of pain symptoms. There is some proof that TENS can relieve the symptoms of chronic back pain. There is, however, no proof that TENS relieves labour pain (1). This said, many women – and many midwives – believe TENS to be of value, particularly in early labour.

When can I use it? If you want to use a TENS machine you will need to hire or buy one in advance. It's also worth trying it out before you go into

HOW A BIRTH PARTNER CAN HELP

- During labour, if she seems to be tensing up with contractions, remind her gently to keep breathing. Breathe with her if necessary.
- Keep your voice quiet and confident. If you find you are becoming snappy and irritable then take a break.
- Don't hush her if she starts making a noise. Just remind her quietly to keep the noise low and throaty.
- Help her relax by stroking down across her shoulders and upper arms, slowly and rhythmically, in time with her breathing.
- Tell her how well she's doing. If she starts saying she can't do this, agree that it's very hard work but she is doing it, and doing it brilliantly!
- Don't keep asking questions: she needs to switch off the thinking part of her brain. Instead, try to anticipate her needs.

labour. TENS machines can be purchased from NCT Sales. Alternatively, you can hired one from www.babycaretens.com who donate a fee to the NCT for each machine hired. (See Useful organizations, page 245.)

Using a birth pool for pain relief

A birth pool is a large tub, much wider and deeper than a domestic bath. It should be filled with warm water and, ideally, equipped with built-in thermostat and water heater.

When can I use it? It is probably best to wait until your labour is well established before you get into the pool. There is some (mainly anecdotal) evidence that labour may slow down or even stop should you immerse yourself in warm water too early (2).

When you are ready, step into the warm water and get comfortable. Experiment with different positions: many women seem to prefer kneeling, legs well apart, with arms and head resting forward onto the edge of the tub. You can use gas and air (entonox), provided somebody is with you. Being in water will not stop the pain of the contractions, but it will probably make them easier to cope with. We are not sure if this is due to the physical effects of immersion in water, the increased freedom of movement, or the privacy and intimacy of the surrounding. It's probably a combination of all these factors (3).

If you feel strongly that you want to get into the water, you may well benefit from using it. If you feel you want to get out of the pool, you should do so. Warm water can help if your contractions are coming quite strongly and frequently, or if your back is uncomfortable and you just want to relieve a feeling of pressure.

If your labour seems to be slowing down in the water, you might try moving into different positions or getting out of the pool for a while. Walking around can help. Squatting, kneeling on all-fours, or going up and down stairs can all help move the baby into a good position for birth.

Can I stay in the water? Doing what "feels right" is often best while you are in labour. You may choose to stay in the pool to give birth, or find, as many women do, that dry land suits you better when the moment arrives.

What are the drawbacks to a birth pool?

- Getting too hot in the pool can cause problems. If your temperature rises, your baby's will also rise and this may cause her to become distressed (4). Your midwife will need to keep an eye on your temperature, the ambient room temperature, and the water temperature. You can help yourself by drinking at least a glass of water every hour and making sure that the water in the pool is not too deep. Your breasts and upper body should be out of the water, to allow normal sweating and cooling.
- You will have to get out of the water for internal examinations.
- Floating in a tub of water is not compatible with electronic fetal

TIPS FOR WATER BIRTHS

- If you hire a pool, it's useful to try assembling it and filling it in late pregnancy, or at least have one dummy run.
- Some pool-hire companies recommend using a new sterile pool liner each time you use the pool. Other companies recommend simply sterilizing the liner yourself.
- Pools generally take about 30 to 60 minutes to fill.
- You can use entonox ("gas and air") in a birthing pool.
- You will usually be asked to leave the pool for any internal examinations (to assess progress in labour).

"Looking back, one of the most rewarding aspects of the water birth was the fact that I was so clear-headed afterwards as I didn't have to recover from the pethidine or a lengthy labour, and I managed to relax during the labour itself. That was all down to the fact I was in the pool."

The comfort of warm water *can make your contractions easier to cope with, and the weightlessness enables you to move around and change position.*

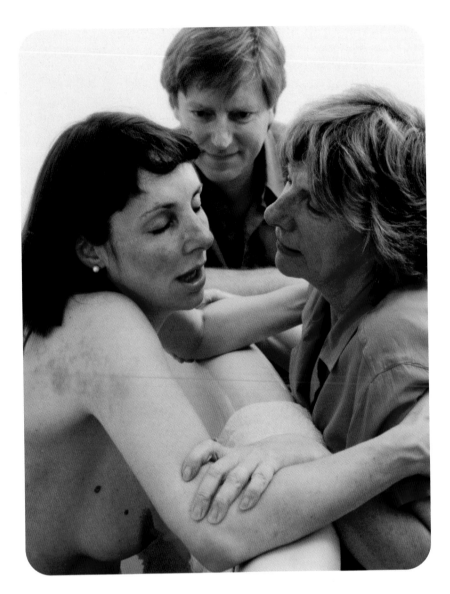

monitoring. You will therefore be advised to get out of the pool should there be any concerns about your baby's well-being – although a hand-held Sonicaid can be used in a birth pool with a waterproof cover.

- You will also be asked to get out of the pool if you want pethidine, because this drug may make you very sleepy.
- Epidural anaesthesia cannot be used with a birth pool.
- Many maternity units have strict policies on the use of water in labour and birth – find out what these are during your pregnancy. There's relatively little research available on the use of water in "at-risk" labours and many units adopt an "if in doubt, say no" policy. Remember, too, that in hospitals, pools are used on a "first-come, first-served" basis and one may not be free when you need it. Many women prefer to plan a home birth and hire their own pool for that reason.

Other ways of using water for pain relief

You can get into a normal domestic bath for pain relief. Run the water as deep as possible (block the overflow with plasticine or Blu-Tack™), then lie or kneel in the water. Alternatively, you can stand under a shower.

Another option is to ask your birth partner to hold a flannel wrung out in really hot water against your lower back and/or belly during contractions. You can use entonox (gas and air) at the same time.

Using entonox for pain relief

Breathing in nitrous oxide "gas" mixed in equal quantities with oxygen, helps to relieve pain effectively. Commonly known as "gas and air", entonox is used by about 80 per cent of women in labour (1). It can be used for a home or hospital birth.

Etonox (gas and air) is normally piped in a hospital, and your midwife will bring a cylinder for a home birth. When choosing your maternity unit, note the length of the entonox pipes in the labour rooms: at least 3m (10ft) means you can move around while using it.

Your midwife will bring *entonox "gas and air" in a cylinder for you to use at a home birth and it's on tap in a birth centre or hospital unit. Warm water in a bath can help too.*

When can I use it? Once again, it's probably best to wait until you are in advanced labour before you start to use it. Once you decide to use entonox, it should be instantly available. You can use either a mouthpiece or a face mask. The gas mixture takes 20 seconds to pass from your lungs, into your blood, and thence to your brain, when it takes effect. This means that you must start to use it right at the very beginning of a contraction. Breathe deeply as the contraction builds up. At the peak of the contraction, you can put the mouthpiece aside and concentrate on quick, light breathing, knowing there is plenty of entonox in your system.

How much will it help? This type of pain relief helps quite a lot – once you get used to it, and provided you use it correctly. You can use gas and air (entonox) standing, kneeling, or on all-fours – provided there is somebody with you. You can use it in birthing pool too.

What are the drawbacks to entonox?

- Most women feel light-headed when they are using it. The effect generally wears off within a minute or so. Some women like this feeling; some don't.
- Many women also feel sick when they first start to use it. The nausea usually only lasts a for a few contractions, so it's well worth persevering for a while.
- It is very important that you hold the mouthpiece or mask yourself. If you breathe too long and too deeply and take too much entonox you will become drowsy. The mask will then slip from your face, so preventing you taking any more.

Using pethidine for pain relief

Pethidine is a powerful morphine-like sedative (sleep-inducing) drug with moderate pain-relieving qualities. It is usually given by injection into the large muscle of the thigh or buttock. The normal dose is 50–100mg. "Pethidine" is in fact a trade name; the correct generic drug name is "meperidine". Pethidine is used by around 30 per cent of women in labour.

When can I use it? Pethidine is best reserved for strong labour. Research suggests that the incidence of Caesarean section birth is increased when powerful pain-killers are given before labour is established (1). Some authorities believe that contractions may slow down after a dose of pethidine, especially if it is given before labour is in full swing.

About half of all women who have pethidine say that it relieves their pain effectively and gives a welcome respite from the full tumult of labour (2). Pethidine seems to take the edge off the contractions, reducing the muscular tension and anxiety that may contribute to the pain, and helps women relax and rest between contractions. Most women find they have to lie down once they have been given pethidine.

"They gave me a small shot of pethidine, which sent me to sleep and made me feel incredibly happy and relaxed."

Other women find that having pethidine makes them feel remote and disassociated from what's happening without actually touching the pain; or they fall asleep only to wake in pain with which they can no longer cope (3). Research on the subject is not very helpful, and concluded only that pethidine is better than a placebo (pretend drug), and no better and no worse than other opioids (4).

How much pethidine do I need? The effect of pethidine, like all drugs, depends on the recipient; 100mg may be appropriate for a plump 20-year-old woman – but too much for a thin 40-year-old. Everyone's experience of the effects of drugs is different although most say pethidine makes them "woozy". If you are undecided about using pethidine, ask for 50mg initially and see how that works.

What are the drawbacks to pethidine?

Perhaps the most significant drawback is the effect of pethidine on babies. Pethidine passes to your baby seven minutes after it is given to you, and reaches its maximum levels in 2–3 hours. The main effect is on your baby's behaviour after birth. Effects are minimal if your baby is born within an hour of you being given the pethidine, or after five hours(5).

Pethidine babies Babies who have been exposed to pethidine may be slower than others to breathe at birth; although the effects can be reversed by repeated doses of the antidote, naloxone hydrochloride (Narcan®). Pethidine babies may also be unusually sleepy for several days after birth. Getting breast-feeding going may be harder than usual(6), though most difficulties can be overcome with patience and good support. Babies whose mothers have had pethidine in labour may also be more prone to getting cold after birth(7). The best way to keep your baby warm is to hold her skin-to-skin. If you are too sleepy to be able to do this, your partner can slip his newborn inside his T-shirt.

Is there anything else I need to know? Pethidine makes two in three women feel sick(8), so midwives often add an "anti-emetic" (anti-nausea) drug to the syringe of pethidine. Many anti-emetics are also potent sedatives, which can increase the soporific effect of pethidine without actually contributing to pain relief. You may prefer to wait until you actually feel sick before accepting an antiemetic.

Complementary therapies for pain relief

The complementary therapies most often used in labour include:

- Acupuncture
- Aromatherapy
- Herbal medicine
- Homeopathy
- Reflexology
- Shiatsu.

All labour intervention should be treated with equal respect and healthy suspicion, and subjected to the same rigorous research standards. The research base for most complementary therapies as applied to childbirth is weak. More recently, however, a study analyzed the effectiveness of five different therapies for labour pain. There was one study each on acupuncture, audio-analgesia (listening to "white noise"), music, and aromatherapy – and three on the effectiveness of hypnosis (9).

It was found that both acupuncture and hypnosis were effective in reducing pain. In the acupuncture study, only 40 per cent of the women who received acupuncture required additional pain relief, while 87 per cent of the control group required it. The three hypnosis studies each had slightly different results, but taken as a whole, the findings suggested that women treated with hypnotherapy are more likely to have a vaginal birth, and less likely to have their labour speeded up. However, the studies of music, audio-analgesia, and aromatherapy treatments showed no difference.

If you want to embrace a single therapy and use it to its full potential to ease your way through labour, prevent, and/or treat complications, you need to contact a registered practitioner. (Always tell your midwife of your plans; some remedies interfere with conventional care, and vice versa.)

"For my first baby I had a lovely lady who gave me reiki and massage during my labour, with special birthing aromatherapy oils. We got on straight away and it was lovely to have her there."

OTHER NATURAL PAIN RELIEF OPTIONS

- Stand up and walk around – the increased pain could be a signal to change your position to help your baby on her journey.
- Request a vaginal examination if you think that knowing how far dilated you are will help.
- Try not to hold your breath for long periods because this lessens the amount of oxygen available for your baby and your uterus. Two phrases to remember are: "If in doubt, breathe out" and "SOS – Sigh Out Slowly". Try to smile as each contraction fades.
- Making a noise can help. Try singing "la la" or groaning.

Birthing your baby

Although there is no sharp demarcation between the first and second stages of labour, many women experience a time of transition: a period of maybe an hour, during which the last circle of cervix melts away and the uterus and vagina merge into one continuous passage.

SUPPORTED BIRTH POSITIONS

You may need to rest *between your contractions if your second stage is very long. Try leaning into pillows or a beanbag, alternatively kneeling up supported by companions can be another good position.*

Transition phase

This is often the most uncomfortable time in labour. Contractions are long and powerful, with very little rest in between. You may lose some blood from your vagina and (if they have not already broken) your waters may break at the height of a contraction. Your body senses that dramatic things are happening; many women are violently sick at this point, others start to shake, some have a fleeting sense of dread or sudden fear. Your midwives will be expecting this and their reassurance will be important to you now.

Don't push too soon Occasionally things can get a bit muddled in transition, and you may get a strong urge to push before your cervix is fully open (it needs to be 10cm/4in dilated). If this happens, your midwife will probably tell you not to push because it is generally believed that if you push against an undilated cervix, the remaining tissue will become very thick and swollen, and even slower to open. Try getting down on all-fours, leaning on your elbows with your bottom in the air; this may help relieve the pressure on the cervix. It's important to keep breathing, emphasizing your out-breaths.

Second stage of labour

Full dilatation (opening) of the cervix does not necessarily mean that it's time to start pushing. Your baby has to be ready (head low and turned), ready for the final part of his journey. The last stage is much easier if you wait for signs that this has happened before you start to bear down. A strong, irresistible urge to push is a good indication. Your midwife will be looking for other clues and will guide you as necessary.

Pushing is not just about gathering your strength and bearing down during a contraction. It's also about letting go, relaxing the muscles around your vagina so that your baby can pass through. This can be difficult: you probably haven't had your bowels open in front of another person for 30 years and pushing your baby out can feel a bit like doing just this. A calm, unhurried atmosphere, privacy, and support from people you trust all help.

Try not to feel under any pressure when you are pushing. Provided you and your baby are well, progress is being made – however slowly – and you are happy to continue, there is no valid reason why you cannot push for up to three hours (1). However, in many hospitals if a woman has not

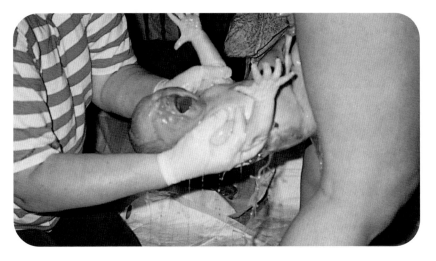

Giving birth standing up, or on all-fours, are both good because if your knees are lower than your hips, your pelvis can open up wider .

delivered her baby after two hours of pushing, she is very likely to be offered forceps or ventouse to help her.

Crowning of the baby's head

As the birth approaches you may be aware of your midwife getting the room ready for your baby. Another midwife may enter the room. If you have decided that you don't want a natural third stage for delivering your placenta your midwife will prepare the hormone injection necessary for "medical management" of the next stage. The injection is given immediately after your baby is born.

Focus on the sensations of your body. Your perineum (the area between your vagina and back passage) will be stretched by your baby's head. It is like foam rubber; soft and very stretchable. Help it stretch slowly by pushing until you feel the area stinging and burning, then ease off. Wait until the burning sensation fades, then push gently once more. You may find it helps to cup the top of your baby's head with your hand as she emerges – or you may not want to.

Your midwife will be close by, ready to suggest what to do should you falter. She may rest her hand lightly on your baby's head in order to control any sudden movement, or she may simply watch and wait; research suggests very little difference in the outcome of either approach (2). Within about five to ten minutes, your baby's head will be born. You can reach down and touch her. It may be several minutes before the next contraction. Your midwife will ask you to push hard and may help by guiding your baby out and up into your arms. You've done it!

"The second stage was amazing, I 'knew' just what to do and when, and the midwives stopped coaching me and just encouraged and reassured me."

EPISIOTOMY

Your midwife may suggest an episiotomy (a cut to enlarge the vaginal opening) for one of three main reasons:
- She suspects your perineum could tear badly
- She thinks your baby is distressed and feels it would be better if she is born sooner rather than later
- She can see that your perineum is unusually tough and unyielding.

Meeting your new baby

The moment you've been dreaming of has finally arrived – your baby is here! Feelings of sheer relief can be overwhelming as you take your her into your arms for the very first time. Be careful as she will be warm, wet, and slippery. Grasp her body under her arms, lift her up, and hold her against your body.

HOW A BIRTH PARTNER CAN HELP

- Take time during pregnancy to talk about what you both want to do immediately after the birth. Can photos and phone calls wait for a while? Try not to rush this precious, never-to-be-repeated time.
- Hold your baby skin-to-skin while your partner is taking a bath or perhaps having stitches if she had an episiotomy or has torn badly; slip her under your shirt and hold her close.
- Help dress your baby. As long as the room is warm, it doesn't matter how long you take.
- If you are in hospital, find out how long you can stay with her and your new baby after the birth. Many hospitals ask partners to leave once the new mother is transferred to the postnatal ward. Think about how you may feel going home alone: who'd you call if you are too tired to drive?
- If your baby was born at home, the midwives will tuck all three of you up into bed before leaving; this is the birth of a new family.

Cuddle your baby

Your baby may not cry immediately and her skin may be bluish. This is normal. Cuddle her close and speak to her. Rub her head and body with a soft, dry towel. Your midwife will be watching closely and may place her fingers on her chest to check her heartbeat. Within a few moments, your baby will take a breath and the blueness will go. She may cry a little, but if she doesn't, it doesn't matter. Keep the lights dim and she will soon open her eyes and gaze up at you. Held in your arms, she can focus clearly on your face. Speak to her; she will recognize your voice.

Some babies need a bit of extra help to start breathing after birth. Home or hospital, your midwife will be trained and have the necessary equipment to clear her airways, administer oxygen, and help her breathe.

First impressions

Your baby may look a little odd immediately after birth. Her head may be misshapen; pushed out at the back or pointed on top. This is due to "moulding" – the normal displacement and overlapping of the soft skull bones. She will look better in 24–48 hours. She may also have a swollen lump on her head, caused by pressure during labour. Her nose may be squashed, her face crooked, her ears crumpled – all this is normal and will soon straighten out. If she is born a little late, she may be covered in dark, tarry meconium. If she is born a bit early, she may be hairy and coated in white, sticky vernix. She may be streaked with your blood. You may not notice any of these oddities as you greet your new baby, exhilarated and, with oxytocin, the natural hormone of love, coursing through your body.

Don't worry if you don't feel exhilarated, though. Your baby may look quite alien to you; completely different from the baby you expected. You may not feel anything much for her. If your labour has been long and hard, you may feel a bit detached and flat. Try not to worry. Hold her skin-to-skin for as long as possible. This will help you feel closer and more loving.

Depending on how you have chosen to deliver your placenta, sooner or later it will be time to cut your baby's cord. You, or your partner, may want to do this. If either of you

"They gave her to me, and it was love at first sight. I just couldn't believe how beautiful she was. She seemed so long. She had all this dark hair that was full of amniotic fluid and meconium, and therefore kind of green."

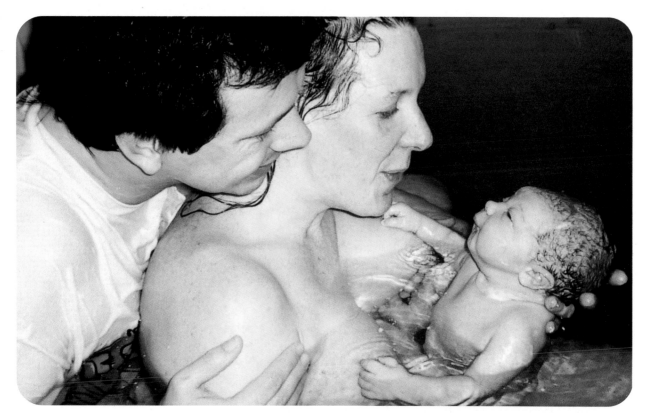

Keep the lights dim *and your baby will soon open her eyes and gaze up at you. She can focus clearly on your face if you hold her in your arms. Speak to her quietly; she'll recognize your voice.*

do want to cut the cord, tell your midwife – she will give you the scissors and will guide you.

Continue holding your naked baby against your bare skin after the cord has been cut and talk to her; hold her close and she will begin to learn your smell. Newborn babies lose heat very quickly after birth and holding her skin-to-skin will prevent this, provided she is dry (particularly her head) and the two of you are covered by a couple of dry towels or a warm blanket. Your midwife will continue to keep a close eye on both of you.

Feed as soon as you can

Breast-feeding your baby within an hour or so of birth helps get feeding off to a good start (1). Cuddling your baby skin-to-skin after the birth means that she is within sight and smell of your breasts. When she starts to look for your nipple, you will be able to respond immediately. However, don't worry if your baby doesn't seem interested in breast-feeding for some time; video studies have shown that, left to their own devices, most babies wait nearly an hour before seeking the nipple (2).

Please don't think that skin-to-skin contact is only for babies that are going to be breast-fed. If you have not yet decided how to feed your baby, cuddle her skin-to-skin and leave her to decide. She may seek your nipple and choose to breast-feed straight away. If you have chosen to bottle-feed your baby, make the first feed special by holding her skin-to-skin.

see also

Delivering your placenta	145–47
Instrumental delivery	160–61
Caesarean birth	162–67
Your feelings after birth	178–79
Your new baby	186–91

Delivering your placenta

Most women don't know that they have a choice when it comes to the delivery of the placenta, because it has become usual in hospital for women to have a "medically managed" third stage of labour. But there is another option.

The third stage of labour

While defining labour in terms of three separate stages may be helpful, there is a danger that you can lose sight of the fact that all the stages are inter-related and combine to form a whole. How your baby's birth unfolds has an affect on the relationship between you and your baby, and how you feel about yourself. This holds true for the third stage as much as any other part of the process, and any approach should be as respectful as possible.

"Active", or medical, management has become the most common way of dealing with the third stage of labour, ever since it was introduced as a precaution against losing too much blood after birth. If you have had any medical intervention, such as a drip to speed up your labour, you will be given a managed third stage, because there is a risk of bleeding. However, this medically managed way of dealing with the delivery of the placenta has become so much the norm that most women don't realize that for those judged to be at low risk of blood loss, there is another, more natural, way of doing it.

Natural delivery of the placenta

The third stage of labour is not just about getting rid of the redundant placenta. This is the time when your baby begins to adapt to life outside your womb and leaving the delivery of your placenta to nature is an integral part in this process.

After birth the umbilical cord is left intact; it is normally just long enough for you to hold your baby. Helped by a final boost of blood from the placenta, she will take her first breath, then another, and another. As your baby's lungs expand, her heart and circulation will make the delicate adjustments necessary for independent life. Slowly, the flow of blood from the placenta will decrease, its job nearly over.

Having your baby enclosed in your arms for the first time is a very special moment for you and your baby. As you cuddle her skin-to-skin, your system will be flooded with oxytocin, the hormone of love and labour. This same hormone will soon cause your uterus to contract, expel your placenta, and start the flow of milk from your breasts.

Cutting the cord After a while, you may sense instinctively that it is time to cut the cord, which will by then have stopped pulsating. Your midwife will first put two clamps in place, then

"After ten minutes of cuddles and suckling we got out and whilst nursing I delivered the placenta sitting in a chair."

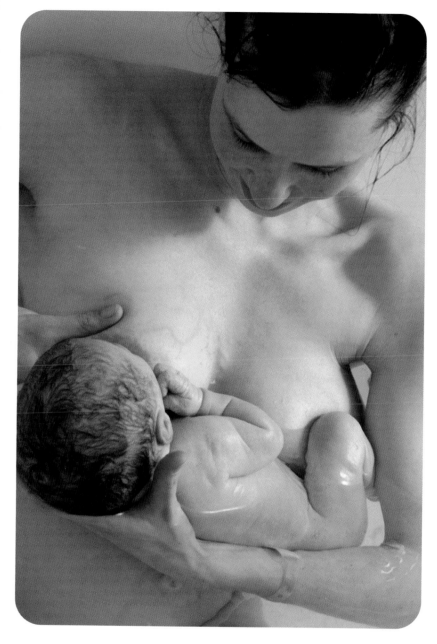

YOUR PLACENTA

Examine your baby's placenta. It's a truly amazing organ – yet so sadly overlooked. The placenta legally belongs to you. You can do what you want with it – although most women ask the midwives or maternity unit to organize disposal.

There is no need *to cut the umbilical cord immediately. Take time to gaze and hold your baby close.*

she, you, or your partner can cut inbetween. You will then probably want to spend time holding and admiring your baby. The room should be kept dim and quiet. It's important that you do not feel tense or watched, or adrenalin may interfere with the natural flow of events. Your midwife should stay close. If you wish, she may examine your perineum to see if you need stitches; she may even do these quickly for you while you are waiting for the placenta.

Your final contractions After a short time (ten to 15 minutes), you should feel your placenta in your vagina and will push it out with a few small

Inside the uterus *your baby was fed and protected by the placenta – the amazing organ that passes oxygen, nutrients, and antibodies from mother to baby and prevents many harmful substances from reaching her.*

contractions. Your midwife will collect it in a container and place a hand on your belly to check that your uterus is well contracted. There will be some blood loss at this stage, and your midwife will know whether or not the amount is normal.

Medical delivery of the placenta

Active, or medical, management of the third stage involves various procedures aimed at reducing blood loss and preventing possible problems with the delivery of the placenta. It generally involves a combination of three factors and the process normally takes about four to seven minutes. These three factors are:

- Administering a drug to the mother as the baby is being born
- Early clamping of the baby's cord, usually immediately after the birth
- Controlled gentle pulling of the cord.

Although these three elements are common, there are different ways that the medical delivery of the third stage can be undertaken.

Different drugs may be used There are a number of drugs that can be used for a medical delivery of the placenta. However, oxytocin and syntometrine are the two drugs most commonly used in the UK. Oxytocin can be given either by an injection into the muscle, or by a drip into a vein via a canula inserted into the back of the hand. Syntometrine is a combination of syntocinon and ergometrine and is given by injection into the muscle. It was thought that the combination of these two drugs gave a stronger more sustained contraction. The drug can be given when the baby's head is crowning, with the birth of the baby's shoulder, or after the birth. In the UK the drug is usually given before the birth so that it can begin to take effect sooner.

Clamping the cord With medical management of the third stage the cord is normally clamped immediately after the birth of the baby, usually within 30 seconds, and before it stops pulsating. The earlier the cord is clamped the less blood will pass from the placenta to the baby by placental transfusion. However, there is also something known as delayed active management, when a drug is not given to the mother until the cord has finished pulsating and been clamped and cut.

Controlled cord traction Your midwife will wait for a few minutes for signs that your placenta has separated. She will then gently draw on the cord to extract the placenta, while maintaining a counter pressure on your uterus with her other hand.

Natural or medical – which way is best?

Medical management of the third stage has two proposed advantages. Firstly, with medical management, you're less likely to lose a significant amount of blood (which means upwards of 500ml/approximately 1 pint).

Secondly, it is faster; an average of eight minutes against an average of 15 minutes for a natural third stage (1) – although at this point you will probably be focussing on your new baby and unaware of the time.

The issue of blood loss may sound alarming, and in a small number of women, it is. However, normal blood loss needs to be put into context in that during pregnancy your blood volume has increased significantly. A healthy pregnant women, therefore, has a reasonable amount of blood to spare after birth. You should be aware though that women can unexpectedly lose large amounts of blood during or after the deliver of the placenta. These women need immediate treatment with drugs to control this abnormal excessive bleeding.

Some midwives think that the emphasis on blood loss at the time of the delivery of the placenta may be misleading, believing that women who had a medical third stage may actually lose the seem amount of blood overall – but they lose more blood in the few weeks following the birth than women who have a natural third stage (2).

Possible contraindications for a natural third stage For some women, there are health risks if they decide to have a natural third stage and for them, medical management has a significant role to play in their care.

- Those who cannot afford to lose even a moderate amount of blood in childbirth are: very anaemic women; the malnourished; unwell or weak; those who have bled heavily during pregnancy.
- Those women who are already at greater risk of an above-average blood loss, and may benefit from the "protection" of a medical third stage are: those having twins or very large babies, women with blood disorders, women who have previously had third-stage problems.
- Finally, there is a group of women who may be steered toward medical management because the type of labour they have had may mean that the uterus does not work so effectively to expel the placenta and control bleeding. For example: women who have had very long and exhausting labours, those who have had very rapid labours (less than an hour), labours that have been started or speeded up with syntocinon, labours where the woman has chosen to have pethidine or an epidural.

Consider all your options beforehand Research shows that women often know little about the third stage of labour. As the issues are complex, you should talk about the third stage with a midwife during your pregnancy and receive full and balanced information. You should not be expected to consider natural versus medical management of the third stage for the first time during labour. All things being equal you should have been able to consider the options and what you decide depends on your circumstances.

- Talk it over with your midwife
- Read *Delivering Your Placenta* a booklet published by the Association for Improvements in the Maternity Services (London: AIMS, 1999).

see also

Your feelings after birth	178–79
Changes in your body	180–83
Your new baby	186–89

A wonderful twin birth in water

"The water was lovely; it didn't take the pain away but helped me to cope. The buoyancy enabled me to change positions, settling into half-kneeling, half-squatting."

A midwife gives birth to two babies in hospital

"I approached the birth of my twins with excitement and trepidation. I had confidence to give birth following a water birth at home with my first child, but discovering that my second pregnancy was twins added a degree of uncertainty. I resigned myself to a hospital delivery. I was lucky to have a wonderful midwife, Carole. I trusted her implicitly and without her support I could never have achieved such a positive experience.

I saw my consultant and emphasized that in the absence of complications, I wished to have privacy, minimal intervention and monitoring, an active birth using water, and a physiological third stage. He was supportive and I was able to look forward to the birth. Both babies were head down.

Labour started two days before my due date. The contractions quickly established between three and eight minutes apart. By 11.30pm, labour was established and Carole arrived to find me kneeling against Ian and concentrating on my breathing. We transferred to hospital where my room was warm, dark, and quiet. The move was unsettling but once there, I switched off from the world and concentrated on giving birth.

The hospital pool was prepared for me

The pool was run and I had the fetal heart monitor held on by Carole, for which I was grateful. I'd hoped my cervix might be 4cm (1½in) dilated and was staggered when an examination revealed I was 9cm (3¾in). The water was lovely; it didn't take the pain away, but it helped me cope. The buoyancy enabled me to change positions, settling into half-kneeling, half-squatting. I appreciated the privacy of the pool as twin deliveries often attract an audience. Carole, a supporting midwife, and my husband were my only attendants; the consultant and paediatrician hovering outside.

My waters broke in second stage and I felt the first baby moving down. I didn't have a strong urge to push, but doing so relieved the pain, and after 20 minutes, my son was born into the water. I brought him gently to the surface. Knowing I had to do it again, the euphoria was overridden by pain and uncertainty.

I left the pool to be re-examined. I was in pain so when I knew all was well, I didn't need asking twice to go back into the pool. The second waters broke spontaneously and I felt the baby coming. In spite of my protests, there was nothing I could do to prevent my daughter being born in two reluctant, but easier, pushes, 17 minutes after her brother. Again I brought her to the surface, but she didn't cry and spent a moment being 'pinked up' with some oxygen. As I had minimal blood loss, I had a physiological third stage and pushed the placenta out nine minutes later. I had achieved a safe, natural twin water birth, which filled me with pride, gratitude to my carers, and love for my babies — it was a truly positive experience."

An antenatal teacher finally births her own baby

"When I woke from the anaesthetic to find my first baby at my breast, I felt wonder at the creature my body had produced, but afterward, started to blame myself for 'failing' by needing a Caesarean. Two more unplanned Caesarean births followed. We decided not to have more children and I had to accept that I would never know what it felt like to birth a baby.

When I found I was pregnant again, my work as an antenatal teacher, and the research I had read, made me certain that vaginal births after Caesareans were not only possible but also safe. I knew that I needed to be at home with a wise woman. I knew of the independent midwife, Mary Cronk, by reputation. Experienced in home births, she is down-to-earth, bolshy with uninformed medics, and very knowledgeable. I resented having to pay for her care, not because I begrudge her, but because I believe this sort of care should be available to every woman.

My previous labours had been long and slow, I couldn't believe this would be different so I was bemused one morning, 18 days overdue, to find I was having strong contractions every five minutes.

I phoned Mary – my going overdue had interfered with her schedule and she had to be at a conference later so she'd reluctantly handed over my care to her colleague, Andrya, but wanted to know when it was happening. I phoned Andrya and then my friend Lesley sat with me while Raymond did the school run. Then Raymond rang Mary who came over until Andrya, and second midwife Sue, could get here.

The midwives supported me

It was lovely to see Mary and soon all three midwives were in attendance. The pain was bearable although the thought of being still or prostrate was agonizing. Andrya's hand-held monitor and pulse-taking assured us that we were well. Eventually I sank into the pool – it felt like being hugged, a comforting and safe place. I rocked through contractions and slumped through the intervals between. I retreated within myself to be with the pain, rocking and breathing.

The pain increased, I felt the presence of God, loving and comforting me. Mary left quietly; though I could still hear her voice, encouraging me. At last the urge to push started and I was doing something other than enduring. I braced myself widthways across the pool, remembering not to grit my teeth but to go with the surges.

In a flurry, Fergus was out: we did it! We did it! It was an affirmation of everything I know about the female body and spirit. On the day, I hadn't needed drugs or props, just my husband, my God, my home, and three wonderful women who understood how birth works and how to help me make the final part of my own birth journey."

A vaginal birth after three Caesareans

"It was an affirmation of everything I know about the female body and spirit."

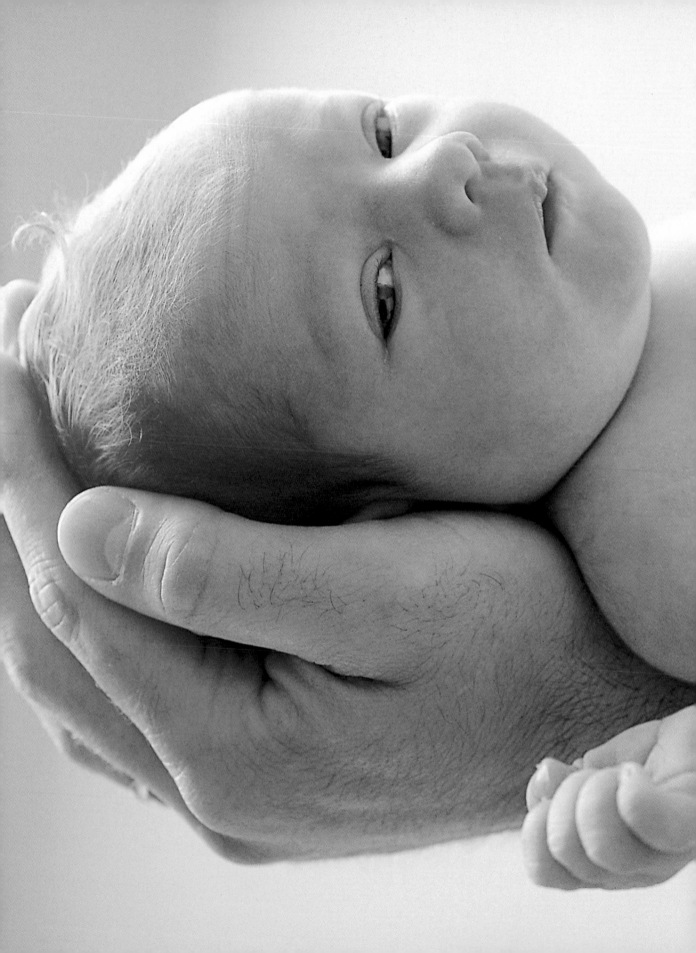

5 Medical intervention

Why extra help may be needed

Birth is a natural process, and women's bodies are designed to have babies naturally. Sometimes, however, things don't go according to plan and medical assistance may be necessary for the health of either baby or mother.

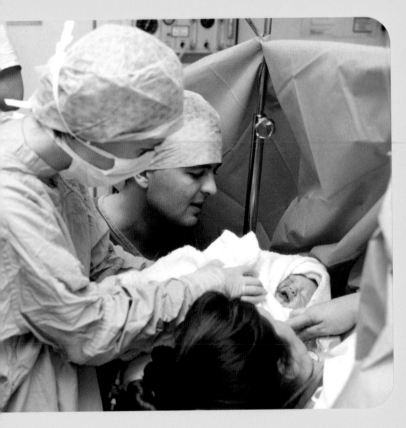

In England fewer than 48 per cent of women give birth without any medical intervention, which can be anything from induction, epidural, instrumental delivery (forceps or ventouse), to a Caesarean (1). It's a fact that simply having your baby in hospital increases your risk of intervention — one study showed that women without complications or high-risk factors who planned to have their baby at home were half as likely as women planning to give birth in hospital, to have a Caesarean section or an instrumental delivery (and their babies were just as healthy as those born in hospital) (2).

your birth year

think through your care options carefully as it can affect likelihood of intervention

find out about medical interventions and their pros and cons

FIRST TRIMESTER												SECOND TRIMESTER													
1	2	3	4	6	7	8	9	10	11	12		13	14	15	16	17	18	19	20	21	22	23	24	25	26

think about possible birth partners you would like to have with you at the birth

if you are planning a hospital birth ask about policy on electronic fetal monitoring

If you were hoping to have a natural birth, accepting medical help can be a disappointment. If you are having your baby at home or in a birth centre, and require medical help, you will almost certainly need to transfer to hospital. Even if you are already in hospital, intervention can change the atmosphere from one of intimacy with your birth partner and midwife, to that of a medical event. On the other hand, it may come as a relief to you that "something is happening" – particularly if you are finding labour a lot more difficult than you imagined.

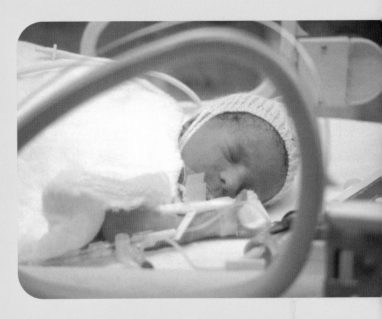

As all forms of intervention have some unwanted side-effects, it is helpful to have a strategy for making decisions when medical help is offered. Try thinking through the "BRAIN" analysis below:

- **Benefits** What are the benefits of the intervention?
- **Risks** What are the risks both to the baby and me?
- **Alternatives** What other options are there?
- **Instincts** What do your instincts tell you?

- **Nothing** What if we don't do anything? Asking yourself, your midwife, and/or your doctor these questions, and thinking through the answers will help you make decisions that are right for you. This in turn should help you to feel more satisfied with the whole birth experience.

The following pages will give you some basic information about common medical interventions: why and how they are done, and what you can do to reduce your chances of needing them.

most babies will have settled head down by now; if your baby is breech, you should be offered external cephalic version (ECV)

you'll have your six- to eight-week check up with your midwife or GP

THIRD TRIMESTER | BIRTH AND FIRST 3 MONTHS

27 28 29 30 31 32 33 34 35 36 37 38 39 40 | 41 42 43 44 45 46 47 48 49 50 51 52

your baby could survive if born now, but would need to go into the neonatal care unit

you can still change your choice of place of birth if you want to

you may be offered an induction from now

Induction and acceleration

Induction means starting labour off by artificial means and may be offered for babies who are "post-term", where the pregnancy has lasted for longer than 41–42 weeks. Although most babies born after this point are fine, a small number seem less able to deal with normal labour and birth – which is why doctors and midwives may strongly recommend induction at this point.

HOW LABOUR CAN BE INDUCED

Sweeping the membranes This is done as a first stage. During a vaginal examination, the membranes are separated from the uterus around the cervix. This procedure, which can be done at an antenatal appointment, can trigger contractions. *If labour does not start within a few days, then the following would be offered:*

Cervical ripening A prostaglandin pessary is inserted into the vagina. This is usually done in hospital and can be enough to start labour.

Breaking the waters (amniotomy) Here your membranes are ruptured using a special plastic hook. It can only be done if the cervix has started dilating.

Synthetic oxytocin (syntocinon) This is an artificial form of oxytocin given via a drip into a vein in your arm. The syntocinon makes the uterus contract. Electronic fetal monitoring is always recommended to ensure that the baby is coping well with your contractions.

What is induction of labour?

Rather than waiting until you go into labour naturally, it may be started or "induced" when:

- There is a problem with you or the baby and an early birth is advisable
- Your baby is "overdue" (41-plus weeks)
- Your waters have broken, but labour has not started.

If you are being offered induction, make sure you fully understand the reasons why it's being suggested. You can choose whether or not to accept the offer – induction of labour is a major intervention and best used only when medically indicated (1). A common reason why a woman with an otherwise normal pregnancy is offered induction is that her baby is "overdue", or post-term. Many doctors are unwilling to let a woman carry on beyond ten days after her due date, while others are happy for the pregnancy to continue for up to 21 days beyond the 40 weeks.

If your waters have broken and you are more than 37 weeks pregnant, but you have not gone into labour after, at most, four days, induction is strongly recommended (2). This is because there's an increased risk of group B streptococcus infection (see page 127).

What are the disadvantages of induction? Your labour can be induced in several ways, see box left, and there are disadvantages to each method.

- Sweeping the membranes increases the chance of labour starting naturally within 48 hours, but there is a risk that your waters could be accidentally broken. If this happens, there is no turning back, and because of the risk of infection, there will be a need to get labour going and for the baby to be born within the next few days.
- Very occasionally women react to prostaglandin pessaries used for "cervical ripening" by having very strong painful contractions. These can be difficult to cope with, which can affect your baby's heartbeat.
- Breaking your waters can cause discomfort, and the contractions following it tend to be stronger and more painful.
- A syntocinon drip can increase the strength, length, and frequency of contractions. For this reason, women who are induced in this way are more likely to have an epidural to cope with the pain and will also need

electronic fetal monitoring. This means, in turn, that there's a greater risk of the labour ending in a ventouse or forceps delivery, or even a Caesarean. This is an example of the "cascade of intervention".

Can I still have a home birth? Apart from sweeping the membranes, all other methods of induction need to be carried out in hospital. Therefore accepting an offer of induction will mean putting aside your plans for a home birth.

What are the alternatives? If, after 42 weeks gestation, an induction has been suggested, you should also be offered, as an alternative, twice weekly monitoring of your baby's heartbeat, and an ultrasound scan to check the depth of amniotic fluid surrounding your baby (3).

What will happen if I am not induced? In an uncomplicated pregnancy, there is a small but definite increased risk of your baby developing health problems after 42 weeks (4). In situations where your waters have broken but labour has not started at term, 91 per cent of women go into labour naturally within 48 hours. Induction is strongly recommended if labour has not started after four days (5). You can try other methods of induction following your due date (see right), however, the evidence for these methods is largely anecdotal.

What is acceleration of labour?

This is sometimes called augmentation. It is a process designed to strengthen contractions and speed up the dilatation of your cervix. It is achieved in similar ways to induction – by breaking the waters (amniotomy) and using a syntocinon drip. If you do choose to accelerate your labour, remember that the benefits of a faster labour in terms of not getting so tired and seeing your baby sooner, have to be weighed against the disadvantages of acceleration.

What are the disadvantages of acceleration? These are similar to the disadvantages of induction – sudden, painful contractions that can be difficult to cope with and you may need epidural anaesthesia. In addition you are also likely to be continuously monitored. All these factors will reduce your ability to move around and adopt comfortable positions. If you do accept syntocinon and are finding the contractions too hard to cope with, you can ask for the drip to be turned down.

What are the alternatives? Any alternatives to acceleration usually focus on helping your body to produce its own oxytocin so that you don't need an artificial supplement. The labour hormone oxytocin is produced in the absence of stress, in other words when you feel safe, nurtured, and relaxed (see box right). Natural stimulation of oxytocin can take some time, so you may need to request being left in private for a while.

AVOIDING MEDICAL INDUCTION AND ACCELERATION

To avoid induction try:
- Sex – semen is rich in prostaglandins; kissing, nipple-stimulation, and orgasm can all increase your natural oxytocin levels
- Eating spicy food or fresh pineapple
- Complementary therapies such as acupuncture, homeopathy, reflexology, or aromatherapy (go to a registered practitioner)
- Gentle exercise
- A vigorous walk.

To avoid acceleration of labour try:
- Getting yourself into a comfortable, upright position
- Moving around between contractions – even pace up and down the room if you feel like it
- Improving your environment – make it dark and cosy
- Relaxation techniques
- Requesting privacy – ask extra people in the room to leave
- Asking your birth partner for lots of positive support: "You can do it!", "You're doing great!"
- Focusing on your baby
- Keeping your energy and fluid levels up
- Kissing and nipple stimulation, which encourages the release of oxytocin
- Staying calm. Don't worry about your labour being slow; it is fine as long as you and baby are coping well.

Fetal monitoring

During labour, your baby's heartbeat will be checked to make sure that he is getting enough oxygen and not "distressed". This can be done with a hand-held ear trumpet (Pinard stethoscope), a hand-held Doppler scanner (also called a Sonicaid), or by electronic monitoring with an abdominal transducer. For the latter you'll be connected to a machine that restricts your movements.

New national guidelines *no longer support an "admission trace", but if electronic fetal monitoring is required, it helps to stay as upright as possible.*

Which type of monitoring is best?

The way you and your baby are monitored can have a profound effect on the progress of your labour. If you and your birth partner are familiar with each type of monitoring it can help with decision-making.

If you are healthy and have had a trouble-free pregnancy, the recommended way of being monitored is at least every 15 minutes using either the hand-held Doppler/Sonicaid or the ear trumpet (see box below). Your baby will be monitored every five minutes in the second stage of your labour (1). The advantage of this type of monitoring is that you are free to move around, or use a birth pool. Research shows that this kind of intermittent monitoring is as effective as other forms of monitoring. If there are no complications, it is the best method of monitoring.

What is electronic fetal monitoring?

Often referred to as EFM, this involves wearing a belt monitor (see box below opposite), which is attached to a machine. It is used when the midwife or doctor wants to follow the pattern of your baby's heartbeat more closely. You could be attached to it for 20 to 30 minutes at a time, or it can be used all the way through labour. There are situations when this may be recommended such as if your baby is distressed (see box opposite).

HOW A BABY'S HEARTBEAT CAN BE MONITORED

- Using an ear trumpet (Pinard stethoscope). This is a tube that allows the midwife to hear the heartbeat just with her ear.
- Using a hand-held ultrasound machine (Doppler or Sonicaid).
- Using an electronic fetal monitor (EFM). This has two receivers held in place by belts around your waist and hips. The patterns of the baby's heartbeat and your contractions are printed out on a piece of paper (the "trace").
- Using a fetal scalp electrode. This is a sensor fastened to the baby's head by a small hook. The sensor is on the end of a wire that is put inside your vagina. Once in place it stays there until your baby is born.

Sometimes, a fetal scalp electrode is used. This will be attached to your baby's head using a metal clip that breaks his skin. The wire from the electrode passes down your vagina, across your thigh to the monitor. It can only be used if your waters have broken.

When is electronic monitoring offered?
- On arrival at hospital (the "admission trace")
- Routinely during labour when there your midwife or doctor are concerned that your baby is not getting enough oxygen
- If you have a particular health problem such as diabetes or pre-eclampsia
- If you are having another intervention such as induction or an epidural
- You are having twins, a breech, or premature baby, or have had a Caesarean.

What are the disadvantages? Usually you need to be lying down for electronic monitoring so continuous monitoring can slow labour and make the contractions more painful than if you could move around. This can make it more likely that your labour will need to be accelerated with the use of drugs, or that you will want an epidural to cope with the pain.

This is especially true of the "admission trace", which is often done when you first arrive at hospital. If you are offered one, ask why. If it's done purely as a routine, you could ask instead for the hand-held monitor to be used.

Another disadvantage of EFM is that being able to read and understand the trace depends on the skills of medical staff. Evidence shows that false readings do occur, which causes an increased incidence of instrumental delivery or Caesarean, with no health benefit to mother or baby.

Is it safer for my baby to be monitored? There is no evidence to support electronic fetal monitoring routinely on arrival at hospital or during labour for low-risk women. Where there is a higher risk of fetal distress, there is some evidence that supports its use (2). You may find that continuous monitoring is reassuring for you. It is, of course, your choice whether you accept EFM or not and your decision will depend on your situation.

WHAT HAPPENS IF MY BABY IS SUFFERING FROM FETAL DISTRESS?

If your baby is not getting enough oxygen, he will need to be born quickly. You may be offered a test called "fetal blood sampling" to confirm the situation. A sample of blood can be taken from the baby's head and tested for oxygen levels. This is an invasive test, and may require that your waters be broken. However, it makes it much less likely that a Caesarean section would be performed unnecessarily.

Sometimes, the pattern of the baby's heartbeat shows unequivocally that he is in distress. In these circumstances a Caesarean section would be strongly advised immediately; babies who are having problems can be delivered very quickly this way. There is no doubt that this operation has saved many lives, but studies also show that electronic fetal monitoring itself increases the Caesarean rate (3).

Remember, most babies come through labour without any problems at all, and you can help to make it easier by "listening to your body". Move around as much as possible and change your position when you feel that you want to.

MANAGING ELECTRONIC FETAL MONITORING

Be sure that you agree that there is a need for electronic fetal monitoring (EFM), and if you're not sure, ask if the department has a telemetric (remote) monitor so you don't have to stay still or request intermittent monitoring. If you opt for it:
- Try to stay upright at the same time – you could either stand or sit, or try sitting the wrong way round on an upright chair, supported by a cushion over the back of the chair
- Ask for the belt monitor to be left on the baby for no more than 30 minutes at a time so you can move around
- Lying on your left side is preferable to lying on your back if you are very tired.

Epidural anaesthesia

An epidural means an injection of local anaesthetic into the lower part of your spine to relieve the pain of labour. It can only be administered in hospital. Although this is a very effective form of pain relief, the benefit needs to be weighed against the increased risk of a longer labour and a greater likelihood of needing instrumental help to birth your baby.

TIPS FOR AVOIDING AN EPIDURAL

- Choose to give birth at home or in a midwife-led unit.
- A birth pool can help you manage the pain of labour.
- Use other types of pain relief that don't affect the physiology of labour, such as TENS, gas and air, massage, relaxation, or homeopathy.
- Have good female support (a supportive midwife, friend, or doula).
- Move around as much as possible during labour.
- Ask for the baby's heartbeat to be monitored intermittently rather than continuously.
- Be aware that any medical intervention, such as having your waters broken or a syntocinon drip, will make labour more painful.
- Write in your birth plan that you will ask if you want an epidural and request that the hospital not offer one first.

How effective is the pain relief?

An epidural usually starts working within 10 to 20 minutes. It has to be given by an anaesthetist. A hollow needle is placed between two vertebrae in your spine, close to the nerves that transmit the pain of labour. A fine tube is then threaded into the needle and the needle is removed. An anaesthetic is fed down the tube, which remains in place for as long as you have the epidural. The anaesthetic drugs can be given in a single dose (which can be topped up), continuously, or by a pump that you control. Because the local anaesthetic numbs the nerves that transmit labour pain, it gives very effective pain relief to most women.

The drugs used vary between hospitals. Some administer a local anaesthetic alone, others mix local anaesthetic with an opiate. When the opiate is combined with a local anaesthetic, the quantity of local used can be reduced: this is called a "low-dose" epidural.

Some hospitals offer a 24-hour epidural service, but in others it depends on the availability of an anaesthetist. If you are hoping to have epidural pain relief, ask your midwife if anaesthetists are readily available in your local hospital .

What are the disadvantages?

There are a number of disadvantages with epidurals that have to be weighed against the benefit of effective pain relief.

An epidural can make your labour longer, and make it more likely that labour will need to be accelerated using syntocinon. It is also more likely that you will need an assisted delivery (1).

Epidurals block the nerves involved in movement and cause you to lose the feeling in your legs. This means that after a conventional epidural you will need to stay lying on the bed for the rest of your labour (or until the epidural has worn off). As a result, you lose the advantages of being able to adopt upright positions and move around, which help labour to progress.

With low-dose epidurals, the mixture of drugs means that you retain some mobility and may even be able to walk with help. However, research has shown that the increased risk of an assisted birth still remains. Other considerations with an epidural are: you may experience problems with

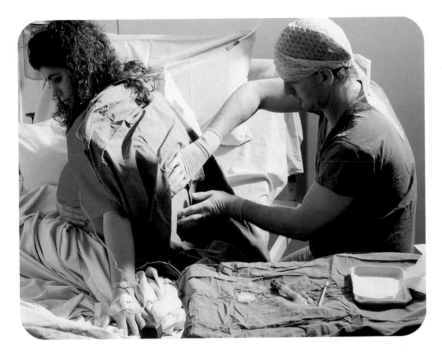

An epidural has to be administered by an anaesthetist in hospital. It usually starts working within 20 minutes, but it increases your risk of having an assisted delivery.

low blood pressure or have a raised temperature, and you may need to have a catheter inserted to empty your bladder.

After labour, approximately one per cent of women who had an epidural experience a "dural-tap" headache. In over half of these women it will be a severe headache. Very rarely a woman has a serious complication as a result of having an epidural. Medical staff on the labour ward are trained to deal with this type of situation.

Can I have an epidural at a home birth?
No. An epidural has to be administered by an anaesthetist in hospital. If you are labouring at home, or you are in a midwifery-led unit, and decide that you want an epidural, you will have to transfer to hospital.

What can I do to avoid having an epidural?
In advance of labour, you can try to ensure that your baby is in the best position for an uncomplicated birth (2). You can also try to arrange your maternity care so that you know the midwife who will be with you throughout your labour (3), and to make sure that you are well supported in labour by a birth partner (4).

Only you will know if you need an epidural. If you had hoped to labour without one, you could try to manage for, say, one more hour, or five more contractions without one and then reassess the situation.

If you find you need an epidural to deal with your labour pain, don't feel guilty, or that you've "failed". Everyone's experience of labour is different – what really matters is that you get the support to make the choice that's right for you and your baby on the day.

Instrumental delivery

The second stage of labour begins when your cervix is fully dilated and ends with the birth of your baby. This, the "pushing" stage, is the most stressful part of labour for your baby, and if you have had epidural pain relief, you may find it harder to "feel to push". For this reason, you might be offered help to give birth to your baby with either ventouse (vacuum extraction) or forceps.

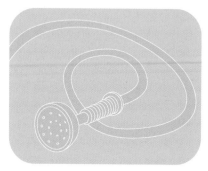

Ventouse

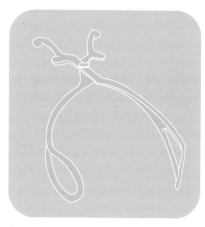

Forceps

A vacuum extractor, or ventouse, *is a silicone cap which fits on your baby's head with suction and helps you push your baby out. As a method of instrumental delivery, ventouse is generally used in preference to forceps (lower picture).*

What is an instrumental birth?

Sometimes when the second stage of labour is very long and a woman is having problems pushing the baby out herself, the process can be helped with the use of either ventouse (vacuum extraction) or forceps. This is also called an assisted delivery.

This type of delivery can usually only be carried out in the second stage of labour when the cervix is fully dilated and your waters have broken. If a ventouse delivery is not successful, forceps may be attempted, or you'll be offered a Caesarean operation. If forceps are not successful, a Caesarean would be offered.

When will it be suggested This procedure might be suggested if you are getting very tired and finding it difficult to push the baby out. It could also be an option if your baby is having a problem moving down through your pelvis. The latter can happen particularly if your baby started labour in a difficult position, such as the "occiput posterior" position, where your baby is lying with him back against your back.

An assisted birth may also be recommended if either you or your baby are having problems coping with the second stage of labour. Unfortunately, having epidural pain relief can increase your chance of needing help with the delivery of your baby .

What happens If you decide to have an assisted delivery, you will be asked to lie on your back and your feet will be put up in stirrups. You may need to have an episiotomy as well, see below.

Ventouse (vacuum extraction) This is a silicone cap attached to a suction pump. The cap is fitted on to the baby's head while it's in the birth canal and is kept in place using suction. The ventouse is then pulled at the same time as you push, to help your baby be born. An episiotomy (a cut in the back wall of the vagina) is not always necessary with ventouse.

Forceps This an instrument that comes in two halves and looks a bit like metal salad servers. These fit together to form a surgical instrument that can help your baby to be born. Each half of the forceps is carefully put round the baby's head while it is in the birth canal and the two handles fit together. The doctor then pulls when you push as for the ventouse delivery. With forceps, it is usual to have an episiotomy or cut in the back wall of the vagina to help your baby out. You would be given an anaesthetic first to numb the area, see below.

What choices can I make?

As with any medical intervention, it is your choice whether you accept help during the second stage of labour or not. If you decide after discussion that you would like to have an assisted, or instrumental birth, you may be given the option of whether to have forceps or ventouse. However, the options will also depend on your particular circumstances, and the doctor involved may have a preference.

Which is best, forceps or ventouse?

Research shows that for most instrumental deliveries, ventouse should be used rather than forceps (1). This is because ventouse is much gentler for the woman than forceps, and an episiotomy may not be necessary.

Women who have had a ventouse delivery also have less postnatal pain than those who have forceps (2). When ventouse is used first, fewer Caesareans are performed, because forceps are the next likely option if ventouse doesn't work (see below).

Will either affect the baby? Both the use of forceps and ventouse can have short-term effects on your baby. Forceps can cause bruising or facial injuries, and ventouse can temporarily affect the shape of your baby's head and may cause bruising. There is not enough research to be able to say which is preferable in the long term.

Some women find that their babies are more unsettled following an assisted delivery. If this is the case, babies may benefit from visiting a cranial osteopath (see Useful organizations, page 245).

Will I need extra pain relief?

If the baby is still quite high up, you will need to have an epidural in place, or a one-off injection called a "spinal". This will give good pain relief to the whole area. If your baby is very low and just needs lifting out, either with a ventouse or forceps, then an injection of local anaesthetic around the perineum will be sufficient.

Can my birth partner stay with me?

Yes, if he or she wishes to. However, once the forceps or ventouse have been applied, the doctor will have to pull quite firmly during the contraction to help the baby be born. Your birth partner may find this distressing to watch, so he or she may prefer to sit near you at the top end of the bed and concentrate on supporting you.

TIPS FOR AVOIDING AN ASSISTED BIRTH

- Opt for non-epidural methods of pain relief.
- Try not to lie on your back during the second stage of labour.
- Relax your pelvic floor.
- Conserve your energy by listening to your body; push only when your body is telling you to, rather than being directed when told to push by someone else.
- Breathe as your body tells you during a contraction, rather than holding your breath and pushing as hard as you can.
- A syntocinon drip can sometimes be used to strengthen second-stage contractions.

Caesarean birth

Birth by Caesarean section is now far more common than it was a few years ago. In some parts of the UK, as many as 30 per cent of births are Caesareans, so it is unwise to assume that "it won't happen to me", or ignore the possibility that your baby could be born this way.

WHY MIGHT I NEED A CAESAREAN?

There are occasions when a Caesarean is needed, other situations where the evidence is less clear cut.

You need a Caesarean if you have:

- Placenta praevia: when your placenta lies across your cervix, the opening into the vagina.
- Placental abruption: when the placenta comes away from the wall of the uterus.
- Pre-eclampsia: which can develop into a serious medical condition of pregnancy.
- Your baby is lying in the oblique or transverse position.
- Medical conditions of the baby.

Indications are less clear if:

- Your baby is lying bottom down (breech presentation).
- The progress of labour is considered to be too slow (failure to progress).
- The baby is believed to be in difficulty (fetal distress).
- You have a history of previous Caesarean deliveries.
- You are carrying more than one baby.

Find out as much as you can

A Caesarean can be an extremely positive experience, when mothers feel confident that it was the right choice for them and that their wishes were respected. It may be planned in advance, called an "elective" Caesarean, or it may have to be agreed at short notice, especially during labour, when it is termed an "emergency" Caesarean.

For some women the suggestion of a Caesarean, or the decision to carry out the operation, will come as a welcome relief. The circumstances of each situation and the information that a woman has been given will combine to reassure her that a Caesarean birth is definitely right for her and her baby at that time.

For other women, the prospect of a Caesarean can be disappointing or distressing. If a woman has not been given enough information, or she is not convinced of the need for or the "rightness" of a Caesarean, then she may feel that she has no option but to agree, despite her misgivings. Under these circumstances a Caesarean can, sadly, be a traumatic experience.

If you do not feel you have been given sufficient information, or you do not understand your circumstances as well as you would like to, do ask for more information. You have a right to a second opinion, and if there is time (for example, if it's an elective Caesarean), you can seek further information from elsewhere such as Caesarean support organizations or the internet. (See also Useful organizations, page 245.)

When would a Caesarean be recommended?

A Caesarean may be recommended at any time during pregnancy or labour. In some cases, there is clear evidence that a Caesarean is needed to save life or to safeguard the health of mother or baby. However, in many cases the best option isn't clear (see box left). Obstetricians can read the same evidence in different ways and hold differing opinions on the need for one.

You may have different priorities when making decisions. There are occasions when the choice is left to the parents – who may feel they have insufficient information on which to base an informed decision.

Can I choose not to have a Caesarean?

As with all interventions in labour and pregnancy, you have to give your consent before you can have a Caesarean. However, if you are uncertain

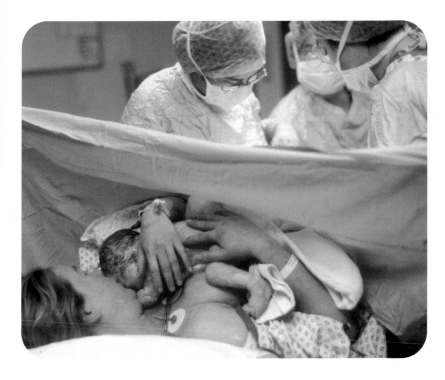

Your baby should be handed *to you straight after the birth. You can get to know him by cuddling him "skin to skin" while the medical team completes the operation.*

about the need for a Caesarean it can be very difficult to disagree with your medical professionals, particularly if you are in labour.

Not all "emergency" Caesareans are dire emergencies. The urgency of a Caesarean (elective or emergency) has been graded into four categories (1):

- There's an immediate threat to the life of the mother or baby
- Mother or baby are in difficulty, but it's not immediately life threatening
- Mother should be delivered shortly, but neither mother nor baby are in difficulty
- Delivery timed to suit the mother and the staff.

Unless the circumstances of your Caesarean fall into one of the first two categories, there should be time for you to seek more information to help you to understand your situation and come to your own decisions. Turn to page 153 for more about using a "BRAIN" analysis to work out what would be right for you and your baby.

What are the main risks of having a Caesarean?

Although a Caesarean is generally considered to be "safe" operation, it is still major abdominal surgery and there are some risks to both you and your baby.

- Vaginal birth is about four times safer for you than having a Caesarean section (2), but in both cases the risk is very small (an elective Caesarean is thought to be safer than an emergency one) (3).
- The mother is at risk of haemorrhage (severe bleeding), wound infection, or small blood clots (thrombosis).
- Recovery will take longer than a vaginal delivery, and varies considerably from woman to woman.

HOW CAN I AVOID A CAESAREAN?

There are ways to make a Caesarean less likely:

- If your baby is breech, you should be offered external cephalic version (ECV) to try to turn him round. You could also consult a homeopath, acupuncturist, or reflexologist.
- In the later part of pregnancy you could try to get your baby into a good position for labour.
- During labour you can encourage things to progress by keeping mobile and trying different positions. Intermittent monitoring of the baby's heartbeat with a Pinard or Doppler (Sonicaid), rather than electronic fetal monitoring, also reduces the likelihood of a Caesarean.
- Mothers who book a home birth are less likely to need a Caesarean.

- One of the long-term effects of the operation is that you will have a scar on your uterus, which may affect future fertility, pregnancies, and births, and complicate any later gynaeocological surgery. A few mothers who have had Caesareans have been known to suffer long-term pain.
- The major risk to babies born by Caesarean is that there's a higher chance of them having breathing difficulties that continue for a while after the birth. The birth process helps a baby to breathe once he is born as labour prepares the baby's lungs for breathing. Babies born by Caesarean – particularly elective – do not go through this and may be more likely to need to be taken to the neonatal baby unit after birth.
- Breathing difficulties due to prematurity can be reduced by waiting until at least 39 weeks of pregnancy to have a Caesarean (2).

What sort of anaesthetic will I have?

If you are having an elective Caesarean, you will be given the opportunity to meet the anaesthetist to discuss your anaesthetic options.

These days, the majority of Caesareans are done with spinal anaesthesia. This is a one-off injection in the lower spine that works quickly and gives sufficient anaesthesia for the length of the operation.

When an epidural has been used for pain relief in labour, this can usually be topped up to provide the anaesthesia required for an emergency Caesarean. An epidural is sometimes used for elective Caesareans but is becoming less common.

Both spinals and epidurals give regional anaesthesia so that you are awake while the operation is being done.

Around ten per cent of Caesareans – both elective and emergency – are performed under general anaesthetic (3). If you have a general anaesthetic you will not be aware of anything going on around you. General anaesthetics are less safe than regional anaesthesia, but may be used for various reasons. For example, you may wish not to be awake during the operation, or you may have a medical problem that prevents the use of a spinal or epidural.

> "We were kept informed of what was happening and the anaesthetist was brilliant. Phillippa was checked over within our sight and then handed to us and tucked up beside me."

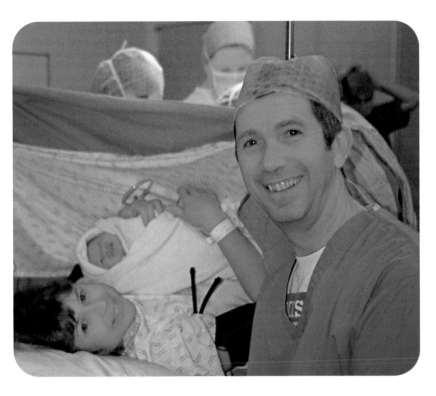

Your baby will be born *during the first five minutes. Stitching up, after the birth, will take around half an hour.*

Preparation for the operation

The exact procedure varies with different hospitals and obstetricians, but in all cases you will be asked to sign a consent form, without which the operation cannot legally take place.

For an elective Caesarean If you are having an elective operation, you will have some routine blood tests done beforehand. You will be asked to go into hospital the night before or early on the morning of the operation. You will be asked not to eat or drink for some hours prior to the operation, and to take an antacid medicine to neutralize your stomach contents.

Before your operation, the final preparations will take place. These will involve: changing into a hospital gown; having a bikini shave if necessary; removing nail varnish, glasses or contact lenses, and jewellery. The nursing staff will put a name-band on your wrist. You may also need to take some clothes to the operating theatre for your baby.

You will then be taken to the operating theatre. If you are having a spinal or epidural anaesthetic, your birth partner will be able to stay with you during your Caesarean, but will have to change into theatre clothes. If you are going to be

"I had a Caesarean. I was surprised at how long it took me to recover. I had an emergency so I didn't have much time to think, but I was frightened and was glad when it was over. The main disappointment was not being able to hold my baby immediately – luckily my husband held him quite quickly afterwards."

IF I HAVE A CAESAREAN CAN I HAVE MY NEXT BABY VAGINALLY?

Vaginal birth after Caesarean (VBAC) is accepted as a safe option for mother and baby. There is a very small risk of scar rupture, but a Caesarean section has risks too. Most mothers who have had a previous Caesarean are able to choose either a between a vaginal delivery or repeat Caesarean with the next pregnancy.

having a general anaesthetic, your birth partner will usually be asked to stay outside the operating theatre.

For an emergency operation If you are having an emergency Caesarean, the same process applies. However, the degree of urgency will determine how much time is available.

What about the operation itself?

The procedure is similar whether the Caesarean is elective or an emergency. There are likely to be a large number of people in the operating theatre with you. The medical staff may include: a midwife, the obstetrician, and an assistant; a theatre nurse and an assistant; an anaesthetist and his or her assistant; and probably a paediatrician (doctor specializing in children).

If you have a spinal or epidural anaesthetic, and you are awake, a screen will be placed near your head so you can't see what is happening. You shouldn't feel any pain at all during the operation though you may be aware of some sensations. Some women describe the feeling as like "someone is doing the washing up in your tummy". If you have had a general anaesthetic, you won't be aware of anything until you wake up.

Your baby will be born very quickly, during the first five minutes, followed by the delivery of the placenta. It will then take around half an hour to have your wound stitched. There are several layers of tissues that need stitching. The stitches in the underneath layers will dissolve by themselves. Your skin will usually have one continuous stitch with beads at either end, or special skin staples that need to be removed later.

When will I see my baby? If you are awake and your baby is well, he will be handed to you straight away. If you have had a general anaesthetic, he can be given to your birth partner outside the operating theatre. If your baby needs any help breathing, or has other problems, he may need to be taken to the special care baby unit.

Your baby should be able to have skin-to-skin contact with either you, or your birth partner, as soon as he is born and some mothers have even breast-fed their babies while still in theatre.

What happens after the birth?

Again, exact procedures will vary between hospitals and obstetricians. Typically, you would be moved out of the operating theatre to another room called a recovery room. A midwife will monitor you to make sure there are no problems until you have recovered sufficiently to be taken to the postnatal ward. If you have had a general anaesthetic, your birth partner and baby should be there with you when you wake up.

After the operation it is usual to be given a painkiller that lasts for several hours. It is also usual to wear tight stockings and/or be given medication to reduce the risk of getting blood clots (thrombosis).

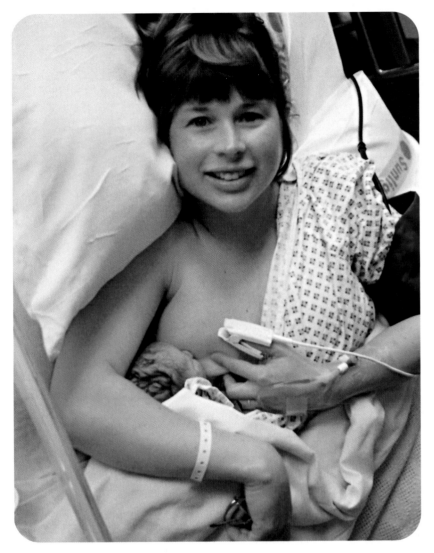

After a Caesarean, *you should still be able to hold your baby and cuddle him. Breast-feeding as soon as possible after the birth, if it's what you would like to do, is possible and some mothers have breast-fed while still in the operating theatre.*

Are there any choices I can make for myself?

Many women are surprised by the scope of options available, even though a Caesarean is surgery. Women who have had time to think about what aspects of birth are important to them, have often found it helpful to think through what they might like to have during their operation and state their preferences while discussing choices at the time.

Your health professionals may be wary of discussing Caesarean preferences until they realize these are not medical requests, but just environmental ones. For example, some women have chosen to have a commentary during the birth, to have music playing, or complete silence; to take photographs or record the birth on a camcorder; see their baby born via a lowered screen or with a mirror; be the first person to greet their baby; discover the sex of the baby themselves or decide who they would like to give them this information.

Premature birth

The UK has the highest rate of low birthweight babies in Western Europe and the proportion of premature and low-weight babies being born and surviving is increasing every year (1). Twenty years ago, only 20 per cent of babies born weighing less than 1kg (2.2lb) survived; nowadays, around 80 per cent survive.

NEONATAL CARE UNITS

Figures show that ten per cent of babies born in the UK spend at least a few days in a neonatal unit, which is an average of 70,000 babies a year. Not all of these babies are early. Some are "term" babies who are unwell and need intensive care, but the proportion of premature and low-birthweight babies being born and surviving is increasing every year. Over the last 15 years, there has been an increase by 40 per cent in live births of babies weighing less than 1.5kg (3lb 5oz) and for babies weighing less than 1kg (2lb 2oz) – an increase of 60 per cent. One in a hundred babies born each year weighs less than 1500g (3lb 5oz)

DEFINITIONS

Term baby	38 to 42 weeks
Premature or preterm baby	born before 37 completed weeks
Very premature	29 to 34 weeks
Extremely premature	24 to 28 weeks

These days, a significant number of babies born prematurely at less than 24 weeks will survive with specialist help.

Premature labour and birth

There's still a lot we don't know about why some babies are born spontaneously very early. About one third of premature births occur for no apparent reason. Reasons we do know include:

- Infection – although whether the infection causes the premature birth, or the other way round, is still open to debate
- Congenital abnormalities
- Multiple pregnancy – twins are often preterm
- Mother who is a heavy smoker
- Mother who has a cervical weakness, where the muscles at the cervix, or neck of the womb, are weak (see page 234)
- Occasionally, history of premature labour, mothers who have already had one may have another
- In some cases, the mother's waters break early (premature rupture of membranes or PROM), starting labour.

If your labour starts while you are less than 35 weeks pregnant, you may be given two sets of drugs. One is to delay the labour for a day or two, while the other is to help the baby's lungs to mature quickly so that they will function better after delivery.

Premature induced or Caesarean birth

Sometimes your baby needs to be born early to avoid risks to the baby's or mother's life, for example, with pre-eclampsia (see page 105). This is a serious disorder that occurs in about one in 14 pregnancies and causes around one third of all premature births. The main symptoms are headaches and swollen feet that are associated with high blood pressure. Although bed rest can help, the only way to stop pre-eclampsia is to deliver your baby, either as an induced birth or a Caesarean section.

In a few cases, an ultrasound scan might show that your baby is not growing well in the womb (described as intrauterine growth retardation). This is usually as a result of not enough blood flowing to and from the placenta. If you have been told that your baby is "small for dates" it can be worrying, but rest assured that he will be carefully monitored. And It may well be that your baby would be safer outside the womb and in this case, a Caesarean birth would be recommended because it puts less strain on the baby than a vaginal delivery.

Hospital care after delivery

Whether your premature baby is born spontaneously, or with a planned induction or Caesarean, it can be hard at first to take in the fact that things have not gone according to plan. A baby born very early may need to stay in hospital for a few weeks or even months, and at times the level of hospital involvement may be so high that your baby may not feel like yours. Occasionally a baby needs to be transferred to another hospital. When this happens, a specialist team provides full intensive-care support throughout the baby's journey.

Premature babies will have to spend their early weeks in a neonatal units. The units are divided into different levels of care:

- Intensive-care unit (ICU) – for very tiny or sick babies. They will be put in an incubator and mechanical ventilation (breathing) may be necessary
- High-dependency unit (HDU) – includes breathing support and intravenous nutrition
- Special-care baby units (SCBU) – continuous monitoring of respiration or heart rate; may involve tube feeding, extra oxygen, or light therapy.

After this babies may receive "transitional" care. This means out-of-incubator care. Babies may still be tube fed and may have phototherapy (light therapy), but they can be out of the incubator.

BREAST-MILK FOR PREMATURE BABIES

Breast-milk is especially suited to preterm babies because their digestive systems are immature. It contains many factors that protect them from infection and allergy, and research has even shown that the milk from mothers of premature babies is better suited to their needs than the breast-milk of mothers of full-term babies. Breast-milk also protects babies from the very serious bowel disease, necrotizing enterocolitis.

Many mothers find it really comforting to provide breast-milk for their preterm baby because it is the one thing they alone can do for their baby. Expressing your milk is hard work and you will need all the support and encouragement you can get – but it's worth it in the long term.

If your baby is premature *he may need to be in the neonatal unit for some time. He may be tube fed and given help with breathing. However, you can still be involved in his care.*

CUP FEEDING

Babies born as early as 32 weeks can be fed expressed colostrum or breast-milk from a special cup (a small plastic medicine cup in fact). Premature babies tend to "lap" the milk in this way.

Babies who have difficulty feeding from the breast for any reason, are often fed breast-milk via a bottle, and then later have to get used to the different sucking style of breast-feeding. The advantage of a cup over a bottle is that your baby won't have to make the difficult switch from bottle to breast, and babies usually enjoy it.

Using a cup can also help when feeding a baby with a cleft palate.

How to cup feed

Hold your baby upright and preferably swaddled to prevent his hands knocking the cup and spilling the precious colostrum.

Have the cup as full as possible but don't worry if there is only a small quantity. Tip the cup so that the rim is directed toward the baby's upper gum and the level of milk is touching his lips. Wait for the baby to take the milk. Do not pour milk into the baby's mouth. His action varies between lapping and sucking.

Keep the cup and the level of milk in place between his feeding bursts. Let your baby pace the feed. He will stop when he has had enough.

Feeding a premature baby

At first your baby may need to be fed using a naso-gastric tube. This is a tube that goes through the baby's nose and into his stomach and is left in place, with sticking plaster over his nose, between feeds. Sometimes the milk is given as a continuous feed with the help of a small electric pump, which makes it possible for your baby to get his food without expending any energy. At the tube-feeding stage you can cuddle him close to give him comfort and stimulation. When he is ready, he can progress to feeding at the breast or, if this is difficult, from a special cup, see box left.

Expressing breast-milk If your baby is very small, or unwell, he may not have strong sucking or swallowing reflexes yet. To give him the benefits of breast-milk, you'll need to express your milk by hand or with a pump. This also means that your supply is kept up for when he is able to breast-feed.

The most common method of expressing milk for a preterm baby is with an electric breast pump, although hand expressing or massage also helps your supply. If you can start pumping as soon as possible after the birth, you'll be able to give your baby more of your valuable colostrum, although you may not be in a fit state to even think about it.

It's best to express your milk frequently and regularly – little and often is more productive; aim to express six to eight times over 24 hours, including a session at night. If you find that expressing from one breast at a time is slow, there are pumps that allow you to express from both breasts at the same time, which is more efficient, and gives your breasts maximum stimulation. Don't forget that every drop of milk that your baby receives is a bonus, so try not to worry if the volume seems small – it can all be frozen.

When your baby is ready to try breast-feeding properly, you can put him to your breast with the nasal tube still in place. If your baby is not strong enough to get all his nutritional requirements at the breast, he can be supplemented later, or at the same time, through the tube.

Getting to know your tiny baby

Although it might seem as though the hospital staff know more about how to care for your baby than you do, there are many things that you alone can do for him. Let the staff keep an eye on the equipment while you and your partner spend time talking to and touching your baby. "Positive" touch (meaning loving touch that does not involve a medical procedure) will be very important to him. However, at the early stages, stroking or patting can over-stimulate a premature baby. Instead, what's called "containment holding" can help. While he lies in the incubator, place one hand firmly but gently on his head, and the other hand on his middle. If your baby is small enough, allow your hands to come together on his middle. This containment holding helps him feel secure, relaxed, and loved.

Kangaroo care for your baby When your baby is strong enough, an effective way of keeping him warm outside an incubator is called

"Kangaroo care". It also helps him feel secure at the same time. It involves skin-to-skin contact. Your baby is placed naked against yours or your partner's bare chest then both of you are covered up. It has been shown that parents' own skin temperature adapts to rises and falls in the baby's body heat. Babies who are given even small amounts of Kangaroo care gain weight more rapidly (and are allowed home earlier) than those in standard special care (1). Kangaroo care can also improve a your milk production, and babies who have it tend to cry less and sleep more deeply.

Preparing to leave the hospital

Planning to take your baby home can cause great anxiety as well as relief. Prepare your move carefully. Once your baby is stable enough not to need the specialist help of the neonatal unit, staff will start to make sure that you can provide all aspects of your baby's care. Staff should give you training in how to perform basic resuscitation and give guidance on "safe sleeping". Resuscitation skills will be useful to have because they will equip you to handle emergencies with your baby.

Some neonatal units have facilities where you can "room in" for one or two nights and practise caring for your baby independently, but within easy access of staff if you have any questions. This can help build confidence for when you get home on your own.

Getting home Over the weeks or months that you and your baby have been in neonatal care, you may have grown used to the high level of support – always having people around to answer questions and help you. At home, you will be much more on your own, although a health visitor should be able to give you support along with your local GP and many pharmacists can also help with issues that may crop up from time to time.

Some areas also have specialized neonatal outreach teams, or possibly community-based paediatric homecare teams who can also provide support. Make sure you know about all services available before you leave.

Giving oxygen at home

A number of babies who need extra help with breathing will go home "on oxygen". This means that the baby still needs to have a supply of oxygen to support his breathing, and the need may continue for several months or even longer. Your paediatrician will tell you how much oxygen your baby needs, what to watch out for, and signs that indicate that he needs more.

The staff looking after your baby in the hospital will arrange a meeting with you before your baby goes home so that you can discuss the future and ask any questions. If there's a community outreach worker attached to the neonatal unit, it's likely he or she will co-ordinate the baby's discharge and provide you with all the information you need about preparing your home, and other practicalities.

You should not be expected to do anything at home that has not been explained and shown to you by a health professional on the neonatal unit.

GETTING HELP

You can find more information and support at BLISS, the charity for the parents of premature babies. They produce a lot of excellent literature, including a Parent Information Guide. Contact details are on page 245.

Once at home a premature baby can feel especially demanding, and it can be difficult to feel able to join in postnatal groups. The NCT can help to put you in touch with other parents who have been through the experience of prematurity, as well as providing an understanding environment in which to take part in activities with your baby. The NCT also has an online support website for parents of preterm babies: http://groups.yahoo.com/group/nct-preterm/

A home birth that became a hospital birth

"Thanks to an amazing midwife who let us continue coping with the contractions, I felt in control, although unable to speak as they were coming every couple of minutes."

A much-wanted home birth doesn't turn out as planned

"I had never considered home birth until I discovered that it was as safe as hospital, in a normal pregnancy. I felt relaxed about the labour even though my baby was in a posterior position and on the fifth day past my due date I went for a walk at 4pm. I had a show and contractions began at 10pm. The midwife discovered that I was 1cm (½in) dilated. The following day, at my antenatal appointment, I felt a gush of water – my waters had broken! Hospital policy was that a woman should deliver within 24 hours of her waters breaking to minimize infection risk, so a doctor was called.

The doctor noticed a slowing of the baby's heart rate and recommended that I stay in. The baby was my priority, but I couldn't see any reason to be in hospital so my partner and I argued, which was stressful, but I stayed. I was then monitored, which was frustrating as I was trying to keep active.

The following day, I had dilated to 2cm (1in) and the next day, 3cm (1½in) – I had progressed just 3cm (1½in) in three days! I was given prostaglandin to move things along and the contractions increased. Thanks to an amazing midwife who let us continue coping with the contractions, I felt in control, although unable to speak as they were coming every couple of minutes. After a few hours, I was put on a syntocinon drip.

This is when I opted for an epidural – after three sleepless nights I decided it would be hard to cope without. This shattered my dream of a natural birth but helped as the contractions became extremely painful.

The baby became distressed

When the midwife examined me, she was amazed that I was fully dilated and the baby had turned into the correct position! I had to allow the contractions to move the baby down, as at this point I had no urge to push. The midwife became concerned that the baby was distressed so the doctor decided that he had to come out by ventouse. My legs were put in stirrups and I pushed with all my might. Liam was born within five minutes.

The cord was around Liam's neck, which probably caused the slowing of his heart rate. He was whisked off for antibiotics. We were transferred to the Transitional Care Ward and spent a week being poked and prodded. Liam had trouble feeding, his blood glucose dropped and he had to be supplemented with formula. Luckily my milk came in the next day and I expressed all Liam's feeds. The doctors tested for meningitis and took Liam for a lumbar puncture. When the results came, nothing was wrong. This was hard to accept after everything Liam had been through.

Eight days after his birth, we went home. Liam is thriving and I can almost see him growing! I do feel disappointed with the birth and given that nothing was wrong – I wonder whether I could have done it at home. Still, I would do it all again!"

A second birth turns out very different from the first

"My first pregnancy was easy and my daughter was delivered vaginally after a 12-hour labour and a few whiffs of gas and air. When I became pregnant again, I thought I had this birth thing worked out. A check at 36 weeks threw a spanner in the works as the midwife discovered the baby was breech. A scan showed the baby was likely to be large. My daughter had weighed 4.1kg (9lb 4oz) and this one looked similar so I was presented with the choice of trying a normal delivery or an elective Caesarean.

The decision wasn't easy; my instinct was for a natural birth but in the end I chose a Caesarean. My husband and I weren't prepared to take the risks that can be associated with breech birth.

Having decided, everything fell into place. We knew the baby's birthday in advance, which felt strange, but enabled us to book grandparents to look after my daughter and my husband knew when to ask for time off work.

The operation went well

On the day of the operation we checked into hospital at 8.30am. I found it unreal. It was only when I heard a baby cry that it hit home why we were there! It was odd getting into a hospital gown and putting a sleep-suit on the radiator to warm when I felt completely normal. The operation went well: there was a relaxed atmosphere in the theatre and the staff were super. My husband saw our son being delivered, albeit accidentally. They asked him if he wanted to see the baby being born, but he didn't catch the last two words! The surgeon told us that Findlay had the cord wrapped around his neck. This would have made a vaginal delivery dangerous so any doubt about choosing a Caesarean was gone.

As the spinal block wore off, I was in a lot of pain. However the pain-killers I was offered were effective and let me catch up on some sleep. I was told that it aided recovery to get up as soon as you can and I believe that's true. I went off for a shower on the morning after the op bent in two, but came back feeling a different person.

I needed three nights in hospital and within a fortnight felt pretty much back to normal. It's 12 weeks since Fin was born and, apart from some numbness above the scar, I feel fine.

I would still much prefer a straightforward vaginal delivery but in the same circumstances would be happy about choosing a Caesarean again. On the ward, the women having the most problems had emergency Caesareans and were exhausted from long labours. I'm happy to say that an elective Caesarean was not like I'd imagined. I'd had time to prepare for it emotionally and was quick to recover from it physically."

A positive planned Caesarean

"I thought I had this birth thing worked out. A check at 36 weeks threw a spanner in the works."

Early daze

Your babymoon

Having a baby is a major life event, something that changes your whole world. It's one of the life transitions known as "thresholds" to anthropologists. When we pass through a threshold, we are allowed to withdraw from the rest of the community for a while into "ritual seclusion".

Centuries ago in England, the period immediately following the birth of a baby used to be a time when mother and her newborn were allowed their own protected space and were cared for by friends and family. In most cultures, seclusions are designed to last 40 days: a sacred period of time; a time to recover, reflect, and readjust(1). Just as a newly married couple enjoy a honeymoon, so a new family can enjoy a "babymoon" together – you, your baby, and your partner at home, preferably in bed for a while, with the rest of the world kept at bay.

In the UK, as new parents, you will receive care from a number of professionals. A community midwife will usually visit you regularly until your

your birth year

colostrum (early milk) is present in your breasts

FIRST TRIMESTER												SECOND TRIMESTER													
1	2	3	4	6	7	8	9	10	11	12		13	14	15	16	17	18	19	20	21	22	23	24	25	26

your breasts are already beginning to prepare for breast-feeding

your nipples and the surrounding area darken to form a "target" for your baby to latch on to later

baby is ten days old (or in some areas, up to 28 days). Some midwives don't come every day, but you can ask for more visits if you need them. Your midwife will give you a phone number where you can contact her, or the team, at any time to answer any questions.

You may have already met your health visitor during your pregnancy. She will visit you at home when your baby is between ten and 14 days old. A health visitor is a qualified nurse with special training in child development and health promotion. In the UK, every family with a child aged under five has a named health visitor who can advise on all health matters as well as all sorts of other issues affecting new parents, from benefit rights to leisure activities. She'll let you know when and where you can visit her at the baby clinic to have your baby weighed, or get advice. She will also leave a phone number with you where she can be contacted if you are worried about anything.

You should be given an appointment to have a check-up at around six to eight weeks after the birth. This is usually with your family doctor but sometimes with your midwife, or a hospital doctor. This provides another opportunity for you to raise any questions or concerns you have about whether your body is returning to normal and about how you are feeling. Remember to write down any questions you have in the days before your appointment, and to take the list with you when you go.

---

investigate the NCT's breast-feeding bra-fitting service: 0870 112 1120

skin-to-skin contact after birth is good for bonding and feeding

you will have your postnatal check around now

THIRD TRIMESTER

BIRTH AND FIRST 3 MONTHS

27 28 29 30 31 32 33 34 35 36 37 38 39 40 41 42 43 44 45 46 47 48 49 50 51 52

colostrum may leak from your breasts in preparation for breast-feeding

if employed, your partner can have up to two complete weeks paternity leave

statutory maternity pay is reduced now and paid at flat rate for next 33 weeks

if you are breast-feeding, it will begin to get a lot easier and confidence in your ability to feed your baby will be growing

Your feelings after birth

It's not surprising that it takes some time to settle into the new role of being a mother. The overwhelming relief and thankfulness that many women feel after giving birth is hard to describe. It's an intensely emotional time – but feelings can be mixed too, possibly even sad.

HOW CAN I BOND WITH MY BABY

You may not feel instant and overwhelming love for your baby. Some women don't. Maybe she doesn't feel like yours yet – or you're just too tired.

- Take each day as it comes
- Keep your baby close to you
- Hold her skin-to-skin
- Feed her, care for her, and sleep with her
- Act out love. It may take several weeks, but it'll soon become a reality.

Talk about your feelings

For many, pregnancy is a very special time, a time when you feel nurtured and unique, on the verge of an exciting adventure. It is normal to feel a sense of regret – even loss – when this phase ends. Give yourself time. Tell other people how you feel, but don't be alarmed if they seem not to understand. Talk through the birth with whoever will listen, or write it all down. The nostalgia for pregnancy will gradually fade and you'll move on.

Some women may feel deeper distress. Maybe the birth was not as you hoped and planned. Perhaps things happened that you didn't want to happen, such as an assisted delivery or unexpected Caesarean section.

"I was bleeding copiously and shaking like a leaf. My baby was very, very sleepy due to the pethidine and I didn't really want to touch her. I was dumbstruck and rather shocked that I had a little girl when all who knew me had told me I was definitely having a boy!"

The overwhelming relief *and thankfulness that many feel when they have their baby in their arms is difficult to put into words.*

Perhaps you feel let down – by your body or by other people. Maybe there were times of great fear and unbearable pain – or perhaps you can't remember much at all.

Talking about your feelings to others may be very difficult. Your family may not understand. After all, you have your baby – so do the circumstances of her birth really matter now? Your partner may even be part of the problem.

If you feel this way, act now. Your distress may fade, but it will probably not go away until it has been faced. Talk to the midwife who is looking after you, tell her how you feel. Ask her to read through your labour notes, and explain what happened, and why. Better still, ask to speak to the midwife and/or doctor who cared for you in labour.

If you cannot talk things through with anybody while in hospital, try to confide in somebody once you are home – your community midwife, maybe, or your GP, health visitor, or antenatal teacher. Perhaps you would find it easier to talk to a stranger – the Birth Crisis Network runs a telephone helpline (see box right).

Your partner's feelings

The early days can be hard for your partner, too. He may also be affected by things that happened during labour, and overwhelmed by the enormity of change. He may feel side-lined by events, ignored by health professionals, or excluded from the closeness developing between you and your baby.

You may feel that your partner has become yet another responsibility. What you had hoped to be a time of shared happiness, becomes a time of increasing distance and tension. And with everything happening, there just doesn't seem to be the time or the opportunity to sort it out.

Tell him that you're having a difficult time – and you know that he is too. Try to use "I" phrases ("I feel let down"); they're more effective and less blaming than "you" phrases ("You're no help"). Try a row, or a cuddle, whichever works best for you, but remember you don't need to shoulder the burden of his feelings.

The "baby blues"

Midwives reckon that 50–80 per cent of all new mothers suffer the "baby blues" – a period of weepiness and irritability that sets in around the third to fifth day after birth and feels like you're "coming down to earth with a bump". Textbooks tell us that these "blues" may last anything from a few hours to seven to ten days. It is sometimes thought that this change in mood is caused by the sudden fall in progesterone that occurs following birth. It may also coincide with the start of mature milk production, your baby becoming more unsettled, and your return home from hospital.

However the "blues" are not inevitable. Women who have a home birth are much less likely to experience them than those who have hospital births. Others have found that the "blues" tend to be worse among first-time mothers – especially if they haven't had much experience of babies.

DIFFICULT BIRTH?

If a "listening" service is not available locally – or if you prefer to talk to somebody not associated with the place where you gave birth – contact Birth Crisis Network, a voluntary service offering telephone support across the country (contact is via the website: www.sheilakitzinger.com/birthcrisis.htm).

Other women may prefer the complete anonymity of speaking with the Samaritans (tel: 08457 90 90 90, e-mail: jo@samaritans.org, website: www.samaritans.org). The Association for Improvements in the Maternity Services (AIMS) is a voluntary organization that has supported many women following traumatic birth experiences (tel: 0870 765 1433, website: www.aims.org.uk).

"I remember on the third day in hospital being inconsolable, crying huge tears. 'What's wrong?' asked the nurse. 'I've got too many blankets on the bed and in the night they kept getting tangled up.' I was still crying when my husband arrived."

see also

After a Caesarean birth	184–85
Organizing your day	224–25
Postnatal depression	226–27

Changes in your body

The female body has amazing powers of recovery. As soon as you baby is born, the dramatic changes of pregnancy are being dismantled as your whole body, having completed its task, is returning to the way it was before you were pregnant – more or less.

Getting back to normal

Within minutes of the birth of your baby and delivery of your placenta, your uterus contracts down to a grapefruit-sized pouch of tight muscle. Squeezed shut in the middle of this muscle is the wound left by your placenta when it detached in the third stage of labour. Already, the area is beginning to heal itself, although you will continue to lose blood in the discharge called the lochia after the birth.

Uterus The soft lining of your uterus is being washed away in your lochia (vaginal loss) and a new lining is being built up. The powerful uterine muscles are beginning to shrink. Within only six weeks of your baby's birth, the weight of your uterus will reduce from 1kg ($2^1/_{10}$lb) to just 60g (2oz). This process is called "involution".

Fluid loss You will probably find yourself going to the loo frequently in the first few days as you lose the 2–8 litres ($3^1/_2$–14 pints) of extra fluid that you carried during pregnancy. At the same time, your heart, lungs, and circulation will be quietly returning to normal.

Hormone changes As your placenta leaves your body, its job finally completed, levels of pregnancy hormones fall rapidly. Smooth muscle tone throughout your body improves quickly – heartburn gets better, constipation is relieved, and varicose veins improve, although backache and the risk of injury remain potential problems for several months.

   As pregnancy hormones fall, so the levels of prolactin rise. Prolactin is the main hormone responsible for milk production. Whether or not you choose to breast-feed, your breasts will begin to make milk to replace the colostrum present throughout most of your pregnancy. If you are breast-feeding, feeding your baby in response to her needs will ensure that your breasts continue production.

Look after your back It takes quite some time for the joints of the pelvis and spine, softened by the hormones of pregnancy, to return to normal; back discomfort and the risk of injury may persist for three to five months after the birth of your baby. Your abdominal muscles, which were stretched to twice their normal length during pregnancy, will regain their tone within

"I feel a new respect for my body which is nothing to do with the way it looks. I'm a much stronger woman now, and that's reflected in all areas of my life."

Take time to get to know your baby. Keep her close to you, hold her skin-to-skin and care for her. If you didn't bond with her immediately, act out love – it will soon become a reality.

a couple of months. Paying attention to your posture and starting regular, gentle exercise that you enjoy, will help build up the strength of these important muscles. In the meantime, be aware of how you move, and always lift things carefully.

Blood loss after childbirth

Your midwife will feel your uterus at each visit to check that it is well contracted, and is involuting normally. You will experience discharge, or loss, called lochia after delivery. This is what to expect:

Days one to three Heavy, dark red discharge that may contain fragments of amniotic membrane and large clots (formed as blood pools in the vagina). This is mainly blood from the placental site. Your loss will be heaviest when you first stand up, after emptying your bladder, and while you are breast-feeding your baby. You will probably have to change your sanitary pad every time you go to the toilet. Call your midwife urgently if your loss seems to be heavier than this, or if you feel dizzy and weak (see box on previous page). You may need tablets or an injection to help your uterus contract down more to stop the bleeding.

You may also experience uncomfortable "after pains" for a few moments every time you feed your baby in these first few days. These "pains" are caused by a surge of the hormone oxytocin, which is stimulated by your baby's suckling. Oxytocin is not only responsible for the "let down" (release) of your milk, it also causes your uterus to contract, and therefore speeds up your vaginal discharge.

CARING FOR YOUR STITCHES

Stitches that result from tears or an episiotomy may cause pain in the first few days afterwards, and you may have some bruising. The following ideas can be helpful:

- Re-start your pelvic floor exercises as soon as possible after the birth. They help reduce swelling and speed healing by improving the circulation to the area. You may find it difficult to feel when you are doing them at first. Start them when you are lying on the bed with your knees bent. You can then progress to practising while sitting up.
- Walking will also prevent stiffness and help reduce swelling.
- To reduce swelling, lie on your side, put an ice pack, or frozen packet of peas wrapped in a tea towel over the painful area for a maximum of 20 minutes. This can ease the pain. Do this in the first three days but no longer, because ice packs do not aid healing and may in fact prevent it.
- When opening your bowels press a clean sanitary pad over the stitches to prevent straining. Sit well back on the toilet. Drink plenty of fluid and eat plenty of high-fibre foods like bran, wholemeal bread, dried and fresh fruit, and vegetables to prevent constipation.
- After emptying your bladder, pour a jugful of warm water over the vulva or use a bidet to help prevent stinging. A few drops of pure essential lavender oil, which is a natural antiseptic, could be added to the water.
- Find a comfortable position for feeding your baby – perhaps lying down in bed on your side.
- If sitting up is uncomfortable, don't sit on a rubber ring as it makes the swelling worse. You can try two pillows, one under each thigh, or better still hire a Valley Cushion. This is a cushion specially designed for women with pelvic-floor pain, haemorrhoids (varicose veins around the back passage), or a sore coccyx (for more information on hiring a cushion, see page 247).
- If you still have problems with stitches after a week or two, ask your midwife or health visitor to refer you to an obstetric physiotherapist.

Days four to ten You will notice the lochia changing to a brownish discharge. The placental site is beginning to heal so there is less red blood and more serum (the watery part of blood).

Days ten to 21 Much lighter, yellowish or clear discharge. The lochia now mainly consist of leucocytes (white blood cells involved in healing and fighting infection) and cervical mucus. Your lochia may be finished by three weeks, or may continue off and on for up to six weeks.

Midwife postnatal checks

Your midwife will check you in hospital if you had a hospital birth, and then visit you at home for about ten days, occasionally 28 days. At each visit, your midwife will check:

- Your lochia to ensure that your loss is normal. In addition she'll feel your abdomen to check the height of your uterus, and make sure it's shrinking back to its pre-pregnant size.
- Legs for signs of thrombosis (blood clots) – the risk of thrombosis is higher if you have had surgery, or you are confined to bed for any reason. Tell your midwife immediately if you experience any pain, swelling, or redness in your legs.
- Breasts for nipple soreness or breast pain, or other signs of difficulties.
- Perineum to monitor the healing of any trauma; at the same time, she will probably ask if you're having any difficulties with passing urine or opening your bowels.
- How you are feeling generally – do use this time to ask questions or talk about concerns.

She may also check:

- Temperature and pulse, as a raised temperature and rapid pulse may be a sign of infection or, more rarely, a thrombosis; a rapid pulse may also indicate anaemia.
- Blood pressure, this is particularly important if you suffered pre-eclampsia during pregnancy; a few women develop high blood pressure for the first time after delivery.

What to eat in the days after childbirth

Eat whatever you feel like eating. Simple nutritious snacks for the early days include sandwiches, bowls of breakfast cereal with milk, bananas, apples, and cheese and crackers. If constipation is a problem, snack on dried fruit and try to drink a lot of water. Breast-feeding is thirsty work and you will probably find you need to drink a lot of fluids; have a glass of water beside you when you are feeding your baby. You may not want to spend a lot of time walking to the loo, but this will help your circulation.

It can take a bit longer to start eating again after a Caesarean section. This is because any big abdominal operation does interfere temporarily with the working of your bowels and it may take some time for your gut to start moving freely again.

After a Caesarean birth

Although births by Caesarean section are far more common (over one in five births), this is still a serious operation and it can help to look at your recovery in terms of weeks and months, not days. Don't feel you have to get better quickly or try to be Superwoman – take your time and be kind to yourself.

MAKING YOURSELF COMFORTABLE

- Whether sitting or lying, experiment with pillows to support you and your baby so you're both comfortable.
- Keep the pressure off your scar with high-waisted knickers, available from NCT Maternity Sales (see page 247).
- Some people find peppermint tea (or ginger) helps to release trapped wind.
- Ring your hospital bell and ask for help if you are in pain when you need to reach or hold your baby.

"I had so much wanted to go into labour again, feel that again, and I wanted our baby to be born when he chose to be born. I was disappointed to have had another Caesarean, but at least I had tried, and we are all so blessed with our beautiful little boy."

What to expect in the first few days

Pain relief will be necessary initially, and different methods include an intravenous drip (you may be able to control this yourself), injections, suppositories (inserted into your back passage), and liquid or tablets taken by mouth. Many women progress quite quickly to taking paracetamol only.

If you feel your pain relief is not strong or frequent enough, discuss this with your midwife. Pain that is allowed to build up can be more difficult to bring under control again. So being "brave" is not a good idea because it can lead to more pain and less mobility.

Ask for help You should have a call bell that you can reach easily. Mothers who have had a Caesarean need more help and you should not feel awkward about asking for help as often as you need it.

Moving about You will usually be encouraged (with help) to get up on your feet very soon after delivery and certainly within 24 hours, to improve blood circulation. To begin with, moving around, getting in and out of bed, standing and walking can be difficult. It is better to try to stand as upright as possible and the more you can move around the easier it will get. Many hospitals have an obstetric physiotherapist who offers specialist advice on postnatal exercises. Ideally, you should be able to see the physiotherapist personally and some units provide post-Caesarean exercise sheets.

Your wound This will be about 15–22cm (6–9in) long, generally on a horizontal line in your upper pubic hair, and covered by a dressing. If you have absorbable stitches, these will be left in place, but your midwife will check your wound. Otherwise, she will remove your stitches or staples after around five days. Postnatal infections are more common after a Caesarean and include infections of the wound, urinary tract, or bladder, and uterine infections. These are usually treatable with antibiotics.

On the postnatal ward

Initially, you may have a catheter (thin tube) draining your bladder that can be left in place for up to 24 hours. Once it's removed, you should be able to pass urine as normal. If you do not have a catheter, you may be expected to use a bedpan in bed. Many women find this difficult. Ask if you can use a commode at the bedside or, better still, be helped to the toilet.

Opening your bowels again for the first time can also be difficult. The timing varies considerably from woman to woman, and often does not happen for a week or more.

Women are often given only fluids immediately after surgery, then a soft diet. However, research shows no disadvantage in allowing women to eat as soon as they are hungry, if they wish to do so.

Most women can go home three to five days after the operation; ask your carers what's best for you.

Lie on your side *to feed your baby so that there is no pressure on your wound.*

Breast-feeding after a Caesarean?

A Caesarean should not alter your choice of feeding or your ability to produce milk. However, you may find it that it is more difficult to sit or lie comfortably and you need to experiment with positions to avoid pressure or strain on the wound. Breast-feeding can be very important for mothers who feel they have been deprived of a vaginal birth, and it can help you feel close to your baby.

Feelings of failure

Many women are able to accept or feel very positive about a Caesarean. Others, however, are left with nagging doubts, or even anger, resentment, or feelings of violation. Some women who experience negative feelings do so straight away, while others may not do so for months or even years.

The way you feel can be very much affected by the circumstances of your Caesarean, including such things as whether you were involved and comfortable with the decisions made, whether you had sufficient information, and whether you were treated with respect. Women often wonder what they may have been able to do differently. For some, a Caesarean may give rise to postnatal depression or post-traumatic stress disorder – these women may need significant support during recovery.

Women cope in different ways: some are able to move on, leaving the experience in the past; others wait until they are ready to deal with their feelings; and others have a need to sort feelings out immediately. Finding the right information and support can be difficult, but may be available from the hospital, your GP or health visitor, from voluntary organizations such as NCT, AIMS, or the Birth Crisis Network (see page 245–7), or via the internet and e-groups. Many mothers who have extreme negative feelings work through the experience to gain new confidence and assertiveness, and many go on to have good birth experiences in subsequent pregnancies.

DRIVING AFTER A CAESAREAN

You will usually be advised not to drive for up to six weeks, although there are no clear restrictions to stop you. If you feel well enough to drive, and you are capable of doing an emergency stop, check that your insurance is valid. You may require medical clearance from your GP or obstetrician.

see also

Your feelings after birth	178–79
Positive elective Caesarean	173
Vaginal birth after three Caesareans	149
Breast-feeding your baby	204–09
Postnatal depression	226–27

Your new baby

Throughout pregnancy, your baby was nourished and sustained by your placenta. Floating in a protective environment, cocooned in warm fluid, sound-insulated, temperature-controlled – all her needs were met in the womb. But at birth, the supply line is cut; and your baby has to adapt to life on her own.

New life

When your baby's umbilical cord is cut, she is immediately forced to adapt to life without the placenta that has provided her with everything throughout pregnancy. The way a baby's body does this is extraordinary: within just a short space of time, her breathing, circulation, and digestion systems are established and she is out there on her own – a separate being.

"It was amazing. I lifted her on to my tummy. I remember her eyes were still full of water from the womb. I bonded with her the minute I looked into her eyes."

Before birth, the placenta acts as your baby's lungs, delivering oxygen and removing carbon dioxide. Although she has been practising breathing movements since the eleventh week of pregnancy, her lungs contain fluid rather than air. This fluid helps keep the tiny air sacs open, ready for her first real breath. As she passes down through the birth canal, your baby's chest is squeezed and this fluid is eased out of her lungs into her mouth and throat. Her lungs are now poised ready to breathe. When her body slips out of yours, the pressure on her chest is released, her lungs expand and air is drawn in. The respiratory control centre in her brain clicks into action and she begins to breathe on her own.

The fluid squeezed out of your baby's lungs will drain quickly away. Some midwives like to use a little suction gadget to remove this fluid, but this can be distressing for the baby, and is generally not necessary.

Immediately she is born, it can be a good idea to keep your baby on her side or front, either across your tummy or in your arms. She may cough and splutter for a few seconds (and she may even swallow some of the fluid) but this won't hurt her. Cover her body with your hands to keep her warm, and you could even try rubbing her back very gently. She will soon be breathing properly.

Your baby's cord stump

The umbilical cord was your baby's lifeline throughout pregnancy. Then, within minutes of her birth, it was clamped and cut. The clamp is there to make sure that no blood is lost from the cord.

Provided the cord clamp has been correctly fixed, it will not slip off. The only way to remove it is to cut through the hinge. Your midwife will remove

Umbilical cord *Your baby's cord will be clamped after birth. The clamp will be removed after about three days, leaving a small stump that dries and falls off about after a week.*

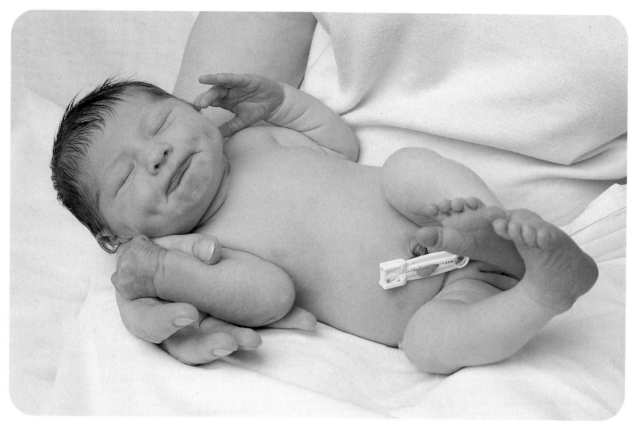

For the first few days *after her birth your baby's body will be curled up as it was in your uterus.*

the clamp when your baby is about three days old, and the risk of bleeding is past. She will also show you how to clean the cord stump. Hospital policies vary but you will probably be told to simply wipe it with cotton wool soaked in cooled, boiled water and dry it with a cotton wool ball each time you change your baby's nappy. You should continue to keep the cord clean until it falls off. Tell your midwife as soon as possible if your baby's cord stump bleeds, looks sticky, or has an unpleasant smell as these may be signs of infection.

If possible, it's a good idea to try and keep the cord stump and clamp outside your baby's nappy. You may have to fold the top of the nappy down to do this. This will stop the stump getting wet with urine – especially if you have a baby boy.

The short length of cord left will dry and shrivel over the next few days, until it detaches when your baby is about a week old. There may be one or two specks of blood when this happens, but it will not hurt your baby. She will then be left with a normal looking "tummy button".

Your baby's health checks

Soon after your baby is born, she will be checked over thoroughly by your midwife. A day or so later a slightly more detailed examination of your baby will be performed by a paediatrician (specialist children's doctor) if she was

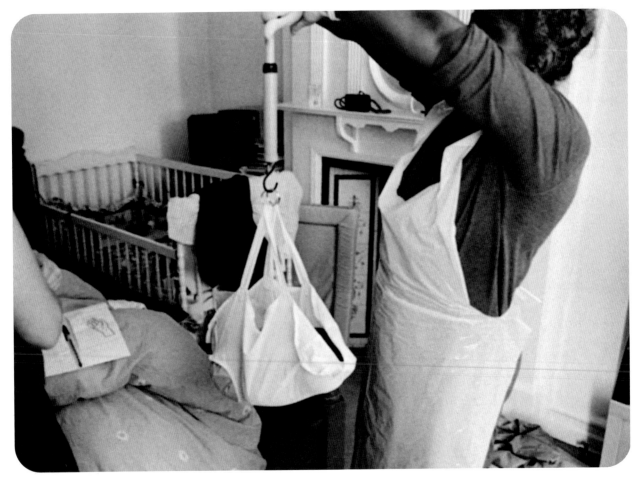

Midwives who visit *you at home will often weigh your baby in a special sling.*

born in a hospital. If your baby was born at home, your family doctor may visit to do this check.

Your baby will probably be examined lying in her cot or on your bed. You should have a clear view and there should be plenty of time for the midwife or doctor to answer any questions your have. It is a good idea to jot down any questions you might have beforehand as this will help you remember to ask them.

Your doctor or midwife will:

- Observe your baby for general signs of good health
- Check for abnormalities
- Listen to her heart and lungs to ensure all is well
- Feel her tummy and check external genitalia (sex organs), for boys the testes will be checked
- Watch her movements and check her reflexes
- Check for congenital dislocation of the hips by gently holding her legs and moving her hip joints
- Ask you about feeding and your baby's behaviour
- Ask you if you have any worries or questions.

Your baby's nappies

Days one to two Your baby has been passing urine for several months while in your uterus. She will urinate for the first time in the outside world within 24 hours or so of birth. If her nappies are still dry after this time, don't panic. It may simply mean that she passed urine during delivery and it was missed in the general excitement. She will probably not pass much urine at all during the first few days.

During this time your baby will also pass "meconium" – a thick, greenish-black, tarry substance. Meconium has been accumulating in her bowel since about 16 weeks of pregnancy. It contains mucus, skin cells, swallowed amniotic fluid, and various digestive products. Oddly enough, it has virtually no smell. Your baby may have one or two very full dirty nappies, or several smaller ones. The colostrum you give your baby also helps her to pass the meconium.

Meconium can be very messy. You may like to apply plenty of barrier cream to your baby's bottom when she is first washed or bathed after delivery. This makes it easier for you to wipe her clean after a dirty nappy.

Days two to five Provided your baby is feeding well, meconium will gradually become greenish-brown in colour. This is because waste products from her food are beginning to pass through her system. Midwives call this a "changing stool". Your midwife will probably ask at each visit what colour your baby's stools are; a changing stool is a useful indicator that your baby is beginning to feed well.

Days five to six onward If breast-feeding is going well, your baby's stools will now be very soft and bright yellow in colour. They will have a sweetish, rather pleasant smell. Once you start producing mature milk, your breast-fed baby will probably pass four to five motions a day initially. (After the first few weeks, and as your baby's digestion matures, she may well have fewer dirty nappies. She may pass just one stool a day – or one every week.) Often your baby's nappy will be wet, rather than dirty. She will now be passing urine regularly. Her urine will be pale in colour. Soft, yellow stools and six or seven wet nappies in 24 hours, are welcome signs that your breast-fed baby is getting plenty of milk.

If you baby is being fed on formula milk her stools will be more solid, bulky, and pale yellowish-brown in colour. They smell rather unpleasant, and at first, are passed less frequently than those of a breast-fed baby. Although a formula-fed baby may have fewer, more solid, stools, she should still have six or seven wet nappies in 24 hours. Formula-fed babies are more likely to become constipated. If your baby is straining and having difficulties filling her nappy, talk to your health visitor; she may need water.

Possible problems Very frequent, greenish stools (after the first five days) and an unsettled baby, may be a sign that your breast-fed baby is not feeding effectively. This may happen if she is not well attached to the

KEEPING YOUR BABY SAFE

- Don't let your baby get too hot (or too cold). Feel her chest or back to check her temperature.
- Don't let anyone smoke in the same room as your baby.
- Be very careful not to have any hot drinks or boiling water anywhere near your baby.
- It's not safe to fall asleep on a sofa with your baby.
- Place your baby on her back to sleep. in the "feet-to-foot" position if she is in a cot or Moses basket so she can't slip any further down.

WHEN TO CALL THE DOCTOR

Contact your doctor immediately if:

- You think your baby is ill, even if there are no obvious symptoms.
- Your baby has a seizure or convulsion.
- She turns blue or very pale.
- Her breathing is quick and difficult, or grunting.
- She is exceptionally hard to wake, unusually drowsy, or does not seem to know you.
- She has glazed eyes and does not focus on anything.
- You see any sign of bruising or bleeding.
- Your baby is not feeding or is reluctant to feed.
- She has a rash that doesn't fade when you press a glass against it.

NEONATAL HEARING TESTS

Experts agree that early diagnosis and treatment of deafness plays a major part in minimizing the problem. Neonatal screening to check newborn babies' hearing is now offered to all newborn babies. This allows babies who have a hearing loss to be identified early. The test only takes a few minutes and the results will usually be given to you at the time of the screening test.

Early detection also means support and information can be provided to the parents at an early stage. Babies who miss the test at birth for any reason will get another opportunity when they are a few weeks old.

What happens

It is called the Automated Otoacoustic Emissions test (AOEA). A small probe is placed just inside the baby's ear and this produces a gentle sound. The "echo", which will be present in nearly all hearing children, can then be measured by a computer. The test is non-invasive and only takes a few minutes. If the first test does not show a strong enough response, the baby is referred for a second screening.

breast during a feed, or she is being taken off the breast before she has had what she needs.

Very infrequent dirty nappies, few wet nappies, and dark, scanty urine may be a sign that your baby (breast- or formula-fed) is not getting enough to eat. It may sometimes be hard to tell whether or not your baby has passed urine because disposable nappies may absorb the urine without leaving a noticeable wet patch. You will soon learn to tell whether she has passed urine by the weight of the used nappy compared to a clean one.

Heel-prick blood tests

When your baby is five to eight days old, your midwife will offer to do a blood test to screen for various metabolic disorders (meaning disorders arising from faulty chemical processes in the human body). If you agree to this test, the midwife will take a small sample of blood from your baby. This will then be sent to a specialist laboratory for testing. The results of the tests will be sent to your health visitor and GP within a few weeks. You will be contacted earlier than this if the test needs to be repeated or a problem has been found. Your midwife will tell you what conditions are screened for in your area. All babies are offered screening for:

- Phenylketonuria (disease resulting from a defective gene that interferes with the regulation of an amino acid)
- Congenital hypothyroidism (a disorder of thyroid activity)
- Sickle-cell disorders (inherited disorders that affect red blood cells).
  Screening for these disorders means that babies can receive early treatment that can help to prevent serious illness and allow the child to live a healthier life.

In some areas screening is also offered for cystic fibrosis and MCADD. Cystic fibrosis is an inherited condition that can affect the digestion and lungs. MCADD is an inherited condition in which babies have problems breaking down fats to make energy for the body. Ask your midwife which conditions are screened for in your area. If a baby is thought to have one of the conditions, she will need further tests to confirm the screening result.

How is the test done Your midwife will take the blood sample by pricking your baby's heel and allowing the blood to drip onto circles of absorbent paper. Your baby may react to the initial prick as it may feel painful for a short time, but the rest of the test should be painless. You can make the test easier for you baby.

- Keep your baby's feet warm with socks until the last moment. This speeds up the collection of the blood. Some midwives use warm water to the same effect.
- Hold her so that her feet are hanging downward; this also makes the blood collection easier.
- Breast- or bottle-feed your baby as the midwife is doing the test. Your baby may stop and cry for a moment when her heel is pricked, but will be instantly comforted by feeding.

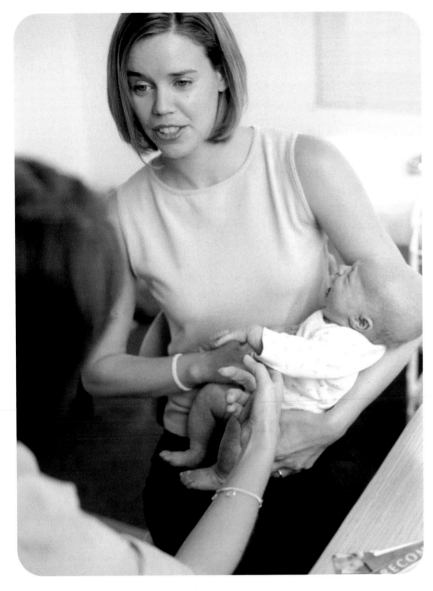

Make a list of questions you want to ask your GP or health visitor in the days before going for your check up.

The six- to eight-week baby check

When you have your postnatal check, which is usually carried out at your GP's surgery, your baby will also be examined. You'll be asked about any concerns or worries you may have, so it's worth writing down a list and bringing it to your appointment. You should have time to discuss any feeding problems. The GP and/or health visitor will:

- Weigh and measure your baby
- Listen to the heart
- Manipulate hip joints again to check for signs of dislocation
- Test your baby's reflexes
- Check that a boy's testicles have descended
- Discuss your plans for childhood vaccinations.

Possible problems with your baby

Your baby will be checked carefully at birth by your midwife and by a paediatrician a day or so later. Problems can range from minor blemishes to more serious physical abnormalities. If you need to know more about a condition, you will find a list of useful organizations at the back of the book.

Talk to your midwife

Spots, rashes, marks, and minor imperfections can all mar your beautiful baby's looks. Your midwife or health visitor should be able reassure you or suggest treatment options if they are necessary.

Birth marks

There are a number of different blemishes, known as birth marks, which can appear on a newborn baby's body.

Mongolian blue spot Dark-coloured, blue-black spots found singly or in groups on the lower back or buttocks at birth, are common in black or Asian children. They fade by the time the child is three or four years old.

Stork marks So-called stork marks (red or purple patches) are found on the forehead, upper eyelids, and on the back of the neck. They are more obvious when the baby is crying. Stork marks, especially those on the upper eyelids, fade within two years. Those on the forehead may take up to four years to fade. The ones on the back of the neck usually persist.

Strawberry marks A strawberry birth mark (haemangioma) is bright red, appears in the first few days after birth and can grow during the first few months. They nearly always shrink and fade after this although the process may take a few years. Approximately one in 20 babies have haemangiomae, and they tend to be more common in girls, twins, and premature babies. Most are best to have no treatment at all and will completely disappear leaving little or no mark on the skin by time the child is about five years old.

Port wine stains These are a darker purple colour and usually don't fade. Recent new advances have revolutionized the treatment of port wine stain with excellent results and minimal side effects.

Physical abnormalities

Some new babies arrive with more marked physical abnormalities, most of which can be dealt with swiftly by experts with specialist knowledge. If you have any concerns talk to the doctor or ask to see a specialist.

Club foot This usually refers to a baby's foot that turns inward and downward, and it can usually be detected on an ultrasound screening test. It can run in some families. Minor degrees of this condition are common at birth and are a result of pressure on the foot while the baby is in the womb. Most babies can be treated by physiotherapy. Babies with more marked deformities may need to have their feet treated by splints and a few may need surgery. All newborns are examined for club foot at birth.

Cleft palate A baby's palate forms in two parts that join together as the she develops inside the womb. Very rarely the palate does not join leaving a gap visible inside the baby's mouth. The condition can also affect the upper lip called a cleft lip; some babies have both a cleft palate and a cleft lip. Clefts of the lip are often picked up at an antenatal ultrasound screening test. There are now centres across the UK specializing in the treatment of this condition and you should be referred to a specialist team.

Treatment involves a series of operations, but in the early days the main problem for the baby is how to get enough milk as the gap interferes with the sucking process especially for breast-fed babies. Formula-fed babies are not so badly affected as the sucking mechanism for bottle-feeding is different. It may be necessary for you to express your breast-milk and feed your baby with a bottle.

Tongue tie A baby with tongue tie cannot make her tongue stick out beyond her lips, because the tongue is "tied" by the frenulum, the membrane that holds the underside of the tongue to the floor of the mouth. Breast-fed babies with tongue tie find it very difficult to suck and it can affect some bottle-fed babies, too. It can be a cause of failure to gain weight in the more marked cases.

Doctors are divided in their opinions on this subject. Traditionally surgery for tongue tie was left until the baby was older, as most cases will partly resolve and don't interfere with speech development. However, it is possible to see a specialist who will divide the frenulum if the tongue tie is interfering with breast-feeding.

Dislocated or unstable hips Your doctor will also examine your baby's hips. This will be to check whether the head of the thigh bone is unstable or lies outside the hip joint, which may indicate congenital dislocation of the hip. While this isn't life threatening, it can have long-term complications if it isn't treated early. Your baby will be examined lying on her back with her hips flexed to a right angle and knees flexed. This is not a painful test but it works best if your baby is relaxed, and she may cry at the movement.

If any dislocation is spotted by the paediatrician, then the recommended treatment will depend on the extent of the dislocation and the shape of the actual hip socket. A baby may be referred to a specialist orthopaedic surgeon for treatment.

see also

Antenatal testing	80–5
Soothing a newborn	214–17
Baby massage	224–7

What your new baby needs

Every baby is born with certain reflexes: the ability to suck, to turn her head if something touches her cheek, to follow a moving object with her eyes, and to close her fist around anything that touches her palm. Without these involuntary responses to stimulation, she wouldn't survive.

Encourage your baby's skills

Did you know that your baby is born with lots of skills to make sure she can survive in the outside world? Did you know that she's even able to start breast-feeding without any help?

If you hold a newborn baby upright, with her feet in contact with something, she'll step as if she's trying to walk. This reflex puzzled scientists for many years, as a newborn baby's neck and back is not strong enough to support her in walking properly. However, scientists in Norway discovered that if a baby is placed onto her mother's tummy after birth, she will "walk" up her tummy until she reaches the breast. Once she gets there, another reflex – the rooting reflex – comes into action, and she turns her head from side to side, with her mouth wide open, looking for your breast. You may have noticed during pregnancy that your areola – the dark skin around your nipple – has got bigger and darker. It's like a target for your baby to aim for. When the baby finds the breast, she latches on, and the third reflex – suckling – comes into play. When the roof of the baby's mouth is stimulated, she starts to move her jaws in such a way that she will "milk" the breast.

Of course these reflexes are for emergency survival, so even though your baby could do it all by herself, you'll want to help her. When she's born, cuddle her close to your breast, and the chances are that she will latch on well during this cuddling time. If she's not in the mood, then simply holding her "skin to skin" will start to stimulate your milk supply, as well as giving you both a chance to get to know each other (1).

Sleep and rest in the first day

Although babies are generally quite alert for the first hour or so after birth (unless affected by drugs you had during your labour, such as pethidine), your baby may well then sleep for long periods in her first day. This is not surprising, really, as birth is also tiring for her. Although you may feel worn out, you may also be feeling "high"

"It was weird – I was so exhausted by the birth I thought I would sleep for days, but in fact I was on such a high that I just stayed awake the whole night, watching my baby! I couldn't believe he was really here at last – it was sort of unreal. The next night I was really tired, yet Billy suddenly started to feed all the time, so the midwife showed me how to feed lying down, and she tucked us up in bed together. It was lovely."

WHY SKIN-TO-SKIN?

Research indicates that when newborn babies are cuddled close to the breast with their skin touching their mother's skin, breast-feeding is more successful. You might want to request this early skin-to-skin contact on your birth plan so that you and your baby stay together.

If you intend to formula-feed, you might still like to have this early skin-to-skin contact, as it will help you and your baby bond (2). It's a way of getting to know each other. (3).

Both you and your partner *can cuddle your baby against your bare skin – it creates all sorts of benefits for all of you.*

and unable to sleep. You might find yourself spending hours just watching your baby – at last you know what she looks like!

This is a great time to rest, recuperate, and cuddle your baby. It's fine to tuck up in bed together if you can; if you are in hospital you can ask the midwife to tuck the bedclothes in around both of you, and to show you how to feed lying down (see pages 218–19 for advice on safe sleeping). You and your baby need to be close, to get to know each other and bond, as well as to build up a milk supply if you're going to be breast-feeding.

Her sleep will seem quite erratic at first; she will not discover the difference between night and day for about six weeks. In the early days

Play with your baby *during her daytime alert periods, but at night-time let her know that sleep is what's required. She'll gradually get to learn the difference between night and day.*

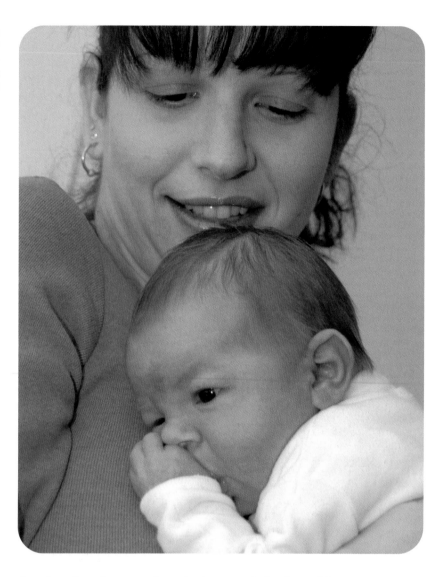

therefore, it makes sense to rest when your baby sleeps, if you can. As you start to recover from the birth, and as your baby becomes more alert, you can begin to show her the pattern of night and day. Keep night-times calm and quiet, avoiding changing her nappy if possible (1).

Early feeds

At first, your baby will feed little and often (2). To begin with, her tiny stomach is only the size of a walnut, so it can't hold much. Secondly, she's learning how to feed and to begin with she'll find this quite tiring. Feeding, especially breast-feeding, in the early days will occupy much of your time until she gets the hang of it.

Don't worry too much if your baby doesn't seem that interested in food at first. Spend as much time as you feel you want to in skin-to-skin contact with each other, offering her a feed during her moments of alertness.

Your midwife may suggest waking your baby to feed her, as sleepy babies can get lethargic and "forget" to feed. You may particularly need to wake a small baby, or one who has been born after a labour with pethidine or other drugs, to make sure she is getting enough to eat (3).

Jaundice is due to an excess of a pigment called bilirubin in the body (see box right) and it's common in newborn babies. To some extent it may even be considered normal. Bilirubin is a by-product of the breakdown of excess red blood cells after birth and often a baby's liver is not quite ready to process this. Breast-feeding or bottle-feeding as often as possible helps jaundice pass, but again you may need to wake your baby to feed as this condition does make a baby sleepy (4). Your midwife will be able to tell whether the jaundice is severe and needs treatment, or whether it is mild.

Unsettled babies

If your baby seems unsettled and unhappy in these first few days, it is worth thinking about her experiences so far. All she has known is the inside of your uterus, where she was held, she was warm, and where she could hear your heartbeat and your voice. She was never hungry, didn't have to worry about keeping warm, or worry if you had left her; she knew you were there. It makes sense, therefore, that the safest and most comforting place for her now that she is born will be cuddled up next to you.

Even though your baby is out in the world, you are still interconnected: she is just as dependent on you and your body as she has been for the last nine months. Not only does she rely on you to feed her, she needs you to watch over her, keep her warm and comfortable, and she needs you to help her feel safe and secure.

JAUNDICE

Many perfectly healthy babies develop this condition two to five days after birth. Their skin and the whites of their eyes will turn a yellowish colour, because their immature livers are struggling to break down bilirubin, a by-product of the destruction of red blood cells no longer needed after birth.

What is the treatment:

If your baby becomes jaundiced, keep feeding her even if she is sleepy. Don't wait for her to cry, offer feeds when she seems interested because it encourages her to excrete bilirubin so the jaundice will start to fade.

Occasionally, babies will need phototherapy (light treatment) that helps their bodies break down the bilirubin. Your baby will be placed in a cot, naked except for a nappy and an eye mask, under the warm light of a phototherapy unit. Treatment lasts from a few hours to one to two days.

YOUR LABOUR CAN AFFECT FEEDING

How your labour progressed, and your pain relief options can affect your baby's ability to feed at first, or even make it harder for you to feed her because you are tired or uncomfortable after surgery, for example.

- If you were given pethidine during labour, especially within a few hours of the birth, it can depress your baby's suckling reflex for several days. This can mean breast-feeding will take longer to get established, so in the meantime, have skin-to-skin contact as much as you can. If you are bottle-feeding, you may need to keep waking your baby to feed as she will be very dozy.
- A Caesarean section shouldn't affect your baby's ability to feed, but your wound may make it harder for you to hold her in the correct position for breast-feeding. You may find an underarm hold works well, and lying on your side can also be comfortable. You also need help to sit carefully after a Caesarean if you are formula-feeding.
- An assisted delivery – forceps or ventouse – can give your new baby a headache, and being held in certain positions or even suckling could be painful for her. She will need you to be patient, perhaps experimenting with different positions.

What a new mother needs

Having a baby can be an overwhelming experience and it's only recently that researchers have really started to look at the impact it has. Your body has gone through massive changes, and you may experience feelings that you weren't expecting. No one adjusts to motherhood overnight – it takes time.

Help in the first days

New mothers need: rest, a good, well-balanced diet, support with feeding, help with looking after the baby, a listening ear, and contact with other mothers. Above all, they need mothering themselves.

Plan ahead Who is going to mother you when your baby is born? Who will cook, clean, shop, wash, fetch and carry, hold your baby while you bathe, shield you from visitors, make endless hot drinks and snacks, dry your tears, give you a cuddle, accept your grouches, tell you you're great – yet expect very little in return? Is this really a one-man job?

Many women describe the early days after their baby's birth as a roller coaster – amazing highs, horrible lows – and no chance at all to get off and just stand still. The days seem to rush by – an endless succession of feeding, nappy changes, visitors, washing, clothes sorting, and tidying. There is so much to do, yet nothing ever seems to get done properly. You may feel selfish and unreasonable wanting it otherwise, yet increasingly aware of the tension and anxiety building within you.

Treat yourself When your baby is asleep, or settled with somebody else, do something that makes you feel good. Often this may be taking a nap yourself. Alternatively, you may feel better if you wash your hair, phone someone who always makes you feel happy, or catch up on your favourite TV programme. Do whatever cheers you up.

Write everything down Make lists – of snacks to eat, questions to ask your midwife, people to phone, items to buy, things to do. Put stars by things that other people can do, and pin the lists up somewhere obvious.

Handling visitors Be firm with company (or, better still, get somebody else to do it on your behalf). State a time limit for their visit at the onset. Be polite but very firm. Tell them that you need to rest. Wearing nightclothes for the first few days at home reinforces this message.

When you're tired If you have an answerphone, use it. Turn the volume on the phone down, let the answerphone take messages, or simply unplug the phone while you feed the baby or take a nap.

Try to relax *when your baby is sleeping. You may be tempted to rush around catching up with housework – but it's better to get someone else to do that.*

Just stay in bed with your baby. It's safe for your baby to sleep with you, unless you or your partner smoke, have drunk alcohol, taken any drugs that affect your sleep, or are extremely tired. Make sure your baby doesn't get too hot, and don't let her head get covered by the bedding.

Don't skimp on your meals. Keep them simple, but nourishing. Sandwiches, fruit, salad and a yoghurt, a bowl of soup with bread and cheese, or baked beans on toast make good, quick meals.

Ask your partner to look after your baby in the evening while you get some sleep – or ask a visiting relative or friend to look after her, so you can both have a rest together.

Help from other mothers

As the sheer hard work of looking after a baby hits home, a typical comment from new mothers is: "I'm now beginning to appreciate how much my mother did for me." There's still a strong tradition that a new mother's own mother should be there to support, nourish, and care for her daughter after birth. She may even do things for you that she hasn't done since you were a child: run you a bath, wash your hair, prepare a favourite meal.

It has been said that motherhood is like a craft, and that all apprentice mothers need a more experienced woman who has had children herself and knows what's involved, to be around and available to support and guide her. Often, this may be your own mother, but if that's not possible, you may find you are drawn to other mothers in your area and seek them out. A new mother needs contact with other mothers. This is not just a social pleasure – it's a psychological necessity.

> "I thought, I'll have the baby, I'll take the maternity leave, and I'll go back to work in six months, no problem. But when it happened it was just like a landslide, a physical and emotional landslide – and nothing prepares you for that!"

HERE ARE SOME IDEAS THAT MAY HELP YOU

- **Lie in the bath** Feed your baby first then get somebody else to hold her, take a piece of fruit, cup of tea, or glass of wine with you, go into the bathroom and shut the door. Run a warm, deep bath and lie back in it.
- **Go for a walk** Exercise stimulates the release of endorphins. A brisk walk will clear your mind of worrying thoughts and niggling anxieties. Carry your baby in a sling, or leave her with somebody else while you walk round the block or go to the corner shop. Swing your arms and breathe deeply. You will come back feeling refreshed.
- **Start a journal** It need not be particularly detailed: just jottings about how you're feeling, what you're doing and how your baby is progressing. If you don't feel like writing, draw little faces to show your mood each day.
- **Have a laugh** It really does help. Watch a funny TV programme, hire a DVD, or chat to a friend who you know will make you laugh. Like exercise, laughter stimulates endorphins, releases muscle tension, and deepens your breathing.

see also

Organizing your day	224–25
Baby massage	220–23
Postnatal depression	226–27
The end of your birth year...	228–29

How breast-feeding works

Before birth, your baby is nourished by your placenta. After the birth, your breasts take over the work of feeding your baby. Breast-milk is the best food your baby can have. It costs nothing and is freely available as long as the interaction between your baby's demands and your body is allowed to work.

ADVANTAGES OF BREAST-FEEDING

- Breast-milk is tailor-made for your baby.
- Breast-milk is convenient and cheap. You can't run out of it.
- Breast-fed babies are less likely to have meningitis, and have fewer gastro-intestinal, respiratory, urinary tract, and ear infections.
- Breast-fed babies have less eczema and asthma.
- A breast-fed baby has less risk of insulin-dependent diabetes, obesity, and high blood pressure in later life.
- Breast-feeding increases babies' intelligence.
- Breast-feeding enhances immunity.
- Mothers who breast-feed have less risk of diabetes, breast, and ovarian cancer.

See "101 Reasons to Breast-feed" on website: www.promom.org

Hormones are in control

Once again, hormones are in charge and direct your body to make milk. Progesterone and oestrogen develop your breasts during pregnancy. The beta-endorphins circulating in your blood to help you during labour, also help the release of prolactin, the milk-producing hormone. In addition, beta-endorphins are present in your colostrum, the early milk you produce in the first few days after delivery (see page 202).

Prolactin and oxytocin work together in a complementary way to make sure your baby gets the benefit of your milk.

Prolactin – the mothering hormone Prolactin is the hormone essential to milk production. It aids the action of progesterone and oestrogen and is essential for the complete development of the milk-producing cells in your breasts. When you put your baby to your breast, her sucking sends messages through the nerves to release prolactin.

The more your baby sucks, the more prolactin is produced. Levels of this hormone start to rise within ten minutes of sucking. This delay in prolactin-release means that when your baby feeds she is in fact "placing her order" for the next feed rather than stimulating milk production for the current one.

Frequent feeding of your baby in the early days is important as, the more the baby sucks, the more prolactin-receptor sites are developed within your breast. Your prolactin levels naturally rise in sleep and night feeds help maintain a high level (1).

Oxytocin – the love hormone The tingly feeling that women describe when they put their baby to the breast is the milk-ejection (or "let-down") reflex and is caused by the hormone oxytocin. This is released in short bursts in immediate response to a stimulation such as thinking about your baby or hearing her cry. This means that milk can spray out of your breast into your baby's mouth before she begins to suck.

In the early days of breast-feeding, it may take several minutes for the first let-down to occur and you may not feel it to begin with. (Some women never feel it.) The pulses of oxytocin, brought on by feeding, stimulate contractions of your womb, known as "after pains". These help your womb to return to its original size after pregnancy. If these pains disturb your baby's early feeds, you could try taking paracetamol half an hour before a feed.

Sexual stimulation also induces the release of oxytocin so you may find that some milk is ejected during orgasm. Feeding your baby before making love will reduce this effect.

Structure of your breast

Each breast is divided into lobes, called alveoli, that look like bunches of grapes. Milk is produced in these lobes, each of which contains 15 to 20 ducts, or tubes, that conduct the milk toward the nipple. The lobes are made up of glandular tissue, each one subdivided into lobules (or "grapes"). Collagen, the connective tissue, acts as a packing material, supporting these glands. The glandular tissue in your breasts is surrounded by fat and it is the fat that determines the size and shape of your breast.

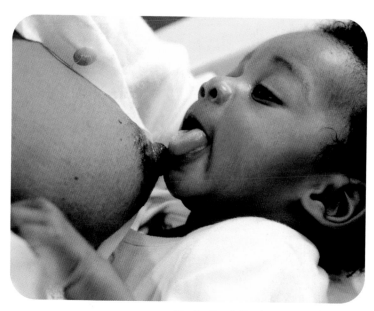

Nipple-stimulation increases the flow of oxytocin in your bloodstream, which in turn triggers the "let-down" reflex and leads to more milk being produced.

Infra-red photos of lactating breasts show that they grow hot in response to a baby's cry, which is when blood rushes to the breasts, bringing blood sugars to the milk glands. With the baby's sucking, oxytocin is released into your bloodstream, causing star-shaped muscle cells around your milk glands to contract and squeeze out sweet-tasting milk. This again, is your "let-down reflex" and it's this reflex that must be stimulated for your milk supply to build up. Soon, baby and breast will work in harmony, with your milk supply matching her hunger.

How your body prepares for breast-feeding

In the first three months of pregnancy, the internal structures of the breast begin to grow, which may make your breasts feel rather sensitive in early pregnancy. Near the end of the sixth month, your body will able to produce early milk or colostrum, but the development of the mature, milk-releasing cells doesn't take place until the last three months. During pregnancy, the pigmentation around your nipple darkens and it has been suggested that this may act as a visual guide or "target" for the newborn baby, to help her latch on. The sebaceous glands around your nipples enlarge. These provide lubrication and protection for the sensitive skin of your nipples. Your nipples also enlarge and become more prominent. Blood-flow to the breasts doubles, so your breasts may look as though they are "marbled" with blood vessels.

What's in breast-milk?

Breast-milk contains exactly the right blend of protein, fat, carbohydrate, minerals, and vitamins needed for the rapid growth and development of your baby. The make-up of breast-milk is individual to you as a mother and changes from feed to feed.

Breast-milk provides immunity for your baby in many ways. For instance, it builds a lining on the walls of her digestive tract, her throat, and her urinary tract, which then protects her from invading organisms. Gastro-enteritis is unusual in breast-fed babies. Because your baby's immune system is immature during her first year and she cannot fight infections as well as you can, your body will also produce antibodies to pass onto her through your breast-milk.

Colostrum This is the first "milk" that your breasts produce in the early days after your baby is born. It is thick and cream to yellow-orange in colour because it contains high levels of betacarotene. It has higher concentrations of sodium, potassium, chloride, protein, and fat-soluble vitamins than mature milk, and has a laxative effect that helps empty meconium from your baby's bowels. (Meconium is a dark substance that forms the first stools of a newborn baby and if this is retained it can lead to jaundice, see page 197.) Colostrum also helps your baby's gut start up slowly after birth and assists with the growth of beneficial bacteria, which compete with harmful bacteria.

> "She knew what to do within ten minutes of being born. I was supremely confident having breast-fed for such a long time last time. Overconfident as it came out. I had forgotten that newborns need to be positioned carefully as their mouths are so small."

Transitional milk This comes after colostrum. It may continue for up to two weeks. Concentrations of antibodies, calories, and protein have decreased while lactose and fat content have increased.

Mature milk This starts to come in as early as three days after your baby's birth and supplies her with everything that she needs. Every feed from now on gives her thirst-quenching foremilk at the beginning and this gradually changes into higher calorie hindmilk. Your baby needs a balance of both foremilk and hindmilk for a satisfying feed. When she latches on, at first she enjoys a drink, and then she gets down to a satisfying meal of hindmilk. If she wants the second breast, she can have another drink and as much hindmilk as she needs.

> "I wasn't sure my baby would know what to do but it did seem she had all the instinct she needed. I just had to make sure I was comfortable and let her feed herself."

An ever-changing "living" fluid

Not only does your milk change during each feed, it also varies with different circumstances. For instance, in very hot weather, if your baby feeds as often as she wants, she will get more foremilk, which allows her to quench her thirst and replace lost fluids without needing to be given bottles of water (1).

Babies are meant to breast-feed often. The volume of milk you produce increases to meet your babies needs and, if you

Get yourself comfortable *with pillows behind your back. If the baby is very small put a pillow underneath her to raise her up to the level of your nipples. (If you are lying down it may help to have a pillow under under your head and if you have generous breasts, you will find it helps to have the short end of a pillow under your ribs – so that your lower breast is not squashed against the mattress.)*

Line your baby up with your breast. When she looks for the nipple and her mouth is open wide, slide her swiftly on to your breast, making sure that her head is not curled forward.

You may need someone to guide you the first few times.

keep feeding, you can go on producing milk for several years. Most studies suggest that the average daily volume of milk produced is about 800ml (1¹/₄ pints), but it varies from person to person, and mothers of twins will produce about twice as much milk.

The World Health Organization recommends that you give your baby nothing but breast-milk for the first six months after birth and then carry on breast-feeding as long as you want, while also giving solid foods (2).

Breast-feeding your baby

There are health benefits for you and your baby with breast-feeding. Breast-milk is more than just a food: it's a living substance that protects a baby from infection as her immune system develops, and contains everything she needs for the first six months of her life. Breast-feeding also protects you against bone disease and certain cancers.

A GOOD LATCH

With good attachment, your baby will feed happily at your breast, quickly at first, to stimulate the let-down reflex, then more slowly as she enjoys the flow of milk. She will stop feeding spontaneously when she's had enough and will be settled afterward (although she may want to feed from the other breast soon). If your baby is well attached:

- Her chin should be firmly in contact with your breast.
- Her nose should be clear of your breast, or lightly touching it.
- Her cheeks will be rounded throughout the feed – her jaw and tongue are massaging the milk out of the ducts behind your areola.
- The whole of her lower jaw will be moving; you will see the muscles working right back near her ears
- It won't be painful for you.

A good latch means she's drawing on your whole breast, not just the nipple.

Getting going

Most babies start feeding soon after birth. All it takes is one really good feed and you and your baby will soon become experts. It's worth getting it right from the start. Ask for help to get you started; your midwife will be happy to show you.

Prepare yourself Before you feed your baby, gather together all the things you may need: a drink for you, tissues, perhaps your telephone, and the TV remote control. New research suggests that choosing a comfortable position for yourself, such as lying back, cuddling and holding your baby so that you are both relaxed, encourages your baby's instincts, such as rooting, and so helps breast-feeding. You'll soon find breast-feeding positions that suit you and your baby. If you prefer to sit up, make sure your back is upright. Pillows on your lap will bring your baby up to the level of your breasts. (You won't need these pillows forever, but they are useful in the first few weeks while you and your baby are both learning and she is small.) Then get your baby calm, and follow the steps opposite.

How much? How often?

Research shows that your body will make the right amount of milk for your baby, if you let her feed when she asks (1). If you try to impose a feeding pattern that suits you, your body will produce the amount of milk you let it, and this may not be enough for your baby. Only your baby knows how hungry she is, and how much breast-milk she needs to satisfy her hunger.

Comfort feeding

Some mothers worry that their baby is "just comfort feeding". They wonder how they can tell when she's sucking at the breast because she really is hungry, and when she's sucking for other reasons, such as wanting some reassurance from you.

For a baby, breast-feeding is not just about nutrition, it is also about warmth and closeness and learning to be a social human being. Researchers notice that breast-feeding babies interact with their mothers, they pause while their mother talks to them, and replying by sucking. They believe that

HOW TO BREAST-FEED

If things aren't going so well, try following these steps.

Calm her If she has been crying, calm her down. Talk to her and tell her what is happening. You may find it helps to wrap her securely in a cot sheet for the first few feeds, but make sure she doesn't get too hot. Later, she'll prefer to have her hands free so she can touch and stroke your breast.

Lie her across your lap Place her on top of the pillow, holding her close and turn her whole body toward you, without twisting her neck. Keep her back and head in a straight line.

Position her nose to nipple Notice how your breast hangs in its natural position and line your baby up so that her nose is level with your nipple. In this position, she will have to tilt her head back slightly to reach for your nipple. This gives her room to open her mouth really wide and get a good latch on to your breast. (Imagine how hard it would be for you to eat an apple with your chin tucked down against your chest.)

Let her head move freely Support her head, but don't have it wedged in the crook of your arm. Your baby needs to have room to tilt her head back and drop her lower jaw so that she can open her mouth wide enough to latch on to the breast.

Touch her lips with your nipple Wait for her to open her mouth as wide as a yawn in response. This may take a few minutes. She needs to open her mouth wide, so that she can take in not only your nipple but a good proportion of your areola (the coloured part around the nipple) as well.

Draw her close As soon as your baby's jaw drops, and her mouth opens wide, quickly draw her closer, moving her whole body, not just her head. Once she gets a good mouthful of breast, with her tongue underneath your nipple, she will draw it further back into her mouth and start sucking. It may take several attempts to get this right. If you don't get "a good latch" your nipples will soon get very sore. Once your baby is latched on, let her feed as long as she needs to.

Pick your baby up and Line her up "nose to your nipple".

Wait for her to open her mouth wide; it may take a few minutes.

Move her swiftly onto your breast with her tongue down.

feeding a baby teaches the give and take of communication and forms the basis of learning human speech (2).

Learning to tell night from day Although your baby has to feed during the night initially, you might also want her to learn how to get back to sleep again quickly. It can help if you:

- Avoid putting on a light – use a low light if you need to see what you are doing.
- Try not to chat or interact with her if possible – low murmurs and gentle, soothing cuddles are best.
- Don't change her nappy unless she is smelly, has a sore bottom, or has wet clothes.
  If you want to start cutting down on the number of night feeds, it's best

FEEDING AT NIGHT

Benefits for your baby
- Your baby needs milk at night because she simply can't store enough food during the day to keep her going when she's little.
- Breast-feeding at night is lovely and comforting, and helps her get back to sleep.

Benefits for you
- Breast-feeding at night in the early weeks helps your milk supply get established. The more you feed, the higher your prolactin levels, and therefore the more milk you make.
- You may well find you wake frequently anyway. It's natural to want to check her when she is so little. Breast-feeding gives you a cosy time together.
- When you breast-feed at night, prolactin helps you get back to sleep: a big advantage over bottle-feeding. You probably found sleeping difficult in the weeks leading up to the birth. This may have been your body's way of preparing you for these disturbed nights. Now you have a good way of dozing off again.

to drop one at a time. It is also better if someone else can go and comfort her until she is used to doing without a breast-feed every time she wakes. Initially, you will need to help her get back to sleep without that feed. Try to become aware of when her cry means "I am tired and want to sleep", or when it means something else, like "I am hungry/cold/frightened".

Common feeding problems and how to solve them

Many women have sensitive nipple skin for the first week after birth, and combined with the unfamiliar, strong sensation of your baby's feeding action, it can feel uncomfortable. As long as your nipples are not damaged or distorted in any way, it will quickly pass. When your baby latches on, wait for 30 seconds, and if you still feel uncomfortable, take your baby off your breast by inserting a clean finger into the corner of her mouth to break the suction, and try again.

Practise relaxation at the beginning of the feed, and try to latch your baby on when she is just waking up and her sucking action is not so strong, before she gets really hungry.

Sore nipples If your nipples become damaged, then it will be painful, although they heal quickly. Now it's even more important to keep asking for help until you find someone who can show you a more comfortable

Bring your baby to breast, *not breast to baby. Don't try to put your breast into her mouth. Wait for her to take it by moving her close, keeping her body and head in line. Put a pillow under your baby to raise her up slightly if you need to.*

position for holding your baby. Continue feeding your baby if you can, as you need to keep stimulating your breasts to maintain your supply. If the pain is worse on one side, it might help to start a feed off on the other side, and swap once your baby is feeding less hungrily. Alternatively, you could hand express milk to feed your baby, as well as to keep your supply going.

It may be suggested that you use a nipple shield to prevent further damage and to protect your nipple, although suction through the shield can still open the cracks. If feeding doesn't feel possible without a one, then a shield may be one option. The main problem is that using them may reduce your milk supply, and it seems to alter your baby's sucking action. Many women find it hard to get rid of nipple shields afterward – their babies sometimes seem to prefer the super-stimulation of this artificial nipple.

If you do have a cracked nipple, you might find it helps to use a pure, hypoallergenic lanolin ointment after feeds until it heals. This ointment prevents scabs forming and keeps the nipple skin moist while it heals. Women also find it soothing. Pat your breasts dry before applying it. You don't need to remove it before the next feed.

Sore breasts Two to five days after the birth, your mature milk "comes in", whether you are breast-feeding or not. Your breasts become hot, swollen, and uncomfortable, and it can be hard for your baby to latch on. This is called "engorgement", but your breasts are not actually full of milk; they are swollen with excess fluid due to your increased blood supply. It usually passes within 24 hours; in the meantime, feeding your baby frequently will help. Many women find putting warm water on their breasts before a feed, or ice cold flannels afterward, brings relief.

If your breasts become engorged when your baby is older, perhaps because she's missed a feed, express some milk to relieve the discomfort, otherwise you could develop a blocked duct, or even mastitis.

As your breasts are always filling up with milk, your breasts will vary in size and shape all the time, and lumps will appear from time to time. These should never last long because whenever your baby feeds she normally drains them. If you have a lump that seems persistent, it may be the beginning of a blocked duct, especially if it feels tender. Feed your baby with her lower jaw as near to the lump as possible – so if the lump is on the outer side of your breast, try feeding underarm on that side. You might also find it helpful to massage the lump gently toward your nipple while your baby is feeding.

Blocked ducts If you are getting recurring blocked ducts, think about where on your breasts they happen, and therefore what might be restricting the flow of milk.

- Does your bra fit well?
- Is something restricting your milk flow during a feed, such as your hand or your baby's hand?

OUT AND ABOUT WITH YOUR BREAST-FED BABY

Some new mothers worry about breast-feeding in public places. While you may feel self-conscious about this at first, within a couple of weeks, you may well find you are both able to feed pretty much automatically, and then it will be easier to go out with your baby. Many shopping centres now have specific spaces for feeding babies, but you don't have to use them. You may find it helps to wear a loose top or drape a scarf around both of you while you feed.

Ring the Breast-feeding Line below or ask your health visitor about breast-feeding support groups where you can meet other mothers.

NCT BREAST-FEEDING LINE
0870 444 8708

You can call the NCT Breast-feeding Line any day of the week between 8am and 10pm and speak directly to an NCT breast-feeding counsellor.

Mastitis Most women have heard of mastitis, but don't worry – not many get it. If you are unlucky enough to develop it, you will feel as if you have 'flu, may have a temperature, and your breasts will be sore. Try to rest and drink plenty of fluids. If you do get it, it's important to keep feeding your baby, as stopping breast-feeding will make the problem worse. Usually, mastitis results from insufficient drainage of the breast, caused by delayed feeds, attachment which is not quite right, blocked ducts, or untreated engorgement. If you can correct the cause of the problem, the mastitis will ease, and you will not require any medication.

Your GP may prescribe antibiotics, but most cases of mastitis are not caused by infection, so antibiotics here are preventive. However, in a few rare cases, mastitis does result from an infection, which can lead to an abscess and this type will require antibiotics. Alternatively, your GP may prefer to prescribe an anti-inflammatory drug to reduce the inflammation. Neither of these will harm your baby, though antibiotics may upset her tummy, and you will also need to watch out for signs of thrush.

If you can identify why you got mastitis, you can probably prevent it happening in the future, so talk it through with a breast-feeding counsellor.

Thrush of the nipples Another, less common cause of sore nipples is thrush (Candida albicans), a fungal infection. Consider this especially if you have had thrush during pregnancy, are prone to thrush, or if you or your baby have recently taken antibiotics. Thrush causes nipple pain, and sometimes deep breast pain. Your nipple skin may look pinker than usual and shiny, and your baby may have white patches on her tongue or in her mouth. Women describe the pain as sharp and stabbing, like needles, and it often continues after feeds. It's important that both you and your baby are treated with anti-fungal treatment, even if only one of you has symptoms, otherwise you can re-infect each other. Talk to your GP or your local pharmacist.

Breast-feeding twins

It's perfectly possible for you to breast-feed two, three, or even four babies concurrently (1) and many mothers of more than one baby breast-feed exclusively or combine breast- and bottle-feeding successfully.

Twins, who can sometimes be small at birth, can enjoy all the benefits of breast-milk and once you've got breast-feeding well established, you too will appreciate the comfort and practicality of having your babies' food instantly available with no bottles and powder to worry about.

Feeding positions Breast-feeding in a "rugby ball" hold works well. Your babies can rest on pillows at either side of you, with their legs pointing behind you, your arms around them and their necks cradled in each of your hands as you hold one at each breast. You'll sometimes want to feed both twins together, sometimes one after the other – it's up to you. Experiment with different set-ups so you feel comfortable and work out which is easier.

You may find you prefer feeding them together, only to discover that at times, one twin is very hungry while the other stays fast asleep.

Accept offers of help It can help to learn to express milk at least occasionally, as this gives you the option, when it's convenient, of allowing one of your helpers to bottle-feed expressed milk to one baby while you breast-feed the other one.

Talking to other parents of twins about what worked for them can help. If you don't know anyone ask your health visitor or ring the NCT. You can also contact the twins association, Tamba (see page 245), as they produce leaflets suggesting ideas to support breast-feeding.

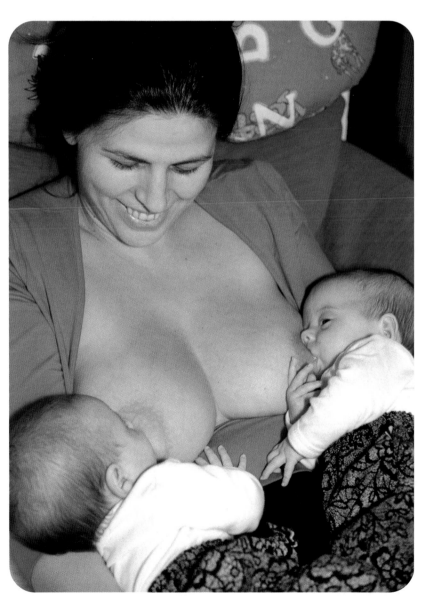

Talk to your babies *while you feed them; they will be communicating with each other at the same time.*

see also

Expressing breast-milk

You may need to express your breast-milk if you or your baby are ill. You may also want to do this if you are returning to work or leaving your baby for any other reason. Try hand expressing first as it's easier because you don't have to keep sterilizing a pump.

USING A BREAST PUMP

All pumps work by drawing the milk through your nipple into a sterilized container. You are really only likely to need a pump if you are expressing frequently, returning to work early, if you are likely to be going out a lot, or if you or your baby are ill, otherwise hand expressing is just as efficient and is free. You can hire an electric pump through the NCT.

Wait until feeding is established

There may be times when you would like to give your baby your expressed breast-milk. It's usually easier to do this after breast-feeding has been established – around six weeks works well. You will need bottles and teats and some method of sterilizing them (see page 212).

If your baby only ever feeds from one breast at a time, it can be a good idea to express from the other side at the same time, using a hand pump or electric pump you can work with one hand. If your baby has long gaps between feeds (three hours or more), try expressing between those times. Alternatively, express what's left after your baby has finished a feed.

You'll need to experiment to find the best time and the best method for you, but you may find it's quicker in the morning and gets easier.

Before you start expressing, there are several things you can do to help:

- Try to be as comfortable and relaxed as possible
- Have your baby, or a photograph of your baby, close by
- Have a warm bath or shower first, or lay warm flannels on your breast
- Gently massage your breast toward the nipple.

Expressing by hand

- Sterilize a wide-necked bottle or bowl to catch the milk.
- Hold your breast, with your thumb on top and your fingers underneath, so that your little finger is against your ribcage, and your first finger and thumb are opposite each other, making a big "C" shape round the whole of your breast.
- Breast-milk comes from deep within your breast, so your finger and thumb need to be well away from your nipple, back behind your areola.
- Squeeze your thumb and first finger gently together, hold and release, and keep doing this without changing the position of your fingers, until you see some drops of milk appearing. This may take a few minutes. You may find you can do this more effectively if you gently push your whole hand back toward the ribcage, before you squeeze.
- If the flow of milk starts to slow down, you can move your hand round, keeping that "C" round your whole breast, so that you are "milking" a different section of your breast each time.
- Swap from one breast to another to increase the amount of milk you express each time.

Benefits for premature babies

Premature babies are often tube-fed to begin with, and many mothers find it very comforting to provide breast-milk for their preterm baby because it's the one thing they alone can do. Expressing milk for a premature baby is hard work though and you'll need all the support and encouragement you can get.

Breast-milk is especially suited to preterm babies because their digestive systems are often immature. Your milk contains factors that protect them against infection and allergy, and research has even shown that the milk from mothers of premature babies is higher in protein and minerals than the breast-milk from mothers of full-term babies. Breast-milk also protects premature babies from the very serious bowel disease, necrotizing enterocolitis that they are prone to (see page 169).

Long-term expressing

If you want to express milk for all your baby's feeds, for example, if she's very premature, or you have to go back to work, you will probably need to buy, borrow, or hire a hospital-grade electric breast pump. When pumping exclusively for a newborn, it's important to imitate a baby's feeding as far as possible. This means pumping about every three hours for the first few weeks, including during the night.

Storing expressed breast-milk

Expressed breast-milk keeps well if refrigerated or frozen. It will last for three to five days stored in the coldest part of the fridge (below 4°C/39°F – usually the back or the bottom of the fridge, and NOT in the door).

Freezing breast-milk Freezing only causes minor changes to the nutrients and anti-infective properties; it should be used within three months. You will need to freeze breast-milk in sterile containers. You may prefer to buy special sterile polybags (available from your chemist) as they contain no harmful chemicals. Label and date the bag, and then pour the milk straight into it from the pump or bowl, if you are hand expressing. As milk expands on freezing, don't fill containers to the top. Chilled expressed milk can be added to milk that is already frozen, as long as you don't add more than half as much again. When feeding expressed milk to your baby, use the fresh milk first, and the oldest batch of frozen milk next.

Defrosting frozen milk Breast-milk is best defrosted slowly. Milk that has been defrosted in the fridge will keep for up to 24 hours. You can thaw milk quickly by standing the container in hot water, but you must use it immediately. The fat in breast-milk often separates as it thaws; just give it a good shake. You can heat frozen milk in a bowl of hot water – don't heat it directly in a pan or microwave; it destroys some nutritional benefits and microwaves heat unevenly so hot spots could scald a baby. Milk does not have to be at body heat – babies don't mind it cool or at room temperature.

Formula-feeding your baby

Breast-milk is the healthiest option for your baby, but there are many reasons why you might not breast-feed. No one should pressurize you to breast-feed or formula-feed – you should be given enough information to help you make your own decision. Feeding your baby, however it's done, should be a source of joy.

Bottle-feeding a baby

The sad fact is that many women who do want to breast-feed end up formula-feeding because of lack of information, support, and practical help. If you are unsure about how you want to feed your baby, it's actually better to start with breast-feeding and see how you feel about it. You can always switch to formula later if it's not for you and your baby. However, it is much harder to switch back to breast-feeding if you start with formula. The one advantage of bottle-feeding is that your partner can enjoy feeding his baby too, but try not to let others share this pleasure at first.

"I wanted to breast-feed, but it all seemed to go wrong, and Sophie just wouldn't latch on. She was given bottles as she was losing weight, and after a couple of weeks, I resigned myself to having to give her formula. She is a happy and contented baby, and we are very close, so although I regret the fact we couldn't breast-feed, I don't think it affected us as much as I thought it would."

What you need

There is a huge choice in formula-feeding – it can be difficult to decide what to buy. You will need about six bottles and teats, some method of sterilizing, plus, of course, the formula. It is probably best to be guided by your health visitor or midwife about which formula to start your baby on. She should also show you how to prepare a bottle at least once, but you must make sure that you read the instructions on the tin of formula milk carefully, as it is important that the ratio of water to powder is correct. Don't ever be tempted to make the milk thinner or thicker than instructed.

Making up the bottles

Formula milk powder is not sterile so the government recommends that feeds are made up as they are needed.

- Wash everything thoroughly, and then sterilize everything you are going to use – bottles, teats, measures, knife.
- Boil more fresh cold tapwater than you need, and allow it to cool to 21°C (70°F) – , which should take no more than 30 minutes.
- Wash your hands and the work surfaces before you make up the feed.
- Fill the bottle to the correct level, using the cooled, boiled water.
- Using the spoon provided in the tin of formula, take a scoop of formula, and level it with the knife. Don't pat it down or compress it. Add the

Bottle-feeding *can be satisfying for you and your baby. Hold her so her head is higher than her body and keep the bottle upright to ensure the teat is full of milk so your baby does not take in air.*

scoops of powder to the bottle, put the top on and shake thoroughly.
- Cool the bottle quickly to the feeding temperature using cold water.
- Check the temperature of the formula by shaking a few drops onto the inside of your wrist. It should feel lukewarm, not hot.
- Throw away any food that has not been used within two hours.

Giving a bottle

Try to feed in a calm and restful atmosphere.
- Gather together all the things you need – bottle, tissues or bib, and a drink for yourself.
- Choose a comfortable chair with good back support. A small footstool or cushions may be useful to level your lap. Pillows under your arms will make you more comfortable.
- Some babies like to be wrapped cosily for feeding. Others prefer to be

able to move their arms, touch, and explore.

- Sit comfortably, and hold your baby close, with her body across your lap, sitting her a little upright if you can. Experiment with feeding positions, but make sure her head is slightly higher than her tummy. You may prefer to hold her tucked in close to you with her head resting in the crook of your arm. Or you may like to hold her, with her head in your hand and her feet touching your tummy – you may both enjoy the more direct eye contact that's possible in this position.
- Touch your baby's lip gently with the teat and wait for her to open her mouth. Don't try and force the bottle into her mouth – she knows when she's hungry.
- Hold the bottle up at an angle so that the teat remains full of milk and she doesn't suck in any air. Don't jiggle the teat around if she stops to rest. Bottle-feeding is hard work for a baby.
- If she starts spluttering, take the teat out of her mouth and sit her upright to catch her breath. When she's calm, start again. Using a slow-flow teat will prevent her being overwhelmed with the flow of milk and will encourage active sucking.
- When she stops sucking and is contented, resist the temptation to make her finish the bottle. If she doesn't want any more, throw away leftovers.

Bonding with your formula-fed baby

It is true that breast-feeding and bonding seem to go naturally together, because you're the only person who can breast-feed, but you will still bond with your baby if you are formula-feeding her. You can formula-feed on demand, which is a way of staying in tune with your baby.

Cuddle your baby skin to skin – with your bare skin next to hers – when feeding her. This will help your baby bond with you, as well as meeting her needs for contact. Don't sleep with your baby, though, if either you or your partner are smokers, you have been drinking or taking drugs, or you are very tired. And try not to fall asleep on a sofa with your baby as this can also be dangerous.

Methods of sterilizing

As your baby does not have a mature immune system yet, and milk allows germs to grow easily, it is important that all the feeding equipment is thoroughly sterilized before it comes into contact with your baby. Otherwise you put your baby at risk of illnesses like thrush or gastro-enteritis. You will need to continue to sterilize everything that comes in contact with milk for at least your baby's first year.

There are two ways to sterilize your feeding equipment; heat or chemical, and both are fairly easy once you've got the hang of them.

Heat sterilizing – steam If you are using a steam sterilizer, just follow the instructions, add water to the unit, plug it in at the mains, and switch it on. The water boils and steam then sterilizes the feeding equipment.

Heat sterilizing – boiling You can also sterilize using heat by immersing all your baby's bottles and teats in a large saucepan of water, bringing it to the boil, and letting the water boil vigorously for 20 minutes. Make sure that everything is completely covered by water.

Heat sterilizing – microwave You can buy special microwave sterilizers, which also work by killing germs through heat. Make sure you follow the instructions, according to the strength of your microwave oven.

Chemical sterilizing Sterilizing tablets are available from any chemist. Dissolve them according to directions, in a deep container of water, leaving everything to soak in the solution for a certain length of time – usually 24 hours. This means you need to have enough equipment to have some soaking and some in use.

WINDING YOUR BABY

Some babies swallow air when they are feeding, which can cause them discomfort, in which case you need to "wind" them to bring up the air. If your baby seems to need to bring up wind sit her upright on your lap with your hand under her chin, keeping her back as straight as possible. Your baby will probably be leaning forward slightly and you will need to support her head at first. Then you can pat her back gently, but quite firmly. Alternatively:

- Put a good absorbent towel over your shoulder reaching well down your back
- Prop her over your shoulder, so she's upright, her chin is resting on your shoulder, and her tummy is stretched out full length against your chest
- Now stroke her back and sides firmly and slowly upward, toward her neck several times. Quite firm pressure is needed, like stroking a cat really hard, backward.

If your baby seems very windy, you could experiment with different types of bottle or teat, perhaps trying a teat that slows down the milk flow. You could also feed your baby in a more upright position, with frequent pauses to allow trapped air to escape.

Soothing a newborn

Most babies have fairly simple needs. They need to be fed, to feel comfortable and safe, they need human company, and they need sleep. Babies cry to let you know there's a problem because that's the only way they can get help, and all they expect is that you will deal with the problem.

BACK TO THE WOMB

Some mammals can get up and walk straight after birth. In comparison, human newborn babies are very dependent on our care. One theory is that evolution has made our brains grow so enormous that we have to be born early, otherwise our heads would be too large to fit through the pelvis.

As a result, some say that all human babies in a sense are born premature. They could do with another three months inside.

It's certainly true that recreating the sensations of life in the womb after the birth can make a baby feel secure. Holding, rocking, and shushing noises can all help soothe a crying baby.

One study compared infants sleeping in an ordinary cot, with those sleeping in a cot specifically designed to feel similar to the womb: it moved, made noises, and held the babies firmly. The babies with the special cots cried significantly less during the study period, slept for longer at night, and slept through the night sooner, too (1).

Respond to crying

It can be hard to find a way of comforting a baby who's not hungry. Your baby won't cry "just to annoy you", or from any other complicated motive. They don't know how, so you should respond to her cry. Most research suggests that babies whose cries are answered, cry less, and grow up to be more independent (2).

Most babies seem to enjoy anything that reminds them of being in your womb, where they were warm, held, rocked, and moved around in constant contact with you.

Most people can *tune out all sorts of noise, but the sound of a baby crying is very difficult to ignore. Your baby's appearance – her smooth skin, big eyes – is designed to make you want to pick her up and cuddle her straight away.*

Babies respond to sound and music You can buy "womb-noise" tapes, but the sound of a tumble drier, extractor fan, running water, vacuum cleaner, or hairdryer works just as well, as does playing the radio when it is not tuned to any station, so you hear the static.

Many babies love music, and we know that they remember the music they heard during pregnancy (3). Playing your favourite music (CDs you listened to during pregnancy) can sometimes help soothe a crying baby (4).

If your baby is not one for loud music, try singing lullabies to her. She will probably particularly like it if you hum or sing softly while resting her head against yours.

Soothing with warm water Get into a warm bath with your baby, but make sure that the water's not too hot. Make sure that someone is around to help you get out.

Babies like movement Babies love motion. You can dance with your baby, jiggling round the room in time to your favourite music, you can take her for car rides, perhaps en route to see other new mothers in a postnatal support group, or to have a good walk in the park or the country with your baby in a sling, backpack, or pushchair. Getting outside for a walk with your baby every day is a good idea. It's healthy exercise, you both get lots of fresh air, and getting out of the house will help you avoid developing postnatal depression.

If your baby wants to be held or jiggled around a lot of the time, get other people to hold her, too. Invest in a good sling; the ones with lots of different positions will probably last you longer, but ask around for recommendations and borrow a few to try out. Some slings don't have enough support for the baby's back or head, and/or your baby may outgrow it very quickly.

Helping your baby to sleep

Young babies are not capable of deep sleep. Many drift in and out of sleep fairly ineffectively, depending on their ability to soothe themselves.

Research into sleep training consistently shows that the most effective strategy early on is to find a way of establishing the difference between night and day (5), and this involves two things:

- When you feed your baby at night, always keep lights dim, don't change her nappy unless it is absolutely necessary, talk to her quietly – avoid too much interaction – simply communicate that this is sleep time.
- Establish a bedtime routine to let her know that it is time to sleep and stick to it every evening.

Bedtime routines It doesn't really matter what you choose to do; a routine is basically about keeping things predictable. It should involve winding down, so perhaps a bath, clean nappy, and a feed and finally, tucking her up in her cot. Never put her in an adult bed on her own (see page 219).

SWADDLING

You can recreate the feeling of the restricted space inside the womb by swaddling your baby, although make sure she doesn't get too hot when wrapped like this.

To swaddle your baby, use a large baby blanket or sheet: lay it in a diamond shape, folding the top point over to create a flat edge for her shoulders to lie along. Fold one side over her body and tuck under her bottom (keep her arms bent up). Then bring the bottom point up to tuck into this wrap, thus immobilizing the feet. Wrap the other top corner around her and secure this corner in the material at the back. Leave her hands free so that she can find them, unless you are swaddling her temporarily so you can feed.

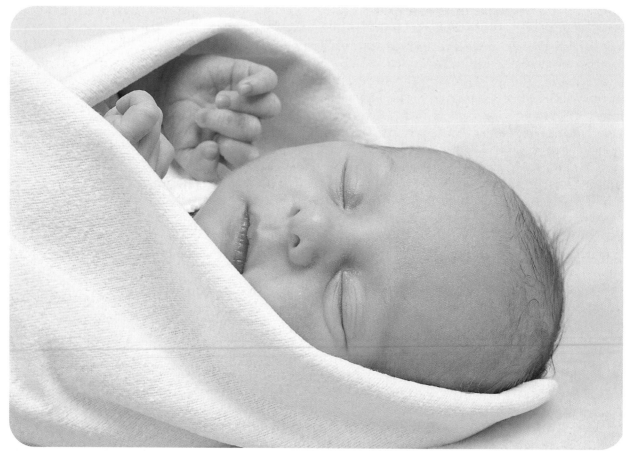

If you "swaddle" *your baby in a cot sheet or blanket, make sure she has access to her hands and don't let her get too hot.*

During the first six weeks, a baby's circadian rhythm, which governs her heart rate, temperature, and activity level, matures. This means that she will begin to develop a pattern that will help her to be more definitely asleep or awake – rather than drifting in and out of these two states as she does in the early days. Somewhere between one and three months of age, she should begin to sleep less frequently, but for longer periods. You will start to learn to anticipate her sleepy times and she will begin to recognize your signals that it's time for bed.

Should babies sleep in a separate room? Some people think that it is better for babies to sleep alone, and that sleeping in separate rooms encourages independence. In fact there is no research evidence to suggest that babies who sleep on their own are more or less dependent on their parents than those who don't.

When scientists have observed bedsharing in the laboratory, they noticed that mother and baby tune in to each other, and their cycles of arousal and sleep come together. Research has also found that when mothers and babies sleep together, they face each other, close enough to inhale each other's breath, suggesting that perhaps the mother is stimulating the baby to breathe more regularly (1). Mothers who share a bed with their baby do wake more often, but overall they actually spend just as much time asleep as mothers whose babies sleep in another room, but they tend to feel less disturbed (2). This is because the baby who sleeps in a separate room has to cry to attract attention, and in the process, gets agitated and upset (3). The mother then has to get out of bed to respond to her baby, so both wake up fully, and thus it takes longer to get back to sleep. In addition, babies will not feed as effectively if they are already crying and upset (4).

The Foundation for the Study of Infant Deaths (FSID) advises having your baby's cot in the bedroom with you for the first six months, as it is safer. The most recent and comprehensive research into cot death in this country.

Sharing a bed with your baby

If you do plan to sleep with your baby research shows these precautions help to reduce the risk.

- You need to make sure your baby can't fall out of bed. You could use a guard-rail if it can be placed flush against the side of your mattress. Alternatively, you can buy sidecar cots, where the side drops down and the cot mattress can be raised to the same level as your bed.
- Always put your baby on her back to sleep.
- Don't put your baby to sleep alone in an adult bed.
- Avoid large pillows or cushions, and don't sleep with your baby on a couch or water bed, as these are too soft. Surfaces should be firm.
- Make sure that your duvet or pillows cannot cover your baby's head.
- Don't fall asleep with your baby on the sofa.

It's better not to bedshare if:

- You or your partner are smokers.
- You have been drinking alcohol or taking drugs (this includes prescribed drugs such as sedatives or strong painkillers).
- You are extremely tired.

Safety in the cot

- Use a mattress completely covered with PVC or another wipe-clean surface. It doesn't have to be a new mattress as long as it's firm, clean, and dry.
- Make sure the mattress fits the cot without any gaps.
- Put your baby on her back to sleep, with her feet at the bottom of the cot so she sleeps "feet to foot".
- Don't use pillows, duvets, or other soft bedding, which could pose a risk of suffocation. Use one or more layers of light blankets for babies less than a year old, tuck the covers in firmly, and make the cot up from the bottom so she can't slide down under the blankets.
- Avoid overheating the room or overdressing your baby.

CRANIAL OSTEOPATHY

This is popular with many parents and there's some evidence that it helps soothe babies who cry a lot (6). Cranial osteopaths look for disturbance in the bones of the skull, and remedy these with gentle massage. The theory is that during labour, the baby's skull is compressed, which causes the skull bones to distort and overlap. Normally this moulding is reduced in the first few days after birth by crying (which raises intracranial pressure) and by suckling, which also moves the bones of the jaw and face.

Difficult births

If the moulding is extreme though, because of a very slow, difficult, or assisted delivery, then the compression stays, making the baby more irritable; perhaps to the extent of giving the baby a headache. She cries a lot and prefers being held upright as this decreases pressure on the head. It is also suggested that the nerve to the tongue can be affected so suckling is less effective, and the baby tires before she has had enough milk, so feeding is frequent and erratic.

Where can I get treatment?

Cranial osteopathy treatments are only available privately. If you do want to try this, it is important that you use a registered practitioner.

Baby massage

During her last weeks in the womb, your baby was firmly held and continually caressed by the muscular walls of your uterus. No wonder then that, now she is born, firm holding and stroking continue to calm and soothe her. Babies need touch as much as they need food.

PROVEN BENEFITS

In 1986, an American study confirmed the benefits of touch for premature babies. Nurses were asked to massage a group of babies in the special care unit for 15 minutes, three times a day, for ten days. At the end of that time, the massaged babies were able to go home almost a full week earlier than the control group, having gained 47 per cent more weight than expected.

One year later, when the massaged babies were examined in a follow-up study, their IQ was found to be higher than that of babies given the routine handling. And in another study by the same team, when healthy, full-term babies were massaged for 15 minutes a day, they cried less, were more alert and socially engaged, gained weight faster, and they had lower levels of stress hormones (1).

"I didn't have a lot of time for my second baby, because my first was still so young. Massage sessions with the new baby gave us time to focus on each other."

Learn how to give a massage

For all ages, the physical touch of massage encourages good blood circulation, relaxes muscles and nerves, improves the functioning of the lymphatic system, and has a relaxing effect on the mind. Your health visitor should be able to give you information about baby massage classes in your area. These provide an excellent way to meet other mothers, bond with your baby, and learn a skill that will enhance your life.

Massage can be tried out at home as well as learned in classes. Many fathers, in particular, find it rewarding to massage their baby. Massage is especially good for a second or third baby who may not get much special time alone with you, apart from feeds. Remember that you don't have to do a full massage every time – if you're in a hurry, just do the favourite bits.

Constant contact Stroking and caressing your baby is something you will probably do almost without thinking from the moment of birth. Massage is most effective in the first six or seven months of life. Once your baby is mobile, she may be too busy to lie still, but massage can still be part of your routine.

It's good for both of you

In a study recently conducted at Queen Charlotte's and Chelsea Hospital in London, a group of depressed mothers attended five baby massage classes. Each showed a remarkable improvement in their mother-baby interaction, and were "back as normal mothers enjoying their babies...and relating to them" after learning how to do the massage (2).

Massage can help postnatal depression The research involved two groups of postnatally depressed mothers who were allocated randomly – to attend either infant massage classes plus a support group – or the support group only. Each group attended five weekly sessions. Measures of depression (the Edinburgh Postnatal Depression Scale/EPDS) and mother-infant interaction (a video recording) were made at the beginning and the end. The Edinburgh scale scores decreased in both groups, but most significantly in the massage group. The massage group also showed marked improvement in mother-infant interaction, which was not apparent in the non-massage group.

Giving a massage

Have everything ready before you start. Find a warm, quiet place where you won't be disturbed and have everything you need to hand – massage oil (a simple vegetable oil such as almond), tissues, a clean nappy, and a clean set of clothes. The massage can be done on the floor, with the baby laid on a towel on top of a changing mat or folded blanket.

Use firm but gentle pressure with either the flat pads of your fingers or the whole palm of your hand. Keep one hand on your baby at all times. If you need to reach for a tissue, for example, keep the other hand on your baby's skin for reassurance.

Prepare yourself Remove any rings or bracelets you may wear; make sure your fingernails are short and wash your hands in warm water. Dry them, then rub them together to make them nice and warm.

Undress your baby Lay her down on her back. Kneel or sit facing her, and

MASSAGE TIPS

- Don't give a massage near feeding time. One hour before or after is best.
- Never wake a baby up for a massage.
- Aromatherapy oils designed for adults should be avoided.
- Never use deep pressure when you massage a baby.
- Always be guided by your baby's response. If your baby's not happy being undressed and massaged, leave it for a while and perhaps try again another day.

Massage is a delightful way *of getting to know your baby. A parent's loving touch shows a child she is lovable, and a happy baby shows parents they're doing it right.*

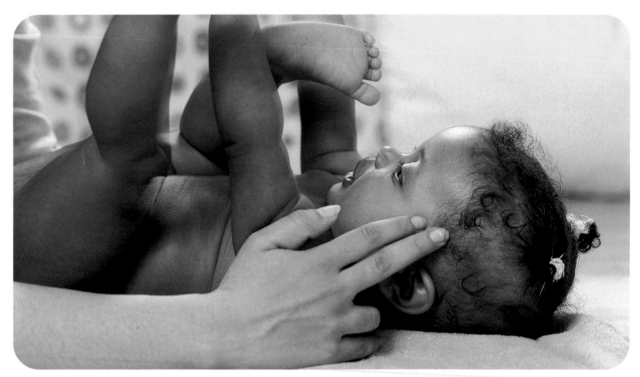

Research shows that *baby massage is good for mother-infant interaction. It's a fun thing to do and can cheer you both up.*

taking about a half-teaspoonful of oil, rub it over the palms of your warm hands. Use just enough oil to let your palms glide smoothly over her skin. Talk to your baby, make eye contact with her, and tell her what you are going to do.

Start with a greeting Place your hands, side by side, palms down flat on the baby's tummy and stroke gently upward around the shoulders and smoothly back down to the toes. Repeat this a few times, talking or singing gently, and letting your baby's response guide you.

Work on chest and arms first Without applying any more oil to your hands, place them together, palms down, side by side on your baby's chest, and gently press them down, around the chest, and up again. From the same starting position, stroke up around the shoulders and down again, stroking the arms down toward the wrists. Repeat this movement two or three times, without getting any massage oil on the baby's hands (it will irritate her eyes if she rubs them).

Massage her tummy Put a little more oil on your hands and make clockwise circles over her tummy with one hand and then, with the pads of two fingers, make small clockwise circles around the colon (beginning just up from the right groin, upward to just under her ribs, across to the other side and down). Repeat this a few times. This technique sometimes helps colicky babies. Then repeat the "hello" strokes you began with, running your

hands around the shoulders and back down to the toes. Then ask your baby if she'd like to turn over, and turn her on to her tummy.

Use a simple vegetable oil *such as almond and a firm, but gentle stroke, letting your baby's response be your guide.*

Massaging her legs Apply a little more oil to your hands if necessary and, starting with your hands at either side of the base of your baby's spine, stroke up to her shoulders and work back down to her toes. Do this a few times before smoothing each leg in turn.

Hold one of your baby's ankles in one hand, and with the other hand, take hold of the top of her leg on the other side. Pull down gently but firmly and as you reach the ankle, move your other hand up to the top of the leg on the same side, pulling down in the same way, while your first hand takes over holding the ankle.

Repeat this "leg pulling" motion several times. Go through the same massage on the other leg. Then run both hands up both legs at the same time and gliding right back down to the ends of the toes. Repeat this finishing stroke a few times.

Stroke her feet With your thumb, rub small circles on the base of your baby's foot (anti-clockwise circles are supposed to be calming). Repeat on the other foot and then rub up and down the legs as before.

Progress to her back Starting with your hands at either side of the base of the spine, stroke up to the shoulders and down to the toes. Glide your hands back up the legs to either side of the base of the spine, and repeat the movement. Do not touch the actual spine itself, just massage along either side. With the flat of your hand, make large anti-clockwise circles around the base of the back. Finish off with a few strong stroking movements, up the back, around the shoulders, and back down to the toes.

Finish off with a cuddle When you have finished the massage, or she has had enough, wrap your baby in a warm towel. Keep talking to her, then pick her up and give her a cuddle.

Organizing your day

Gradually, after the first few weeks, a pattern will emerge and you will begin to feel as though things are settling down. The initial excitement may fade, but you'll start to find time for simple pleasures like taking a shower that lasts longer than two minutes, or eating a meal without a baby at your breast.

The chaos of the early days passes

Everyone will tell you that the chaos of the first weeks with a new baby does not last long – so remember that when you're finding it hard. Anyway, you may find that you love this stage, when your baby's greatest pleasure is to be cuddled in your arms and gaze up at your face. If you lower your standards, and you've got the right support, you can relax and really enjoy this special time. At this stage, a little organization can help a lot.

Rationalize your home:
- Keep a "baby-changing station" with nappies, wipes, and a change of baby clothes in every room you use on a regular basis.
- Hang a stocked-up baby-changing bag ready to go by the front door. Include nappies, wipes, nappy-cream, a change of clothes, changing mat, hats, toys, and anything else you'll need.
- Pack away your fancy clothes and just keep easy-care separates to hand – comfortable trousers, tops that don't need ironing, stretchy skirts, and comfortable shoes.
- Keep one complete outfit including tights, shoes, and fresh underwear, hanging up in a dry cleaner's bag in your wardrobe so that you can slip it on if you need to look good in a hurry.

Get help if you can:
- Accept all offers of help – ironing, cooking, and shopping – and promise to do the same for your friends when it's their turn.
- Ask visitors to stop off and pick things up for you on their way over – a loaf of bread, milk, nappies – whatever you need.
- Perhaps you could find a neighbour or local teenager to pop in a couple of times a week to help you with washing or cleaning, and use some of your new Child Benefit to pay for it.
- Contact your nearest college of further education and see if there are any trainee nursery nurses who would like to get some work experience by helping you out.
- Get to know your health visitor. Every new mother in the UK has a named health visitor to give support and friendship. Health visitors are ideally placed to form a relationship of trust with mothers. Research has shown that, if you're feeling overwhelmed, a health visitor can be more

> "I think it's really important to get out and see as many different people as you can, because there are certain people you click with and others who you don't. I go to all the groups on offer."

Getting out of the house and meeting new people is good for you. All mothers need to find time to be with other new mums.

help than a psychologist (1). Let her know how you're feeling. She will understand what you're talking about, and can offer useful ideas.

- Contact HomeStart, an organization that provides help on an as-needed basis. It's a voluntary organization that has over 200 branches across the UK offering support and practical help to families with preschool children. They send experienced mothers out to help and support new mothers and it doesn't cost a thing. For contact details, see Useful organizations, page 245.

The talking cure

It always helps to talk through how you're feeling. If you don't have someone close you can talk to, seek out other new mothers through your local baby clinic or NCT branch. New mothers, and first-time mothers especially, can get very lonely when they stop work, and it can feel worse if you have mixed feelings about being at home with your baby. If you can make friends with other women in the same situation, it's good for you and the whole family. A happy mother with a social outlet of her own is a definite asset to her baby, who in turn will thoroughly enjoy her mother's happiness and the variety of new faces that she'll see.

In the early weeks it can sometimes seem to be an achievement to get the curtains open by lunchtime, let alone get out of the house and socialize with a whole new group of people, but as soon as you are able to, making friends with other mothers can help to reduce loneliness. You might find that problems you thought were unique to you are in fact shared by many others, and that discovery alone – plus the opportunity to take the long view – puts things into perspective.

FEELING STRESSED?

- Make time to do at least one of your favourite things every day. Even small things like wearing your favourite perfume, playing some music you love, or doing some gardening will help keep your spirits up.
- Rest whenever your baby sleeps.
- Get into bed with your baby to breast-feed her.
- Get someone (your partner, mother, or a friend) to take your baby out for an hour or two in the buggy to give you a break. If this is a success, make it a regular arrangement.
- Go out to a mother and toddler group, even if the other babies are much older than yours. A new baby is always a conversation opener and it's good to talk to other mothers who will understand how you're feeling and will be able to sympathize.
- Light some candles and run a warm bath. If your baby has been fed and she still won't sleep, have a candle-lit soak in the tub with her. (Ask someone else to bring you warm towels.)

see also

What your new baby needs	194–97
What a new mother needs	198–99
Soothing a newborn	216–17
Baby massage	220–23
Postnatal depression	226–27

Postnatal depression

Postnatal illness was once a taboo subject – but now it's recognized that motherhood can turn a woman upside down. New mothers are expected to adapt to their new life and carry on as though nothing has changed, when in reality their lives have changed forever.

LEARNING TO BE A PARENT

Girls are not born to be mothers any more than boys are born to be fathers. Looking after a child is a skill we have to learn like any other. You get thrown in at the deep end when you have your first baby and it's not surprising that you may find this hard.

Sometimes it can feel as though you'll never cope, but remember that the time when your baby is very new really does pass by in a flash. Enjoy it as much as you can because when it's gone there's no way of turning back the clock.

Positive changes

All life-changes mean extra stress and strain, but they also offer enormous potential for growth. A time of change is both a period of heightened vulnerability and of increased potential. If you can be aware of how you are changing, and can reflect on what you are doing, thinking, and feeling at this time, it can help you grow in strength.

What is postnatal depression

Postnatal depression (PND) is more than just feeling low some of the time after the birth of your baby. After all, "off" days are a part of normal life and no one expects sunshine every day. Postnatal depression is longer lasting. It usually presents within the first six weeks after the baby's birth and 60 per cent of women with it will experience symptoms before six months, although it may be a long time before it is recognized. A practical definition of postnatal depression is that it is a depressed mood that lasts, overwhelms more positive feelings, and becomes evident in the first weeks and months after childbirth.

Textbooks on the subject generally quote studies that put the numbers of women affected at between ten and 15 per cent of all new mothers. However, other studies reveal higher totals of as much as 27 per cent (1).

Have I got postnatal depression?
It is possible you have postnatal depression if:
- You are often sad, and find it hard to see the funny side of things – some women feel so low they avoid meeting people, and some cry easily
- You feel you are the only mother who can't cope
- You feel a failure, and guilty because of it
- You feel anxious and irritable, maybe worried over world problems you can't influence
- You find coping with your baby's crying very difficult
- You can't get to sleep even though you are exhausted, or you endlessly crave sleep
- You feel as if you hardly ever have enough energy to do things
- Making decisions, even about simple things, is very hard.

How is postnatal depression diagnosed?
The Edinburgh Postnatal Depression Scale (EPDS) is a brief questionnaire given to mothers normally at six to eight weeks after the birth and/or six to eight months after the birth of her baby if the GP or health visitor are concerned about them. It asks a mother what her moods and feelings have been in the last week. It's simple to use and doesn't pry into personal experiences but does identify women who could do with help, and enables GPs and health visitors to get assistance for them.

Caring for someone with postnatal depression

Living with a depressed partner places a considerable burden on the other partner, whatever the cause of the depression – new motherhood or anything else. Fathers who are trying to support a partner who is very needy can feel desperately lonely themselves. So it's important for supporters to get help too, and if friends or family members are not able to provide what you need, your GP will be the best person to talk to.

The right medical help The good news is that postnatal depression responds well to treatment, especially if you seek medical help early. Health visitors, too, are trained to spot signs of postnatal depression and can offer counselling as well as practical support and suggest medication. Your GP may prescribe antidepressants, so do ask about any possible side-effects, to help you decide whether or not to take them. Tell your doctor if you are breast-feeding. There are several different types of antidepressants and some are safe to take while breast-feeding; others aren't.

For many women, antidepressants have helped their unpleasant symptoms fade until they have gone completely. Women come off them gradually, as they recover.

Other strategies that really do make a difference include spending regular short periods of time away from your baby, doing things you enjoy. And relaxation tapes can be helpful. Ask your health visitor if she has tapes she can recommend. Talking to a supportive friend or counsellor can make a real difference, too, but not all women will find this works for them.

You can help a friend with postnatal depression

If you know some with this condition, you can help her:
- Show you care – without feeling loved, she may find it hard to get better
- Listen, let her tell it in her own way – she may need you to listen to the same story many times before she can make sense of it all
- Let her express her bad feelings as well as the good ones – don't say things like "you don't mean that"
- She may worry she doesn't have feelings for her baby, but these will emerge as her depression lifts, and you can reassure her
- Persuade her to give time to herself, she needs it; you could offer to look after the baby for her
- Encourage her to seek help if she hasn't already done so.

Puerperal psychosis

This is a very serious illness that affects two or three women in every 1,000 after childbirth. It usually starts within the first six weeks of birth with a dramatic change in personality. Often a woman becomes extremely agitated, her thoughts race, and her ideas are chaotic. At other times she is severely depressed. It's important to get medical help straight away for puerperal psychosis, as it can worsen if untreated. With the right treatment most women make a full recovery.

"I had postnatal depression with my first baby, but it took a long time to acknowledge that's what it was. I just didn't feel like myself: that all this was happening to someone else. I found it hard to cope at times, but getting out was better than staying at home. I remember hiding my utter horror when others cooed over newborn babies... for me having a new baby was absolute hell in every way possible..."

see also

Your feelings after birth	178–79
After a Caesarean birth	184–85
What a new mother needs	198–99

The end of your birth year...

Becoming a mother has turned everything on its head. It's now 12 months since conception and the last year has seen you develop enormously as a person, as you and your partner faced the challenge of new parenthood. The years ahead will have their challenges too.

Strengthening your body

In her first year of life, your baby moves rapidly from dependent newborn to active toddler, and you may find you have trouble keeping up. If you're planning to go back to work, this next year will probably be the busiest of your life to date and will stretch your organizational skills to the limit. However, you and your partner will also find life immeasurably richer now that you both have the responsibility of your baby to care for.

As at any other challenging period in life, it's important to eat well, stay fit, and take care of yourself. Keep up your postnatal exercises to get your yourself back into shape. A month or two after your baby's birth, you could ask your health visitor or a local sports centre if there's a postnatal exercise class being run near you. Make sure the class is run by a teacher with a recent qualification (last three years) to teach postnatal exercise.

Exercising with your baby can be fun for both of you. She'll enjoy "playing" with you, and you start to get your body back into shape. Start with gentle exercise at first.

KEEP FIT CAUTION

Pregnancy hormones will have loosened your ligaments to accommodate the growing baby and for some time after the end of pregnancy, your joints will remain loose and prone to injury.

- When you exercise, never lie flat on your back and lift both legs in the air. This can do damage when you've just had a baby and your muscles are still weak.
- Avoid "sit-up" or "curl-up" type exercises as these are likely to give you neck, shoulder, and back pain, and make your abdominal muscles bulge out.

Avoid high-impact exercise initially Don't start any high-impact exercise, such as running and jumping, until at least three months after your baby is born – no matter how fit you were before you became pregnant. High-impact exercise puts a great deal of strain on your pelvic floor and this is an area you will want to get back into condition as soon as possible. Continue with your pelvic floor exercises until you feel that those muscles are completely back to normal. The exercises will help stitches to heal more quickly too. Doing them for the rest of your life will help prevent problems later on, such as a prolapsed uterus or bladder.

Strengthening your relationship

After the birth of a child, the majority of couples experience a change in their sex lives, usually for the worse. Tiredness, physical discomfort, and loss of libido are just some of the problems that impact on sex. But simple caresses help a lot – whether you're being stroked and cuddled or doing the stroking, both ways make you feel better.

A new baby obviously needs an awful lot of nurture from her mother. This puts a big strain on you and means you'll want more love and attention in turn, from your partner. On the other hand, he may feel deprived of your usual emotional support during this time, and if he can't cope with a lot less cherishing than he's used to, he can't help you when you most need it.

Keep talking, spending time together, listening to each other, and considering each other. You are parents now: you depend on each other and need to take care of each other as well as your child.

It can be helpful to think of your ability to give love and affection as an "emotional cupboard" that needs to be kept stocked up if you are to draw from its supplies. Who's filling up your cupboard? Everyone needs love and support from different places – from friends and family as well as their partner. Spread the load and remember that no one can really give love unless they're getting it too.

Is there sex after childbirth?

The National Childbirth Trust ran a survey to see how well couples were able to adjust their sex lives in the year following the birth of their new

THE KEYS TO HAPPINESS

Researchers in the USA collected data from 21,501 couples, some happy with their relationship and some not. They gave all the couples a list of 195 statements and asked them to tick the ones that most applied to them. When the mass of data was analyzed, the researchers discovered that a few statements were ticked a lot more by happy couples, so these could well be goals worth working toward in your relationship:

- I am very satisfied with how we talk to each other – 90 per cent.
- My partner understands my ideas and opinions – 87 per cent.
- We are both equally willing to make adjustments in the relationship – 87 per cent.
- We find it easy to think of things to do together – 86 per cent.
- Our sexual relationship is satisfying and fulfilling – 85 per cent. (1)

baby. The questionnaire was returned by 864 people and the results make interesting reading.

According to the survey approximately 29 per cent of women said that they had resumed sex within one month of giving birth – almost 30 per cent resumed within twelve weeks. But over 40 per cent took longer to feel ready, including three per cent who waited for over a year.

The time taken to recover from labour and resume lovemaking depends on the type of birth you had. In the survey:

- The women most likely to resume sex within a month or two were those who had a normal birth with no tears or stitches.
- Women who had a forceps delivery were more likely to wait six months.

Six out of ten women said that they resumed intercourse at what felt like the "right time" for them (59 per cent), but just under one in five said that that they had resumed intercourse too soon (18 per cent). Just over one in five said that they had resumed intercourse "a little late" (23 per cent).

You don't need to wait for your six- to eight-week check to make love provided that both you and your partner feel ready. (Remember though that breast-feeding may not give you full contraceptive protection.) As the survey showed, many women wait several months before making love with penetration. Stitches can be problematic. Your doctor will check your stitches at the six- to eight-week check, but if they continue to give trouble after that, make another appointment to have them looked at.

Better or worse In the survey, about half of all new mothers said that they had sex less frequently than before they had their baby. But one-fifth made love just as frequently, and over one third had sex more often.

However, although they may have been having sex less frequently, quality is as important as quantity. One third of women said sex was just as good as before and 42 per cent felt sex had improved post-baby. One tenth of women felt a stronger bond with their partner and experimented sexually more than before. So things can change for the better.

Breast-feeding may affect your libido The survey revealed that women who breast-feed:

- Are less likely to resume sex quickly after birth
- Are more likely to say they have sex less frequently than before the birth (if they breast-feed for more than six months).

While you're breast-feeding, levels of oestrogen stay low to prevent you ovulating and becoming pregnant. One effect can be vaginal dryness. If this is the case, you may want to use lubrication and also take it slowly. Low oestrogen levels may reduce desire in some women. In the survey, leaking milk during sex was a key reason breast-feeding mothers gave for not wanting to make love. Feeding your baby before sex will make your breasts less likely to leak and your baby more likely to sleep soundly.

"After nine months of breast-feeding I felt I had done all I wanted to, so stopped, and three days later my sex drive returned like a storm."

You're parents now *and your relationship is the root out of which your future happiness will spring. This in turn helps you give your children all the security they need in order to grow and flourish.*

Talk to each other Intimacy can be achieved in many other ways than sex. It's important to talk to your partner about your feelings, and listening to your partner talk about his or hers, is of course another way of getting close. Most happy couples would probably put their success down to "being there for each other", simply making time to listen to each other as well as sharing their hopes and concerns.

Look at how far you have come

As your birth year closes, think back to where you were at this time last year and reflect on how much has changed since then. An enormous physical, emotional, and spiritual shift has taken place and you have emerged from that upheaval, transformed into deeper, stronger people who know that now you are parents, life can only get better.

see also

Caring for your pelvic floor	84–5
Your feelings after birth	178–79
Organizing your day	224–25
Postnatal depression	226–27

A–Z glossary of terms

The following list covers many pregnancy, and childbirth-related terms and conditions. If you have any queries, your midwife or antenatal teacher can give information too. Cross references to other entries are given in italics.

AFP TEST A *screening* blood test carried out between 16 and 18 weeks of pregnancy. This measures the amount of alpha-fetoprotein (afp) present in the mother's blood to assess the risk of the baby having spina bifida or Down's syndrome.

AFTERBIRTH *see placenta*

AFTERPAINS Contractions occurring in the first few days after the baby is born. Can be painful, especially during breast-feeding. More common after second babies than first. They help the uterus regain its pre-pregnancy size.

AMNIOCENTESIS A *diagnostic test* that can be carried out between 16 and 18 weeks of pregnancy. A needle is passed through the mother's abdominal wall and a small amount of amniotic fluid is withdrawn from her uterus. Cells that have come from the baby can be extracted from the fluid and used to diagnose *spina bifida*, *Down's syndrome*, and other genetic abnormalities.

AMNIOTIC FLUID The fluid surrounding the baby during pregnancy. Also called "waters" and "liquor". At eight months, there is about 0.5 to 1.5 litres (1–2pints). Too little amniotic fluid (oligohydramnios) may indicate problems with the baby's urinary tract; too much (polyhydramnios) could indicate problems with the oesophagus or spinal cord.

AMNIOTIC SAC The "bag" that contains the baby and the waters. It consists of two membranes lining the uterus: the chorion and the amnion. Also known as a fetal sac.

ANAEMIA An iron deficiency of the blood that causes tiredness, breathlessness, and pallor. Can be treated by eating a diet containing foods rich in iron and/or by taking iron tablets.

ANALGESIA *(see also entonox, epidural, pethidine)* Medical word for drugs or treatments that provide pain relief.

ANTENATAL CLASSES Classes run by midwives, health visitors, physiotherapists, and childbirth educators to prepare women and their partners for labour and parenting. Classes are often provided in early pregnancy and then during the final two months of pregnancy.

ANTERIOR POSITION When the baby is lying with the back of his head toward the front of the mother's pelvis at the end of pregnancy. The technical term is *occiput anterior* or OA. Labour tends to be shorter and less painful when the baby is in the anterior position.

ANTIBIOTICS Drugs that are used to fight bacterial infections, but cannot be used against viruses. Antibiotics must be prescribed with caution during pregnancy as they may have adverse effects on the baby.

ANTIBODIES Proteins made by the body to fight off infections. The mother's antibodies cross the placenta and provide the baby with protection against infections such as *rubella* (German measles) and chicken pox (varicella) during the first few months of his life.

APGAR SCORE A score indicating how strong the baby is at birth. The midwife assesses the baby's heart rate, breathing, muscle tone, reaction to stimulus, and skin colour on a scale of zero to ten. Typical Apgar scores might be seven at birth and ten, five minutes later.

AREOLA The coloured circle of skin around the nipple. Raised areas on the areola are called Montgomery's tubercles and secrete substances that keep the nipples supple.

ARNICA A homeopathic remedy that promotes healing, and helps reduce swelling and bruising, derived from arnica montana. Always consult a qualified homeopath.

AROMATHERAPY The use of essential oils made from plants to treat pain, illness, and states of mind. Essential oils can be inhaled, used for massage, or added to the bath. Many are dangerous during pregnancy and labour, so always consult a qualified aromatherapist.

BIRTH BALL A large ball, similar to those used in gymnastics, which the mother can sit on or kneel over during labour to help her keep mobile.

BLOOD PRESSURE *(see also pre-eclampsia)* An important indicator of the mother's and baby's health during pregnancy. The blood pressure consists of two readings, recorded as a higher figure over a lower figure (for example, 120/70). Raised blood pressure may be due to pre-eclampsia.

BRAXTON HICKS CONTRACTIONS Contractions of the uterus that may be felt in late pregnancy. The mother's tummy goes very hard, but the contractions are not painful. Some women have frequent Braxton Hicks, while others don't feel them.

BREECH POSITION When the baby's bottom, rather than his head is in the pelvis at the end of pregnancy.

BROW PRESENTATION When the baby's head is tipped backward, so that his brow would be born first. This can make labour very difficult because the brow is much wider than the back of the baby's head, which normally comes first. A Caesarean section may be necessary.

CARPAL TUNNEL SYNDROME The carpal tunnel carries nerves from the wrist to the hand. Fluid retention during pregnancy can narrow the tunnel and this puts pressure on the nerves, causing pins and needles and numbness in the fingers. Exercising the hands and wearing wrist splints can help. The condition usually disappears after birth.

CEPHALIC Describes a baby who is lying upside down, with his head in the mother's pelvis. The usual position at the end of pregnancy; it may be written in medical notes as ceph.

CEPHALO-PELVIC DISPROPORTION (CPD) When a baby's head is too big to pass through the pelvis; he will have to be born by Caesarean section.

CEREBRAL PALSY A condition involving varying degrees of physical and mental disability caused by lack of oxygen during pregnancy or at birth.

CERVICAL WEAKNESS This is when the muscles that close the *cervix*, the neck of the uterus, are weak. The weight of the baby may cause the cervix to open in the fourth or fifth month of pregnancy. A stitch called a *Shirodkar suture*, can be put around the cervix in the early stages of pregnancy to keep it closed.

CERVICAL MUCUS Lubricates the vagina. The mucus changes in quantity and consistency during the *menstrual cycle*. Women can be taught how to examine their mucus to determine when they are fertile.

CERVIX The neck of the uterus. It is long, hard, and tightly closed during pregnancy. At the start of labour, it becomes softer and shorter and then opens to 10cm (4in) to allow the baby to be born.

CHLAMYDIA A sexually transmitted infection that can be treated with antibiotics. Although the mother may have no symptoms, the presence of the bacteria in the vagina can lead to premature labour and the baby may become infected.

CHLOASMA A slight darkening of the mother's forehead, nose, and cheeks during pregnancy, which makes it look as though she has a butterfly-shaped mask on her face. Disappears after the baby is born.

CHORIONIC VILLUS SAMPLING (CVS) A *diagnostic test* that can be carried out from 11 weeks of pregnancy to find out whether a baby has Down's syndrome or another genetic abnormality. A needle is passed through the mother's abdomen under ultrasound guidance, and a tiny sample of the placenta taken. This is analyzed in a medical laboratory.

COLOSTRUM The milk that is in the mother's breasts immediately after birth. It is thick, yellowish and rich in antibodies that protect the baby from diseases such as rubella. Colostrum is replaced by mature milk after about three days.

CONSTIPATION A common problem in pregnancy, caused by hormones slowing down the passage of food through the large bowel. Iron tablets can make it worse. Treatment includes eating plenty of fresh fruit, vegetables, and whole-grain cereal.

CONTRACTIONS Sometimes called labour pains. The muscles of the uterus tighten to open up the *cervix*, the neck of the *uterus*, and push the baby out through the *vagina*.

CORDOCENTESIS Specialized *diagnostic test* that involves taking blood from the baby's umbilical cord under *ultrasound* guidance between 14 and 24 weeks. The blood is examined to see if the baby has haemophilia, *anaemia*, problems with his immune system, or other abnormalities.

CRAMP Leg cramps are common during pregnancy. Drinking plenty of milk may help reduce the frequency of attacks. Flexing the foot at the ankle and then circling the ankle vigorously relieves the spasm.

CYSTITIS An infection of the bladder that makes passing urine painful, with a burning sensation. There is a need to pass urine much more frequently than usual. Cystitis should be treated with antibiotics to prevent the infection from spreading to the kidneys.

DEEP TRANSVERSE ARREST A problem that can occur during labour. The baby cannot get past the two bony projections (the ischial spines) that stick into the pelvis. Changing the mother's position can help, but sometimes forceps may be used to help the baby's head pass the spines, or a Caesarean is necessary.

DIABETES Condition where the pancreas does not produce enough insulin, or the body cannot use the insulin produced. This causes sugar to accumulate in the blood, leading to extreme thirst, drowsiness, and eventually unconsciousness. Some women develop it during pregnancy (gestational diabetes). Babies born to mothers with diabetes can be large.

DIAGNOSTIC TEST A test such as *chorionic villus sampling* or *amniocentesis* that can confirm whether the baby has a congenital abnormality such as spina bifida or a genetic condition such as Down's syndrome. It is offered after a positive *screening test*.

DOULA A Greek word meaning "wise woman". Used to describe an experienced mother who supports another woman during labour, and helps her care for her baby during the first few days at home.

DOWN'S SYNDROME Sometimes called Trisomy 21, this syndrome is caused by the presence of an abnormal twenty-first chromosome. People with Down's syndrome are of below-average intelligence, and may have heart and lung problems. The degree of disability varies greatly.

DUE DATE The date the baby is "due", also called estimated date of delivery (EDD). It is calculated as nine months and one week from the first day of the woman's last menstrual period. Only five per cent of babies are born on their due date.

ECLAMPSIA A serious medical condition, sometimes called toxaemia of pregnancy, in which the mother has major seizures, or fits. It is usually preceded by *pre-eclampsia*. The fits can occur during pregnancy, labour, or in the postnatal period. Both mother and baby are at risk.

ECTOPIC PREGNANCY One in which the *embryo* develops outside the uterus, either in the Fallopian tube, or occasionally, in the abdomen. If it is in the Fallopian tube, the mother may experience severe pain on one side of her abdomen and shoulder pain. If an ectopic pregnancy is suspected, the mother should contact her midwife or GP immediately.

EMBRYO The name given to an unborn baby in the first weeks of pregnancy.

ENDOMETRIUM The innermost layer of the uterus. The endometrium is shed each month during a menstrual period and then regenerated.

ENGAGEMENT When the baby's head or bottom sinks down into the pelvis during the last month of pregnancy. If the baby is four-fifths engaged, the midwife can feel only one-fifth of his head above the "cage" of the pelvis.

ENGORGEMENT When the breasts feel hot, hard, and uncomfortable. In the first two to five days after the birth it can be caused by excess fluid in the mother's system. Later on it may occur if, for example, a baby misses a feed. Engorgement is generally only a problem during the first weeks of breast-feeding, after which the breasts adjust to make the amount of milk required by the baby.

ENTONOX Also known as gas and air, this is a mixture of 50 per cent oxygen and 50 per cent nitrous oxide, which can be inhaled during labour for pain relief.

EPIDURAL An anaesthetic injection into the spine that numbs the nerves supplying the uterus and cervix so that the mother can no longer feel contractions. Also removes sensation from the legs and feet. Some hospitals administer *mobile epidurals*.

EPISIOTOMY A cut made through the tissue stretching between the back wall of the vagina and the back passage (*perineum*). Helps the baby to be born more easily. May be necessary to put forceps around a baby's head.

EXTERNAL CEPHALIC VERSION (ECV) A procedure carried out in the final weeks of pregnancy to turn a baby who is in the *breech position* into a head-down position. The doctor places one hand on the baby's head and one on his bottom and pushes him round. It is now considered best practice to try to turn breech babies because it reduces the likelihood of the mother needing a Caesarean section.

FALSE LABOUR This is *Braxton Hicks contractions*. It can easily be interpreted by the woman as the start of labour. However, labour is not diagnosed until the contractions are regular and painful, and the cervix is opening up.

FETAL SAC *see amniotic sac*

FETAL SCALP ELECTRODE A tiny monitor that is clipped onto a baby's head during labour to check that he is not becoming distressed.

FETUS The term that is used to describe an unborn baby after ten weeks of pregnancy.

FIRST STAGE The first part of labour from when the cervix begins to open, until it is fully dilated (10cm/4in). It may last a few hours or a few days, but generally takes 12 to 18 hours for a woman having her first baby.

FLUID RETENTION Sometimes called *oedema*. The blood volume and the amount of fluid in a woman's tissues increase considerably during pregnancy. Her ankles, hands, and face may become puffy. A small amount of swelling is generally normal, but should be mentioned to the midwife as it is occasionally a sign of pre-eclampsia.

FOLATE This is the naturally occurring form of *folic acid*.

FOLIC ACID Vitamin supplement that helps prevent spina bifida. Women are advised to take 400mcg a day from the time they start trying to conceive to three months after becoming pregnant. Women who have previously given birth to a baby with spina bifida should take a higher dose when trying for their next baby.

FORCEPS Sometimes described as stainless steel "salad servers", these are used to help the baby be born when he is lying in an awkward position and the mother cannot push him out. They may also be used if a mother's pushing is ineffective because she has had an epidural or is very tired.

FOREMILK The thin, watery milk that comes at the beginning of a feed. The foremilk is designed to quench the baby's thirst.

FUNDUS The medical term for the top of the *uterus*. The fundus reaches the mother's belly button by 20 weeks of pregnancy, her diaphragm by 36 weeks, and then drops down again as the baby *engages* in the pelvis.

GAS AND AIR *see entonox*

GENITAL HERPES Painful ulcers (similar to cold sores) that can develop on the cervix, vagina, and vulva. If the ulcers are "active" and weeping at the end of pregnancy, it is safer for the baby to be born by Caesarean rather than vaginally as the ulcers may infect his eyes, causing blindness.

GERMAN MEASLES *see rubella*

GINGIVITIS Medical term for inflammation of the gums. Common in pregnancy and can lead to tooth decay. Flossing between teeth can help prevent this.

GLUCOSE TOLERANCE TEST A test for *diabetes*. Blood is taken after the mother has fasted for six hours. She is then given a glucose drink and a repeat blood test. The blood sugar level should rise and then quickly return to normal.

GUTHRIE TEST A blood test performed around the fourth day of the baby's life to detect a rare disease called *phenylketonuria*. The baby's heel is pricked with a needle and a small drop of blood squeezed onto a specially prepared absorbent card.

HAEMOGLOBIN The iron-containing part of the blood that makes it red. Lack of haemoglobin causes *anaemia*, although it's normal for haemoglobin levels to drop slightly during pregnancy. Haemoglobin levels are tested at the first pregnancy visit, and at 28 and 36 weeks.

HAEMORRHAGE Medical term for excessive bleeding. Bleeding may take place before the baby is born, when it is called an antepartum haemorrhage, or postpartum haemorrhage after the baby is born. A postpartum haemorrhage can occur when the placenta is being delivered or up to ten days after the birth.

HAEMORRHOIDS These are varicose veins in the back passage (also called piles). They can be extremely painful and may bleed heavily. Constipation makes them worse, so it is advisable to have a diet rich in fibre and to drink plenty of water. Ointment can be prescribed to help shrink them.

HINDMILK The creamy, satisfying milk that comes after the *foremilk*, with the "let-down" reflex, after the foremilk.

HOMEOPATHY An alternative therapy based on the theory of treating like with like. Remedies derived from plants, minerals, and animal sources are given in minute quantities. In large quantities, these remedies would cause the symptoms they are designed to treat. Consult a qualified homeopath before taking any remedies in pregnancy.

HUMAN CHORIONIC GONADOTROPHIN (hCG) The hormone measured in antenatal tests. From 16–18 weeks of pregnancy, the level of hCG in the mother's blood can be used to estimate the risk of her having a baby with Down's syndrome.

HYPNOTHERAPY An alternative therapy that induces a state between waking and sleeping, when emotional problems and irrational fears can be more easily understood and overcome. Women can be taught self-hypnosis as a means of controlling pain during labour.

IMMUNE SYSTEM *(see also antibodies, immunization)* The immune system is a complex defence mechanism that operates throughout the body to protect against infections and toxins. The bone marrow, thymus, spleen, and lymph nodes are important parts of it.

IMMUNIZATION A method of preventing serious diseases such as polio, diphtheria, and tetanus, by injecting into the body a modified form of the organisms that cause the disease. Immunization is not offered in pregnancy because there is a risk to the unborn baby.

INCOMPETENT CERVIX *see cervical weakness*

INCONTINENCE Partial or complete loss of control over the bladder or bowels. Forceps and ventouse deliveries and pushing for a long time in the second stage of labour can sometimes cause incontinence.

INDUCTION Starting labour off by doing a "*sweep*", inserting a *pessary* containing *prostaglandins* into the vagina, breaking the waters, or giving the mother a hormone drip (*syntocinon*).

INVOLUTION The process by which the *uterus* shrinks after childbirth and returns to its pre-pregnancy size and position. Takes about six weeks.

KEGEL EXERCISES *see pelvic floor exercises*

KETONES Substances produced if the body starts burning fat to meet its energy requirements. A mother's urine is tested for ketones during labour to ensure that she has enough energy to keep her contractions going.

KICK CHART A chart used during pregnancy for the mother to record the movements made by her baby. Too few movements in the space of 12 hours might mean that the baby is distressed.

LINEA NIGRA This is a dark line that appears down the middle of the abdomen during pregnancy. It fades after the baby is born.

LISTERIOSIS An infection caused by the bacterium *listeria monocytogenes*, found on unwashed fruit and vegetables, in soft cheeses made from unpasteurized milk, undercooked chicken, some cold meats, and shellfish. It is not dangerous for a pregnant woman, but can be life-threatening to her unborn baby, and may lead to premature delivery.

LITHOTOMY POSITION A position in which the woman's legs are raised and held apart in stirrups to enable medical procedures such as an internal examination, forceps delivery, or stitching the perineum to be carried out.

LOCHIA The name given to the discharge, or heavy period, that occurs in the first weeks after birth. Some women "bleed" for as long as six weeks.

LOW BIRTHWEIGHT A baby that weighs under 2.5kg (5$^{1}/_{2}$lb) is considered to be of low birthweight. Low birthweight babies may be weak and are vulnerable to infection.

MASTITIS Infection of the breast, treated with antibiotics. Breast-feeding women are often incorrectly diagnosed with mastitis when the problem is simply a blocked milk duct.

MECONIUM The baby's first bowel movement that is black, sticky, and tar-like. If the baby opens his bowels in the uterus during labour, the "waters" will be meconium "stained", which may also be a sign that the baby is distressed.

MENSTRUAL CYCLE The female cycle during which the uterus is prepared for pregnancy, an egg is released from the ovary, and is expelled from the body with the lining of the uterus during menstruation. An average cycle lasts 28 days, but cycles lasting from 21 to 35 days are not uncommon.

MINERALS Substances such as iron, calcium, magnesium, and zinc that are found in dark green vegetables, wholemeal bread, unrefined cereals, dairy products, and fish. Minerals are important for a healthy pregnancy.

MOBILE EPIDURAL An anaesthetic injection into the spine (*epidural*) that aims to numb the pain of contractions while leaving the mother some mobility. May involve a combination of drugs. Not available at all hospitals.

MOXIBUSTION A technique used in Traditional Chinese Medicine for turning *breech* babies into a head-down position. A herb called "moxa" is burned close to acupuncture points on the mother's feet. Success rates are reported to be as high as 90 per cent.

NAUSEA Feeling of sickness, common in the first three months of pregnancy. Nausea can also be caused by drugs given for pain relief in labour, for example, *pethidine*.

NOSEBLEEDS Quite common during pregnancy because the increased volume of blood in the woman's circulation places extra pressure on the tiny vessels in the nose.

NUCHAL TRANSLUCENCY SCAN A screening test carried out at around 12 weeks of pregnancy. A high resolution ultrasound scanner measures the fold of skin behind the baby's neck. The thickness of the fold combined with the mother's age are used to estimate the risk of Down's syndrome.

OBSTETRIC CHOLESTASIS A serious complication of pregnancy involving the liver and bile duct. The main symptom is itching over the whole body. Both mother and baby are at risk, and the affected pregnancy needs careful monitoring in a hospital consultant unit.

OBSTETRICIAN A doctor specializing in the care of women who have complications during pregnancy, labour, and the early postnatal period.

OCCIPITO-ANTERIOR (OA) POSITION *(see anterior position)*

OEDEMA Medical term for swelling in any part of the body.

OESTROGEN The female hormone that is responsible for growth of the uterine muscle during pregnancy, and for the development of the milk glands in the breasts. At the end of pregnancy, oestrogen levels increase, precipitating labour.

OPERCULUM *see show*

OPTIMAL FETAL POSITIONING (OFP) Refers to the positions the woman can use during pregnancy and labour to help her baby go down into the pelvis in an *anterior position*. The term was coined by a New Zealand midwife called Jean Sutton.

OVERDUE Going beyond 40 weeks of pregnancy. Most hospitals induce labour when the mother has reached 40 weeks and 10 days of pregnancy, in a process known as *induction*.

OVULATION The release of an egg from the ovary; usually occurs 14 days before the start of menstruation.

OXYTOCIN The hormone that makes the *uterus contract* during labour. It also causes milk to be squeezed out of the milk reservoirs in the breasts during breast-feeding.

PASSIVE IMMUNITY The immunity a baby acquires from the *antibodies* passed to him by his mother during pregnancy and breast-feeding. It helps protect the baby from infection.

PAEDIATRICIAN A doctor who specializes in the care of babies and children.

PELVIC FLOOR EXERCISES Sometimes called Kegel exercises, these exercises are designed to strengthen the muscles of the pelvic floor and so reduce the risk of incontinence and prolapse later. They are often taught at *antenatal classes*.

PERINEUM The tissue between the back of the vagina and the back passage. Some research shows that massaging the perineum with oil regularly during late pregnancy can help to protect it from tearing during childbirth.

PESSARY This is a soluble tablet that is inserted directly into the body. *Prostaglandin* pessaries can be inserted into the vagina to induce (bring on) labour if the *cervix* is not "ripe" (ready for labour). The pessary melts at body temperature releasing the drug that stimulates *contractions*. Pessaries can also used to treat *thrush*.

PETHIDINE Synthetic form of morphine used for pain relief in labour. Given by injection into the thigh. Side-effects include drowsiness and sickness; it also passes to the baby and can affect his breathing at birth.

PHENYLKETONURIA A metabolic disorder affecting one in 10,000, babies in which a baby cannot break down proteins, and toxic substances accumulate in the brain causing mental disability. If diagnosed early using the *Guthrie test,* a special diet is prescribed that enables the baby to develop normally.

PILES *see haemorrhoids*

PLACENTA A large organ, weighing about 500g (1lb) by the end of pregnancy, which passes oxygen, food, and *antibodies* from the mother to the baby, and removes waste products from him. While it acts as a barrier to many harmful substances, it cannot stop alcohol, drugs, nicotine, and viruses from reaching the baby.

PLACENTA PRAEVIA Condition in which the *placenta* is situated very close to, or lies across, the *cervix*. May mean that the baby has to be born by Caesarean section.

PRE-ECLAMPSIA *(see eclampsia)* A condition that is not well understood. It seems to be related to the early development of the *placenta*, although it does not generally cause a problem until the second half of pregnancy. The symptoms are high blood pressure, protein in the urine, and sometimes swelling. It can develop into life-threatening *eclampsia*.

PREMATURE BABY This is a baby born before 37 completed weeks of pregnancy. Premature babies may have difficulty breathing, maintaining their body temperature, and sucking, and often have to be looked after in a neonatal unit, sometimes for several weeks.

PRESENTATION The term used to describe the part of the baby that is most deeply engaged in the pelvis and which will be born first. The most usual presentation is *cephalic* or *vertex* (head first).

PRE-TERM *see premature birth*

PROGESTERONE Hormone that is vital to maintain pregnancy. Progesterone relaxes the muscles of the uterus to prevent the baby being born too early, and the muscles of the gut and urinary tract, which can sometimes lead to indigestion, *constipation*, and urinary infections.

PROLACTIN Hormone that stimulates the breasts to make milk.

PREMATURE RUPTURE OF THE MEMBRANES (PROM) This describes the situation when the "waters" break early; it can lead to premature birth.

PROSTAGLANDINS Hormones, or chemical messengers, produced in almost all tissues of the body, that have a variety of actions. They can also be used artficially induce labour and/or control bleeding in the *third stage*.

PTYALISM Overproduction of saliva experienced by some women during pregnancy.

PUDENDAL BLOCK An anaesthetic injection given via the vagina or through the *perineum* to numb the lower part of the *vagina* and the *perineum*. May be used for a forceps delivery if the mother has not already had an epidural.

PUERPERAL PSYCHOSIS Serious mental illness affecting two to three women in every 1,000 after childbirth. Symptoms include hallucinations and insomnia. Sufferers lose touch with reality and may harm themselves or their babies. Treatment in a special unit is necessary.

PUERPERIUM The six weeks following the birth of a baby.

RASPBERRY LEAF The raspberry leaf plant has been used for centuries to tone up the uterus and shorten labour. It is usually taken as tea or in tablet form from about 36 weeks of pregnancy.

RELAXATION Relaxation techniques are often taught in *antenatal classes*. Being able to relax during labour helps conserve energy, and maximize the oxygen supply to the baby.

RELAXIN A hormone that, in animals, softens the pelvic ligaments and the cervix in readiness for labour. It's uncertain whether it plays any part in human pregnancy and labour.

RETAINED PLACENTA This occurs if the placenta remains in the uterus after a baby has been born. Normally, the placenta is delivered within a quarter of an hour of the baby; if retained, surgery is required to remove it.

RHESUS POSITIVE/NEGATIVE If a person has the gene for the Rhesus factor, they are said to be Rhesus positive because their red blood cells have a special protein attached to them. Women who do not have this protein are Rhesus negative. If the baby they are carrying is Rhesus positive, there is a risk that their blood will attack the baby's blood cells and destroy them.

RUBELLA The medical term for German measles. If a woman contracts rubella during early pregnancy, the development of her baby's heart, eyes, and ears may be affected. If contracted later in pregnancy, the baby is less at risk though his hearing may be damaged.

SALIVA TESTS These are used to diagnose whether a person carries the cystic fibrosis gene. If both the mother and father are carriers, there is a risk that their baby will have the disease.

SALMONELLA A bacteria often found in chickens that causes food poisoning. Infection is usually the result of eating contaminated food, poor kitchen hygiene, and inadequate cooking.

SCREENING TEST A test that assesses the baby's risk (for example, one in 25 or one in 250) of having a condition such as *spina bifida* or *Down's syndrome*. It cannot say for certain that the baby is affected; this can only be determined by a *diagnostic test*.

SECOND STAGE The middle part of labour from when the *cervix* is 10cm (4in) dilated, to the birth of the baby.

SHIRODKAR SUTURE A stitch tied round the cervix to prevent it from opening too early in pregnancy. Can sometimes help women who have had repeated miscarriages because of a weak cervix. The stitch is inserted at 14 weeks and removed at 37 weeks.

SHOW Also known as the operculum, this is when the mucus plug sealing the neck of the *uterus* during pregnancy comes away, sometimes with a little blood. This can be an early sign of labour.

SPINA BIFIDA A condition in which the bones of the baby's spinal column have not closed properly around the spinal cord so that the nerves are damaged. In severe cases, the baby may be paralyzed from the waist down; in other cases, there may be very few symptoms.

STILLBIRTH When a baby is born who shows no signs of life.

STITCHES These may be used to repair a tear in the perineum, following an episiotomy, or to close a Caesarean section wound. Stitches need to be kept clean and dry while the wound heals. Some women find that taking arnica tablets helps the wound heal.

STRETCH MARKS Red lines that appear on the abdomen and thighs during pregnancy due to tearing of the tissues beneath the surface of the skin as it stretches. After the baby is born, the marks fade and become silvery.

"SWEEP" A method of induction of labour. The midwife inserts a finger into the cervix and gently separates the membranes from the edge of the uterus, triggering the release of hormones that initiate labour.

SYNTOCINON A synthetic form of oxytocin, the hormone that stimulates contractions. It is used in a drip to *induce* or speed up labour.

SYNTOMETRINE Drug given by injection into the thigh as the baby's shoulders are being born, to speed up the delivery of the placenta in a medically managed *third stage*.

TENS This stands for Transcutaneous Electrical Nerve Stimulation; a method of relieving pain in labour. Pulses of electricity are channelled through four pads placed on the mother's back that are conected to a machine. The electrical pulses override the pain signals coming from the uterus and cervix, and stimulate the body to release its own pain-killing substances known as endorphins.

THALASSAEMIA A genetic abnormality of the blood affecting people from Africa, Asia, the Middle East, and the Mediterranean. Symptoms include anaemia and attacks of severe pain. Regular blood transfusions are required. All pregnant women are now offered a blood test to check for the possibility of thalassaemia.

THIRD STAGE The final part of labour when the placenta is delivered. A drug (syntometrine) can be given to speed the process (medically managed), or the mother may prefer to wait for the placenta to be delivered naturally.

THRUSH Fungal infection that can affect the mouth, vagina, or nipples. It is often a side-effect of taking *antibiotics*. Sometimes mothers pass thrush to their babies during breast-feeding. Both mother and baby then need to be treated, and the mother should continue to breast-feed.

TOXAEMIA *see eclampsia*

TOXOPLASMOSIS Infection caused by a parasite that is endemic in cats. If a pregnant woman becomes infected, the development of her baby's eyes and brain may be affected. To minimize the risk, gloves should be worn to handle cat litter trays, and vegetables and fruit should be washed thoroughly to remove any traces of soil.

TRANSITION The bridge between the first and second stages of labour when the *cervix* is almost fully dilated and the mother starts to feel the urge to push. Symptoms may include vomiting, shivering, and aggressive behaviour.

TRANSVERSE LIE A term used by midwives to describe a baby who is lying across his mother's uterus so that neither his head nor his bottom is in her pelvis. If the baby stays in this position, a Caesarean section is necessary.

ULTRASOUND SCAN Reflected sound waves that can be used to build up a picture of the organs inside the body. During pregnancy, scans are used to estimate the due date, to see whether the baby is developing normally, and to show where the *placenta* is situated.

UMBILICAL CORD The lifeline that links the baby to the placenta. The average length is 50cm (20in). It contains two arteries and one vein and is covered in a jelly-like substance (Wharton's jelly) that prevents it from becoming tangled.

URINE TESTING An important part of pregnancy care. Protein in the urine may point to *pre-eclampsia*, or a urinary infection. Sugar in the urine could indicate gestational *diabetes*.

VACCINATION *see immunization*

VACUUM EXTRACTION Also known as ventouse, this is a device that can be used to help a deliver a baby if the mother is having a difficult second stage. A silicone plastic "cup" is placed on the baby's head, air is sucked out, then the doctor "pulls" on the cup during *contractions* to deliver the baby.

VAGINA The passage leading from the *uterus* to the outside world. Its walls are elastic so that they can stretch to accommodate the baby.

VARICOSE VEINS Painful distended veins in the legs or back passage (*haemorrhoids*). They are common in pregnancy because the weight of the baby obstructs the circulation of blood around the mother's body.

VENTOUSE *see vacuum extraction*

VERNIX The white coating that covers the baby during the last months of pregnancy to help protect his skin, and make him slippery so that he can travel more easily down the birth canal during labour. Vernix is absorbed into the baby's body after birth.

VITAMINS Naturally ocurring nutrients needed in small quantities that are found in a variety of foods, essential for a healthy pregnancy. Vitamin A is important for night-time vision and for healing. The best source for pregnant women is from vegetables. Too much can be toxic, so only take vitamin supplements if recommended by a doctor. Vitamin K helps the blood to clot. It used to be given by injection to new babies. Research carried out in the 1990s questioned whether this was safe and some hospitals and parents now prefer it to be given by mouth.

VULVA The external genital area, composed of thick layers of skin that form outer and inner lips or labia. The colour of the vulva changes from pink to purple during pregnancy.

ZINC A mineral that is important for the normal development of the baby in the uterus, and to help strengthen the uterine muscles. Found in high-fibre foods such as bran cereals, hard cheese, and meat.

ZYGOTE The name given to the unborn baby in the very earliest stage of his development.

Useful organizations

EXERCISE AND THERAPIES IN PREGNANCY

The Aquanatal Register
Tel: 01628 661961
www.aquanatal.co.uk
Safe exercise in water during and after pregnancy. Classes are run locally.

Body Control Pilates Association
Tel: 020 7636 8900
www.bodycontrol.co.uk

The British Acupuncture Council
Tel: 020 8735 0400
www.acupuncture.org.uk

British Homeopathic Association
Tel: 0870 444 3950
www.trusthomeopathy.org

British Wheel of Yoga
Tel: 01529 306851
www.bwy.org.uk

Guild of Pregnancy and Postnatal Exercise Instructors
www.postnatalexercise.co.uk

The International Federation of Professional Aromatherapists
Tel: 01455 637987
www.ifparoma.org

Pilates Foundation UK Ltd
Tel: 07071 781859
www.pilatesfoundation.com

The Pilates Institute
Tel: 0870 111 0166
www.pilates-institute.co.uk

PROBLEMS IN PREGNANCY

Action on Pre-Eclampsia (APEC)
Tel: 020 8863 3271
www.apec.org.uk
A UK charity set up to prevent suffering from pre-eclampsia.

Antenatal Results and Choices (ARC)
Tel: 020 7631 0285 (Helpline)
www.arc-uk.org
Non-directive support and information.

BackCare
Helpline Tel: 0845 130 2704
www.backpain.org

Baby Life Support Systems (BLISS)
Tel: 0500 618140 (Parent Support Helpline Freephone)
www.bliss.org.uk
Making sure that more babies born prematurely or sick in the UK survive.

General Osteopathic Council
Tel: 020 7357 6655
www.osteopathy.org.uk
Find a registered osteopath.

Hyperemesis Gravidarum Support Group (Blooming Awful)
www.hyperemesis.org.uk
Information for those with very severe pregnancy nausea, and their families.

Obstetric Cholestasis Support
Tel: 0121 353 0699
www.ocsupport.org.uk

Pre-eclampsia Society (PETS)
Tel: 01286 882685
www.pre-eclampsia-society.org.uk
Support and information for women, who themselves have suffered from pre-eclampsia.

Symphysis Pubis Dysfunction
Tel: 01235 820921
www.pelvicpartnership.org.uk

Toxoplasmosis and pregnancy
Tel: 0870 777 3060
www.tommys.org
Information on toxoplasmosis.

EXPECTING MORE THAN ONE BABY

The Multiple Births Foundation
Tel: 020 8383 3519
www.multiplebirths.org.uk

Twins and Multiple Births Association (TAMBA)
Tel: 0870770 3305
www.tamba.org.uk

PLANNING YOUR BIRTH

Active Birth Centre
Tel: 020 7281 6760
www.activebirthcentre.com
Gives advice on pre- and postnatal yoga classes, preparation for birth, and birth-pool hire.

Association for Improvements in the Maternity Services (AIMS)
Tel: 0870 765 1433
www.aims.org.uk
Working to get women the best care.

Association of Radical Midwives
Tel: 01695 572776
www.radmid.demon.co.uk
Supporting midwifery.

Baby Tens
Tel: 0845 230 9737
www.babycaretens.com
Makes a donation to NCT for each TENS machine hired.

BirthChoiceUK
www.birthchoiceuk.com
Helping you make choices about where to have your baby.

British Doula Association
Tel: 020 7244 6053
www.topnotchnannies.com
Sets professional standards of practice.

Caesarean Support Network
Tel: 0870 241 3449
www.findsupport.co.uk

Find a Doula
tel: 0871 433 3103
www.doula.org.uk
UK-wide database of doula services.

Gentle Water Birthing Pools
Tel: 01273 622 001
www.gentlewater.co.uk
Water birth and pool hire.

Home Birth Reference site
www.homebirth.org.uk
Information about home birth.

Independent Midwives Association
Tel: 0870 850 7539
www.independentmidwives.org.uk
Information about, and support for, independent midwives.

Splashdown Water Birth Services
Tel: 09456 123 405
www.waterbirth.co.uk
Information on water birth and pool hire.

BREAST-FEEDING

The NCT Breastfeeding line
tel: 0870 444 8708
Puts you straight through to an NCT
Breastfeeding Counsellor any day of
the week, from 8am to 10pm.

**Association of Breastfeeding Mothers
(ABM)**
Tel: 0870 401 7711
www.abm.me.uk
Counselling and telephone support
for breast-feeding mothers.

La Leche League (Great Britain)
Tel: 0845 120 2918
www.laleche.org.uk
Aim to help mothers to breast-feed
through mother-to-mother support.

POSTNATAL

*The National Childbirth Trust runs local
postnatal groups in all areas where new
parents can get to know each other.*

Association for Post-Natal Illness
Tel: 020 7386 8885
www.apni.org
Aims to provide support to mothers who
are suffering from postnatal illness.

Birth Crisis Network
www.sheilakitzinger.com/BirthCrisis.htm
The website provides details of a
helpline that women can ring to talk
about a traumatic birth.

Depression Alliance
Tel: 0845 123 2320
www.depressionalliance.org
Helps mothers suffering from post- or
antenatal depression and their families.

Home-Start
Tel: 0116 233 9955
www.home-start.org.uk
Trained volunteers visit families regularly.

Meet-A-Mum Association (MAMA)
tel: 0845 120 3476
www.mama.co.uk
Provides friendship and support.

Positively Women
Tel: 020 7713 0222
www.positivelywomen.org.uk
Support for women with HIV and AIDS
and their families.

Samaritans
Tel: 08457 90 90 90
www.samaritans.org.uk
A UK charity offering support to people
who are suicidal or despairing.

**Trauma and Birth Stress after Childbirth
(TABS)**
www.tabs.org.nz
A New Zealand-based organization
supporting parents with post-traumatic
stress disorder after giving birth.

Working parents
Daycare Trust
Tel: 020 7840 3350
www.daycaretrust.org.uk
National childcare charity, campaigning
for quality affordable childcare.

Parents at Work
Tel: 020 7253 7243
www.parentsatwork.org.uk
Helps children, working parents, and
their employers find a better balance
between home and work.

BABY LOSS

Ectopic Pregnancy Trust
Tel: 01895 238025
www.ectopic.org
UK charity providing information about
symptoms, diagnosis, and treatment.

**Foundation for the Study of Infant
Deaths (FSID)**
Tel: 020 7233 2090
www.sids.org.uk
Charity working to prevent infant deaths
and promote baby health.

The Miscarriage Association
Tel: 01924 200799
www.miscarriageassociation.org.uk

Stillbirth and Neonatal Death (SANDS)
Tel: 020 7436 5881
www.uk-sands.org
Support for parents and families whose
baby is stillborn or dies soon after birth.

SUPPORT FOR BABIES WITH PROBLEMS

**Association for Spina Bifida and
Hydrocephalus (ASBAH)**
Tel: 0845 450 7755
www.asbah.org
ASBAH provides advice and practical
support to people with spina bifida and
hydrocephalus, their families, and carers.

Birth Defects Foundation
www.birthdefects.co.uk

Cleft Lip and Palate Association (CLAPA)
Tel: 020 7833 4883
www.clapa.com

Contact a Family
Tel: 020 7608 8700
www.cafamily.org.uk
Helping families of disabled children.

Cystic Fibrosis Trust
Tel: 020 8464 7211
www.cftrust.org.uk

Disabled Parents Network
Tel: 08702 410450
www.disabledparentsnetwork.org.uk
National organization of and for disabled
people who are parents or who hope to
become parents, and their families.

Down's Syndrome Association
Tel: 0845 230 0372
www.downs-syndrome.org.uk

REACH
Tel: 0845 130 6225
www.reach.org.uk
Working with children with hand or arm
deficiency.

SCOPE
Tel: 0808 800 3333
www.scope.org.uk
Scope is a UK disability organization
whose focus is on people with cerebral
palsy and their carers.

Sickle Cell Society
Tel: 020 8961 7795
www.sicklecellsociety.org
Information, counselling, and caring for
those with sickle-cell disorders.

SoftUK
Tel: 0121 351 3122
www.soft.org.uk
SoftUK provides support for families
affected by Patau's and Edwards'
syndrome and related disorders.

UK Thalassaemia Society
Tel: 020 8882 0011
www.ukts.org

All about the NCT

Since it started in the mid-1950s, The National Childbirth Trust (NCT) has worked successfully to improve the experience of childbirth in the UK. Through its antenatal classes, postnatal groups, support for breastfeeding, and national campaigning, the charity has furthered its goal of ensuring that all parents have an experience of pregnancy, birth, and early parenthood, which enriches their lives and gives them confidence in being a parent.

Powerful at a local and national level, the NCT has over 350 branches, run by parents for parents. Every postcode is covered by a branch that may offer:

- Antenatal classes
- Breastfeeding counselling
- Early days groups
- Bumps and babies groups
- Open house get-togethers
- Support for dads
- Working parents' groups
- Nearly-new sales of baby clothes and equipment
- Other social and fundraising events

You'll be able to meet and make friends with others going through the same life changes as you. You may also be able to hire a breast pump or a Valley Cushion locally after the birth. To find the contact details of your local branch, or if you have a question about antenatal classes, or if you are looking for postnatal support, please phone our Enquiry Line on 0870 444 8707 or email **enquiries@nct.org.uk**. You can also check the branch details on **www.nct.org.uk**

If you have pregnancy and birth queries, ring the Pregnancy and Birth Line: 0870 444 8709 or log on to **www.nct.org.uk**

To get support with feeding your baby, ring the NCT Breastfeeding Line: 0870 444 8708

To find answers to pregnancy and parenting queries, ring the Enquiry Line or log on to: **www.nctpregnancyandbabycare.com**

To buy excellent products to help you and your baby through pregnancy, birth and early parenthood, have a look at what nctsales can offer. There is a wide range of items including books and information, maternity and feeding bras, and essentials for early parenthood and toys. All profits help fund the NCT's work to support parents. Contact NCT Sales on **www.nctsales.co.uk** or tel 0870 112 1120.

To join the NCT, just call 0870 990 8040

You can access the services and support of the NCT whether or not they are a member, but as a charity membership helps us to fund our work to support all parents and be more influential in campaigning for better services.
National Childbirth Trust, Alexandra House, Oldham Terrace, London W3 6NH.
Tel 0870 770 3236. Fax 0870 770 3237

"Join us and help make the UK a better place for all new parents."
Gail Werkmeister, President, The National Childbirth Trust

References

Chapter 2 Choices in your care
Page 29
1 Importance of support during labour:
Hodnett ED. *Continuity of Caregivers for Care during Pregnancy and Childbirth* Cochrane Database of Systematic Reviews 2000, Issue 1 www.library.nhs.uk/default.asp.

2 Most women with the right support can give birth without medical assistance:
World Health Organization: Care in Normal Birth: a Practical Guide. Report of a Technical Working Group. Geneva: WHO, 1996.

Page 33
1 Hodnett ED 2003 ibid.

Page 36
1 Hodnett ED 2003 ibid.

2 MIDIRS. *Support in Labour – Informed Choice for Professionals*. MIDIRS, 2005. www.infochoice.org

3 Breart G, Mlika-Cabane N, Kaminski M *et al.* Evaluation of Different Policies for the Management of Labour. *Early Hum Dev.* 1992; 29: 309–12.

4 The continuous support for women during childbirth.
Cochrabne Database of Systematic Reviews 2003 Issue 3.
www.library.nhs.uk/Default.aspx

Pages 38–9
1 Robertson A. *The Midwife Companion – The Art of Support During Birth*. Camperdown: ACE Graphics, 2004, 2nd edition, p.55.

2 A woman "labours best when she's undisturbed and has privacy":
Robertson A. (ibid) p.22.

3 Most women simply want their birth partner "to be there":
Singh D, Newburn M. *Access To Maternity Information and Support. The Experiences and Needs of Women Before and After Giving Birth.* London: National Childbirth Trust, 2000.

4 Support acts as a buffer against stress:
Cobb S. 1976. Cited McCourt C, Percival P. Chapter 12: Social Support in Childbirth. In: Page LA, Percival P (eds) *The New Midwifery – Science and Sensitivity in Practice*. Edinburgh:

Churchill Livingstone, 2000, pp.245–68.

5 What is a doula?
WHO (1996) ibid.
Hodnett ED 2003 ibid.

Page 46
1 Squier M, Chamberlain P, Zaiwalla Z et al. Five cases of brain injury following amniocentesis in mid-term pregnancy. Dev Med Child Neurol 2000;42(8):554-60.

Pages 48–9
1 Campbell R, McFarlane A.*Where to be Born?* Oxford: National Perinatal Epidemiology Unit, 1994.

2 Hodnett ED 2000 ibid.

Pages 50–1
1 Campbell, McFarlane 1994 ibid.
Hodnett ED 2000 ibid.

2 First labour is particularly suitable for home birth: Dr Rick Porter, *Pregnancy and Birth magazine*, Sept 1998; p77.

Pages 52–3
1/2 Transfer rates from home to hospital:
Home Births – The report of the 1994 Confidential Enquiry by the National Birthday Trust Fund, The Parthenon Publishing Group, 1997.

3 Women rate home birth as less painful:
Home birth and hospital deliveries. *Res Nurs Health June 1988*; 11(3): 175–81.

4 Home birth at least as safe as hospital for healthy women with normal pregnancies:
National Birthday Trust Fund (1997) ibid.

5 *BMJ* 23 Nov1996; 313 (7068).

6 Campbell, McFarlane 1994 ibid.

7 Very few home-hospital transfers are due to real emergencies:
National Birthday Trust Fund 1997 ibid.

Pages 54–5
1 Study of 29 midwifery practices in the US:
Murphy PA, Fullerton J (Department of Obstetrics and Gynaecology, Columbia University College of Physicians and Surgeons, New York, NY10032).

2 In an earlier UK study of 285 women... 9.4 per cent were transferred during labour:
Ford C, Iliffe S, Franklin O. *BMJ*;14 Dec1991; 303(6816):1517-19.

3 Transfer rate of 16 per cent:
National Birthday Trust Fund (1997) ibid.

Pages 56–7
1 Warm water helps pain of labour:
The Royal College of Midwives Position Paper no. 1a: *The Use of Water in Labour and Birth*, Oct 2000. Reviewed 2005. www.rcm.org.uk

2 Beneficial effects of water:
RCM Position Paper no. 1a, ibid.

3 Study showing fewer babies born in water admitted to special care:
Gilbert R, Tookey P. Perinatal mortality and morbidity among babies delivered in water: a surveillance study and postal survey. *BMJ*; 21 Aug 1999 319: 483-87.

4 Babies less stressed at water birth:
Geissbuhler V, Eberhard J. Waterbirths. *Fetal Diagnosis and Therapy* 2000; 15(5): 291–300.

5 Water must be kept at or below 37°C:
Garland D, Jones K. Waterbirth: supporting practice with clinical audit. *MIDIRS Midwifery Digest* 2000; 10(3): 333–6.
Royal College of Obstetricians and Gynaecologists (RCOG), Royal College of Midwives, Joint Statement no. 1 Immersions in water during labour and birth, 2006.

Page 58
1 Water must be kept at or below 37°C:
Garland D, Jones K. Waterbirth: supporting practice with clinical audit. *MIDIRS Midwifery Digest* 2000; 10(3): 333–6.
Royal College of Obstetricians and Gynaecologists (RCOG), Royal College of Midwives, Joint Statement no.1 Immersions in water during labour and birth, 2006.

Pages 62–3
1 Benefits of continuity of care:
Hodnett ED 2000 ibid.

2 World Health Organization (1996) ibid.

3 The Edgware Birth Centre:
Saunders D, Boulton M, Chapple J, Ratcliffe J *et al. Evaluation of the Edgware Birth Centre.*

London: Commissioned by Barnet Health Authority, 2000.

4 Women giving birth at home were more satisfied with their care:
Singh D, Newman M, 2000. Cited NCT *All-Party Parliamentary Group on Maternity Briefing*. London: NCT, 2001.

Page 66
1 Monitoring in labour:
National Institute for Clinical Excellence. *The use of electronic fetal monitoring*. London: NICE, 2001: www.nice.org.uk/pdf/efmguideli-nenice.pdf

Chapter 3 Self-care in pregnancy
Pages 84–5
1 Water birth and perineum:
Brown L. The tide has turned: audit of water birth. *BJM* 1998; 6(4): 236–43.

2 Evidence to support perineal massage:
Eason E, Labreque M, Wells G. Feldman P. Preventing perineal trauma during childbirth: a systematic review. *Obstet Gynaecol*, 2000; 5(3):464–71

Page 91
1 Alcohol in pregnancy: 2 units a week - RCOG 1–2 units once or twice a week. MIDIRS. *Alcohol and pregnancy – Informed Choice for Professionals*. MIDIRS, 2005. www.infochoice.org

2 Caffeine intake during pregnancy:
Food Standards Agency. www.eatwell.gov.uk

Page 93
1 Air travel in pregnancy:
Kingman CE, Economides DL. Air travel in pregnancy. *The Obstetrician and Gynaecologist* 2002; 4: 188–92.

2 Air travel and deep vein thrombosis:
Royal College of Obstetricians and Gynaecologists. Advice on Preventing Deep Vein Thrombosis for Pregnant Women Travelling by Air. Scientific Advisory Committee Opinion Paper 1 Oct 2001.

Pages 94–5
1/2 Pregnancy nausea linked to a larger placenta and lower rate of miscarriage:
Huxley RR. Nausea and vomiting in early pregnancy. *Obstet Gynecol* 2000; 95: 779–82.

Page 111
1 Nolan M. Modern Midwife, January 1997, Vol7 No.1

Pages 112–13
1 Success rate for moxibustion:

Francesco Cardini MD; Huang Weixin, MD. Moxibustion for Correction of Breech Presentation A Randomised Controlled Trial. *J Am Med Assoc* 1998; 280(18): 1580–4.

2 Caesarean birth considered safer than vaginal birth for a breech baby, according to international trial:
Term Breech Trial Collaborative Group. *Lancet* 2000; 356: 1375–83. Glezerman M.

3 Five years to the term breech trial: the rise and fall of a randomized controlled trial. Am J Obstet Gynecol 2006;194(1):20-5.

4 External cephalic version, success rate:
Hofmeyr GJ, Kulier R. External cephalic version for breech presentation at term Cochrane database of Systematic Reviews 1996, Issue 1. www.library.nhs.uk/default.aspx

Bewley S, Robson SC *et al*. Introduction of external cephalic version at term into routine clinical-practice. *Eur J Obstet Gynaecol Reprod Biol* 1993; 52: 89–93.

Zhang J, Bowes WA *et al*. Efficacy of external cephalic version – A review. *Obstet Gynaecol* 1993; 82: 306–12.

Page 115
1 Guidelines on induction from the National Institute for Clinical Excellence:
NICE 2001: About Induction of Labour – Information for pregnant women, their partners and their families. www.nice.org.uk/pdf/inductionoflabourinfo-forwomen.pdf

Chapter 4 The birth
Page 122
1 Odent, M. *The Scientification of Love*. London: Free Association Books 1999.

Page 125
1 Taking painkillers too early may increase chance of Caesarean: Ontario Women's Health Council. Attaining and maintaining best practices in the use of Caesarean section. Ontario: Ontario Women's Health Council (Caesarean section working group), 2000. www.womenshealthcouncil.com

Pages 126–27
1 Labour pain stimulates hormones:
Page LA. *The New Midwifery: Science and Sensitivity in Practice 2nd Edition*. Edinburgh: Churchill Livingstone, 2006.

2 Endorphins in mother-baby bonding:
Odent M (1999) ibid.

Page 129
1 Enkin M *et al*. (2000) ibid., p486.

Pages 134–35
1 Enkin M *et al* .(2000) ibid., p319.

2 Beneficial effects of water: RCM Position Paper, No.1a (2000) ibid.

3 Benefits of a birth pool in labour:
Garland D. *Waterbirth: An Attitude to Care* (2nd edition). Oxford: Books for Midwives, 2002.

4 Getting too hot in a pool can cause fetal distress: Garland D. (2002) ibid.

Page 137
1 Use of entonox during labour:
Garcia J, Redshaw M, Fitzsimons B *et al*. *First Class Delivery: A National Survey of Women's Views of Maternity Care*. London: Audit Commission/National Perinatal Epidemiology Unit,1998.

Pages 162–63
1/2 Taking painkillers too early may increase the chance of a Caesarean: Ontario Women's Health Council (2000) ibid.

3 Women's views of pethidine:
Fairlie F, Walker J, Marshall L, *et al*. Intramuscular opioids for maternal pain relief in labour. *Br J Obstet Gynaecol* 1999; 106: 1181–7.

4 How pethidine compares with other opioid drugs in labour:
Jordan S. *Pharmacology for Midwives: The Evidence Base for Safe Practice*. Basingstoke: Palgrave, 2002.

5 Effect of pethidine on baby after birth:
Crowell MK, Hill P, Humenick S. Relationship between obstetric analgesia and time of effective breast-feeding. *J Nurse-Midwifery* 1994; 39(3): 150–6.

6 Nissen E, Lilja G, Matthiesen A, *et al*. Effects of maternal pethidine on infants' developing breast-feeding. *Acta Paediatrica* 1995; 84(2): 140–5.

7 Clyburn P, Rosen M. The effects of opioid and inhalational analgesia on the newborn. In: Reynolds F. *Effects on the Baby of Maternal Analgesia and Anaesthesia*. London: Saunders, 1993.

8 Pethidine and sickness: Jordan S. *Pharmacology for Midwives: The Evidence Base for Safe Practice*. Basingstoke: Palgrave, 2002.

9 Smith CA, Collins CT, Cyna AM *et al.* Complementary and alternative therapies for pain management in labour. Cochrane Database of Sytemtic Reviews 2006, Issue No.4. www.library.nhs.uk/Default.aspx

Pages 140–41
1 Length of stage two: Janni W, Schiessl B, Pescherrs U, *et al.* The prognostic impact of a prolonged second stage of labor on maternal and fetal outcome. *Acta Paediatrica et Scandinavia* 2002; 81(3): 214–21.

2 Midwife's role during "crowning": McCandlish R, Bowler U, van Asten H, *et al.* A randomised controlled trial of care of the perineum during second stage of normal labour. *Br J of Obstet Gynaecol* 1998; 105(2): 1262–72.

Page 143
1 Breast-feeding immediately a good idea: De Chateau P, Wilberg B. Long-term effect on mother-infant behaviour of extra contact during the first hour postpartum. *Acta Paediatrica et Scandinavia* 1997; 66; 145–51.

Righard L, Alade MO. Effect of delivery room routines on success of first breast-feed. *Lancet* 1990; 336: 1105–7.

Widstrom A-M, *et al.* Short-term effects of early suckling and touch of the nipple on maternal behaviour. *Early Human Dev*, 1990; 21: 153–63.

2 Most babies wait an hour before seeking the nipple: Widstrom AM. *Breast-feeding: The Baby's Choice.* (video) 1996.

Page 146–47
1 Syntometrine versus syntocinon: McDonald S, Abbott JM, Higgins SP Prophylactic ergometrine-oxytocin versus oxytocin for the theird stage of labour. Cochrane Database of Sysytematic Reviews 2004, Issue 1. www.library.nhs.uk/Default.aspx

2 Iron levels in mother after birth: Thilaganathan B, Cutner A, Latimer J, *et al.* Management of the third stage of labour in women at low risk of postpartum haemorrhage. *Eur J Obstet Gynaecol Reprod Biol* 1993; 48(1): 19-22.

Chapter 5 Medical intervention
Page 152
1 Statistics on birth intervention: Department of Health: NHS Maternity Statistics, England: 2004–05. Bulletin 2006/08/HSCIC.

www.ic.nhs.uk/pubs/maternityeng2005/maternitystats06/file

2 Women giving birth at home half as likely to have medical intervention:

Home Births – The report of the 1994 Confidential Enquiry by the National Birthday Trust Fund, The Parthenon Publishing Group, 1997.

Page 155–56
1 Induction of labour is best used only when medically indicated: Enkin M *et al* (2000) ibid., p.375, p.495.

2 Induction after waters have broken: Royal College of Obstetricians and Gynaecologists: Induction of labour. RCOG Press, 2001. www.rcog.org.uk/index.asp? Page ID 697

3 Recommended alternatives to induction: RCOG (2001) ibid.

4 Gulmezoglu AM, Crowther CA, Middleton P. Induction of labour for improving birth outcomes fpr women at or beyond term. Cochrane Database Systematic Reviews 2006, Issue 4. www.library.nhs.uk/default.aspx

5 Induction is strongly recommended after four days: RCOG (2001) ibid.

Page 156–57
1 Recommendations for EFM: National Institute for Clinical Excellence: The use of electronic fetal monitoring. London NICE 2001. www.nice.org.uk/pdf/efmguideli-nenice.pdf

2 Fetal distress and electronic fetal monitoring: NICE (2001) ibid.

3 Use of EFM increases the Caesarean rate: Enkin M *et al.* (2000) ibid., p279.

Page 158–59
1 Howell C, Anim-Somuah M, Smyth R,: Epidural versus non-epidural analgesia or no analgesia in labour: Cochrane Database of Systematic Reviews 2005, Issue 4. wwwlibrary.nhs.uk/Default.aspx

2 Try to get your baby into the best position: Sutton J et al. *Understanding and teaching optimal foetal positioning.* New Zealand: Birth Concepts, 1996.

3 The benefits of support in labour: Hodnett ED 2000 ibid.

4 Hodnett ED 2003 ibid.

Pages 160–61
1 Ventouse rather than forceps: Enkin M *et al.* (2000) ibid., p.401.

2 Less postnatal pain with ventouse: Johanson RB, Menon V. Vacuum extraction versus forceps for assisted vaginal delivery Cochrane Database of Systematic Reviews 1999, Issue 2. www.library.nhs.uk/Default.aspx

Page 163
1 The urgency of a Caesarean is graded into four categories: Thomas J, Paranjothy S. The National Sentinel Caesarean Section Audit. London: RCOG Press, 2001.

2 Vaginal birth is safer for the mother: Lilford RJ *et al.* The relative risks of Caesarean section (intrapartum and elective) and vaginal delivery. *Br J Obstet Gynaeco* 1990; 97(10): 883–92.

3 An elective Caesarean is thought to be safer than an emergency Caesarean: Lilford RJ *et al.* (1990) ibid.

Pages 164–65
1 Use of EFM increases the Caesarean rate: Enkin M *et al.* (2000) ibid., p279.

2 Waiting until at least 39 weeks: Morrison JJ *et al.* Neonatal respiratory morbidity and mode of delivery at term: influence of timing of elective Caesarean section. *Br J Obstet Gynaecol* 1995; 102: 101–6.

3 Department of Health: NHS Maternity Statistics, England: 2004–05 Bulletin 2006/08/HSCIC. www.ic.nhs.uk/pubs/maternityeng2005/maternitystats06/file

Page 168
1 See the Bliss Parent Information Guide and their website: www.bliss.org.uk

Page 171
1 Conde-Agudelo et al Kangaroo Mother care. Cochrane Database of systematic Reviews 2003, Issue 2. www.library.nhs.uk/default.aspx

Chapter 6 Early Daze
Page 176
1 For more about traditions of care: Jackso D. *Baby Wisdom.* London: Hodder Mobius, 2002.

Pages 194–95
1 Skin-to-skin stimulates milk supply:
World Health Organization. *Evidence for the Ten Steps to Successful Breast-feeding*, 1998. www.babyfriendly.org.uk

2 How skin-to-skin contact after birth enhances breast-feeding:
Righard Alade. Effect of delivery room routines on success of first breast-feed. *Lancet* 1990; 336: 1105-7 In: Mohrbacher N, Stock J. *The Breast-feeding Answer Book*. La Leche League, 2003.

3 Elliot L. *Early Intelligence*. London: Penguin, 1999 – cites several studies to support bonding enhanced by smell and skin-to-skin contact. See in particular p.166.

Pages 196–97
1 Show your baby that night-time is not for playing:
Nikolopoulou M, James-Roberts I. Preventing sleeping problems in infants who are at risk of developing them. *Arch Dis Child* 2003; 88(2): 108–11.

Pinella T, Birch L. Help me make it through the night: behavioural entrainment of breastfed infants' sleep patterns *Pediatrics* Feb 1993; 91(2): 436–44.

2 At first your baby will feed little and often: Frantz 1985: Frantz 1983: In: Mohrbacher N, Stock J. (2003) ibid.

3 Effect of pethidine on breast-feeding: Nissen E *et al*. Effects of routinely given pethidine during labour on infants' developing breast-feeding behaviour. *Acta Paediatr* 1997; 16(2): 201-8, In: Mohrbacher N, Stock J. (2003) ibid.

4 Breast-feeding helps jaundice pass: Yamauchi,Yamanouchi. Breast-feeding frequency during the first 24 hours after birth in fullterm neonates *Pediatrics* 1990; 86: 171–75. In: Mohrbacher N, Stock J. (2003) ibid.

Page 200
1 Stanway P, Stanway A. *Breast is Best*. Pan, 1996 p17.

Pages 202–03
1 Breast-feeding in hot weather:
Nylander. Unsupplemented breast-feeding in the maternity ward. *Acta Obst Gyn Scand* 1991; 70: 205-9, In: Mohrbacher N, Stock J. (2003) ibid.

2 The World Health Organization recommends: See www.who.int

Pages 204–05
1 Renfrew M, Fisher C, Arms S. *The New Breast-feeding*. Celestial Arts, 2000, p67.

2 For more about feeding as the first social relationship, see:
Trevarthen C. Communication and co-operation in early infancy: a description of primary intersubjectivity. In: Bullowa M. (ed.) *Before Speech*. Cambridge: Cambridge University Press ,1979.

Page 208
1 For more on breast-feeding multiples:
Multiple Births Foundation. *Feeding Twins, Triplets and More*. 1999, p1.

Page 216–17
1 Gatts JD, *et al*. Reducing crying and irritability in neonates. *J Perinatol*. May/June 1995; 15(3): 215–21.

2 Babies whose cries are answered, cry less: Bell SM, Ainsworth MDS. Infant crying and maternal responsiveness. *Child Dev* 1972; 43: 1171–90.

3 Babies remember music from the womb: Hepper PG. Fetal soap addiction. *Lancet* 11 June 1988; 1347–48.

4 Playing your favourite music can sometimes help soothe a crying baby:
Frederic GF, *et al*. *Music Therapy and Pregnancy*. MIDIRS June 2002; 12:2;197–201.

5 Nikolopoulou M, James-Roberts I. Preventing sleeping problems in infants who are at risk of developing them. *Arch Dis Child* 2003; 88(2): 108–11.

Page 218–19
1 Cycles of arousal and sleep come together: McKenna J, *et al*. Experimental studies of infant-parent co-sleeping. *Early Hum Dev* 1994; 38:187–201.

2 Bedsharing mothers disturbed less:
3 McKenna J, *et al*. (1994) ibid.

4 Baby sleeping in a separate room cries more and gets more upset: Cory A. Mermer response to Blair *et al*. 1999. http://bmj.com/cgi/eletters/319/7223/1457

5 Keeping your baby's cot in your room halves the risk of cot death: Blair *et al*. *BMJ* Babies sleeping with parents: case-control study 1999; 319: 1457–62.

6 Cranial osteopathy research:
Hayden CJ. Towards an understanding of osteopathy in the treatment of infantile colic.

J Manual and Manipulative Therapy. 2002, p162.

Page 225
1 A health visitor can help:
Seeley S, Murray L, Cooper PJ. The outcome for mothers and babies of health visitor intervention. *Health Visitor*, April 1996.

Page 226
Ballard CG, *et al*. Prevalence of postnatal psychiatric morbidity in mothers and fathers. *BJP*, June 1994.

Page 224
1 Onozawa K, Glover V, Kumar C, *et al*. Infant massage improves mother-infant interaction for mothers with postnatal depression, *J Affect Disord* 2001; 63: 201-207.

2 Proven benefits of massage:
Field T. Interventions for premature infants *J Paediatr*. 1986; 109.
Field T, *et al*. Massage stimulates growth in preterm infants: A replication. *Infant Behaviour and Development* 1990; 13.

Page 230
1 Olson, Fournier, Druckman. The Enrich Couple Inventory. Psychology Today magazine, May/June 2002.

Index

About the authors

Sue Allen-Mills, long-time NCT antenatal teacher, wrote on self-care in pregnancy. **Tricia Anderson**, currently a Senior Lecturer in Midwifery at Bournemouth University and independent midwife, read manuscripts and contributed the introductions. **Anna Berkley** registered midwife wrote about choices for your care. **Suzy Colebeck**, NCT antenatal teacher, collected and edited NCT members' birth stories. **Caroline Deacon**, journalist and NCT breast-feeding tutor contributed the practical information on breastfeeding and baby-soothing. **Miranda Dodwell**, who wrote on medical intervention, has a PhD. in Genetics and is an NCT antenatal teacher. **Hannah Hulme Hunter** is a practising midwife and supervisor of midwives. She wrote the information on straightforward birth and early days with a new baby. **Penny Lane** contributed the section on from girl to mother and information on the role of hormones in birth and breast-feeding. **Mary Nolan** read the manuscript and wrote the A to Z glossary. She is a long-time NCT antenatal tutor and writer on childbirth issues, with a PhD in antenatal education.

Grateful thanks are due to Roz Collins content consultant on the first edition and Julie Frohlich, midwife, and to the following members of The National Childbirth Trust who assisted by reading and commenting on manuscripts: Lynn Balmforth, NCT information officer and librarian; Debbie Chippington-Derrick, NCT Caesarean and VBAC co-ordinator; Moira Clark, Fitness instructor; Cynthia Clarkson, Chair of NCT Research Networkers Panel; Rosemary Dodds, NCT Policy Research Officer; Juliet Goddard, NCT postnatal tutor; Gill Gyte, Advanced teacher and research networker; Gina Lowdon NCT Caesarean and VBAC co-ordinator; Heather Neil, NCT breast-feeding counsellor; Louise Pengelley, NCT antenatal tutor.

For help with information about premature birth and the early days with a new baby: Bonnie Green and Shanit Marshall of Bliss; Nicola Jones; Bridie Keyse, Health Visitor. For help with information on antenatal testing, Elizabeth Dormandy, King's College, London University.

Acknowledgments

ILLUSTRATIONS Kenny Grant, except pp.130–33 and 140 which are by Patrick Mulrey

IMAGES The publishers would like to thank the following organizations for permission to use images: **Getty Images:** Photographer's Choice/Nancy Brown 10; Hola Images 13; Taxi/Superstudio 15 ;Johner Images/Susanne Kronholm 54; Stone/Brooke Fasani 73; Photodisc 86, 87.; **Mother and Baby Picture Library/EMAP:** 17, 18, 19, 28, 40, 43 (top), 57, 65, 145, 152, 153, 176, 191, 203; **Alamy:** David Hancock 29; Janine Wiedel Photolibrary 30; John Angerson 51; Janine Wiedel Photolibrary 163; Photopia 209; **Science Photo Library:** Hattie Young 136; Mark Thomas 169; **Corbis Photo Library:** 81; 95; Larry Williams 181; David Raymer 213; **Mitchell Beazley/Ruth Jenkinson:** 72, 120, 228; **Bubbles Photo Library** 82; **Prima Baby Magazine** 204–5; Photodisc 6, 174; **MIDIRS Photo Library:** 156, 159
Andrew Florides: 21, 26, 33, 37, 61, 126, 128, 188, 231; **Michael Bassett:** 88, 195, 196, 221–3; Jackie Chapman: 201, 206, 216, 225; **Independent midwives:** 141, 178; **Anne Green-Armytage:** 150, 185, 186–7, 218; Saskia van Rees: 23, 38, 118; **Hannah Clements:** 146, 165, 167; **Tracy Grant:** 43, 143; **Lynn Walford:** 89, 101; **Persil:** 115, 125; **Daniel Ward:** 8, 75; **Antonia Robinson:** 58; **Victoria Dick:** 63; **Megan Oxberry:** 66; **Louise O'Gorman:** 70; **Plus3 Productions Ltd:** Caitlin Bishop 11; Emma Ryves in labour 54; **Phil Bishop:** Jane's birth 121; **Steve Collins:** Roz Collins with Lizzie 177; **Susy Greaves:** Emma with Dominic 196.

First published as *Your Birth Year*, in 2004 by Mitchell Beazley

This revised edition published 2007 by Mitchell Beazley an imprint of Octopus Publishing Group Ltd, 2–4 Heron Quays, London, E14 4JP
www.octopusbooks.co.uk
An Hachette Livre UK Company

Text copyright © NCT 2004, 2007
Design copyright © 2004, 2007 Octopus Publishing Group Ltd

ISBN: 978 1 84533 349 2

A CIP catalogue copy of this book is available from the British Library.

Colour reproduction by Spectrum Colour Ltd, England
Printed by Graficas Estella, Spain

Commissioning Editor Hannah Barnes-Murphy
Senior Art Editor Juliette Norsworthy
Production Sue Fox

Revised edition created for Mitchell Beazley by **Cooling Brown Ltd**
Art Director Arthur Brown
Editor Jemima Dunne
Design Tish Jones
Production Peter Cooling
Proofreading Constance Novis
Index Hilary Bird

Publisher's note: Before following any information or exercises contained in this book, it is recommended that you consult your doctor. The publishers cannot accept responsibility for any injuries or damage incurred as a result of following the information given in this book.